The Good Bishop

The Life of
Walter F. Sullivan

PHYLLIS THEROUX

ORBIS BOOKS
Maryknoll, New York 10545

Founded in 1970, Orbis Books endeavors to publish works that enlighten the mind, nourish the spirit, and challenge the conscience. The publishing arm of the Maryknoll Fathers and Brothers, Orbis seeks to explore the global dimensions of the Christian faith and mission, to invite dialogue with diverse cultures and religious traditions, and to serve the cause of reconciliation and peace. The books published reflect the views of their authors and do not represent the official position of the Maryknoll Society. To learn more about Maryknoll and Orbis Books, please visit our website at www.maryknollsociety.org.

Copyright © 2013 by Phyllis Theroux
All photos used courtesy of Bishop Walter F. Sullivan

Published by Orbis Books, Box 302, Maryknoll, NY 10545-0302

Manufactured in the United States of America

Library of Congress Cataloging-in-Publication Data

Theroux, Phyllis.
   The good bishop : the life of Walter F. Sullivan / Phyllis Theroux.
     pages   cm
   Includes bibliographical references and index.
   ISBN: 978-1-62698-024-2
    1. Sullivan, Walter F., 1928-2012. 2. Catholic Church–United States–Bishops–Biography 3. Bishops–United States–Bishops–Biography. I. Title.
   BX4705.S8825T49 2013
   282.092–dc23
   [B]   2012046773

"What is it, in the end, that induces a man to go his own way and to rise out of unconscious identity with the mass as out of a swathing mist? Not necessity, for necessity comes to many, and they all take refuge in convention. . . . It is what is commonly called vocation: an irrational factor that destines man to emancipate himself from the herd and from its well worn paths."

—C. J. Jung, *The Development of Personality,* vol. 17

Contents

Introduction

In May 2011, I received a phone call from Fletcher Lowe, a retired Episcopal priest in Richmond, Virginia. He was looking for a writer to do an oral history of his friend and colleague Bishop Walter Sullivan. I had heard of Bishop Sullivan. Not even a former Catholic who only reads the local Richmond newspaper to find out what's playing at the movies could be completely unaware of his existence.

There were, for example, the bells. One evening I took part in a candlelight vigil protesting the death penalty outside St. Ann's Church in nearby Ashland. Another Virginia prisoner was being put to death that night, and at some point during the vigil the bells began to ring in St. Ann's steeple. Bishop Sullivan had asked that the bells in every Catholic church in the diocese be rung at 11:00 p.m. on the night of an execution.

Then in 1996 I went to hear Sister Helen Prejean, author of *Dead Man Walking*, speak against the death penalty in downtown Richmond. Sacred Heart Cathedral was packed to the rafters. For over an hour the brilliant, soft-spoken New Orleans nun held a thousand people in her hand as easily as a cup of coffee at the kitchen table.

Helen Prejean was as controversial as she was popular. Not every Catholic diocese would allow her to speak for fear that she might stray from her topic and expound upon unsecured subjects that could get a bishop in hot water. I looked

1

down at my program to see who sponsored the event. Bishop Sullivan had invited her.

One positive experience in a Catholic cathedral is not a trajectory back into the Catholic faith. But in the intervening years, whenever I thought about stepping beyond the circumference of my own life to do something for other, less fortunate people, the name of Bishop Sullivan would come to mind. Now, a week after The Reverend Lowe's phone call, I was sitting across the table from him at Aunt Sarah's Pancake House on Broad Street in Richmond. Bishop Sullivan loves Aunt Sarah's pancakes. And the waitress who brings them to him. And the two Protestant clergymen, his old friends Fletcher Lowe and Jim Payne, who were sitting in the booth alongside him.

It was Fletcher Lowe and Jim Payne's idea to have this oral history done. At eighty-three, Bishop Sullivan would not be with them forever. At seventy-nine and eighty-one, respectively, Lowe and Payne were not in the shank of their youth either. It was now or never. The meeting at Aunt Sarah's was to determine whether the chemistry between the bishop and his potential oral historian was good enough.

From my side of the table, I wondered whether this small, smiling Irishman in a button-down shirt and Mr. Rogers's cardigan sweater would be an honest interview. The pancakes had not yet arrived before I had concluded yes. Doing an oral history of Bishop Sullivan would be my pleasure. What I didn't know, until I got down to work, was that it would not be enough.

Traditionally, the subject of an oral history is like the nave in a cathedral, the longest part of it. If family members or close friends are interviewed they serve to reinforce the structure, like flying buttresses. I had not proceeded more than a month before I realized that such a straightforward, lightly edited approach to Bishop Sullivan's life would not be appropriate. His life was less like a cathedral than the sprawling Denver airport. His friends, who ran the gamut from death row prisoners to wealthy Jewish philanthropists, were too important in their own right to fit into a traditional nave/buttress oral history pattern.

Scrapping that approach, without quite knowing how I would replace it, I continued with my research. I traveled up to Washington, D.C., down to the Tidewater region of Virginia, and went in and out of Richmond multiple times to interview Bishop Sullivan at his house, where we would sit and talk as if we had known each other all our lives. In some ways, we had.

Both of us were products of a pre–Vatican II Catholic education. Both of us had studied theology and philosophy, although in my instance it was a comparatively once-over-lightly treatment at a Catholic women's college,[1] whereas the bishop had studied intensively in two seminaries and gone on to get a doctorate in canon law at Catholic University. But we spoke the same language, understood the same cultural influences, and appreciated the long and twisted history of an ancient Church whose Founder frequently got lost in the bricks and mortar of the institution.

There was another odd coincidence that tied us loosely together as well. Bishop Sullivan was born several blocks away from where I once lived in the same heavily Catholic neighborhood in northwest Washington, D.C. The discrimination he felt from the Church when he was a young boy after his parents were divorced was felt, to a lesser degree, by me thirty years later when my own marriage fell apart.

Most of *The Good Bishop* takes place between 1953, the date of Walter Sullivan's ordination as a priest, and 2003, when he turned seventy-five and retired as the bishop of Richmond. It is a fifty-year period that covers tremendous upheavals in the old order: a cultural revolution, the civil rights movement, the assassination of one president, the resignation of another, a rise in feminist consciousness, the war in Vietnam, and, in the Catholic Church, a reinvigoration of its people by the Second Vatican Council, followed, decades later, by a massive sexual abuse scandal that has not yet ended.

Like all large institutions, the Catholic Church puts a high premium upon internal discretion. The backstage politics of the Curia or, closer to home, the diocese, are usually hidden from public view. But the deeper I got into my research, the more that curtain thinned. As the facts of Bishop Sullivan's life unfolded, so too did the Church behind him. I found it fascinating and hope the reader will, too.

After much thought, it seemed to make more sense to present the bishop according to the issues that defined him. He was at the center of a large world, filled with numerous challenges and interests that overlapped one another. Simply to follow behind him from one year to the next would be too confusing, like trailing behind a chef as he moves between dozens of different dishes being simultaneously prepared in a restaurant kitchen.

It also seemed important to reserve space for the groundbreaking Second Vatican Council, which took place in Rome over a four-year period from 1962 to 1965. Without some understanding of its importance in the Church and beyond, it is difficult to understand in full what motivated Bishop Sullivan and many of the people around him who were interviewed for this book. All of them were part of that same period of hope and turbulence, although some had never given the Catholic Church a second thought, except to dismiss it as isolationist, irrelevant, or, worse, an enemy. Crossing paths with Bishop Sullivan changed them, usually for the better. But not always.

When early on in the project I mentioned to a Catholic neighbor that I was writing a book about Bishop Sullivan, she lowered her eyes to her lap and said softly, "Oh, I'm sure he's very nice . . . beneath it all." Virginians tend to have fixed views and fine manners that join hands to control each other. Only on the editorial pages of the *Richmond Times-Dispatch* did that clasp loosen.

The bishop didn't seem to mind criticism. Particularly in the 1980s, when he became known as a "peace bishop" and the barbs began to fly, being disliked was the price of preaching the Gospel. What did get his attention was when he felt that unfairness or dishonesty was the motivating force behind an attack.

Writing in response to a March 1986 newspaper editorial taking the clergy to task for getting political, Bishop Sullivan promptly and angrily wrote back: "The church's teaching is not determined by a poll of Sunday churchgoers. Christian teaching is not intended to make people comfortable or to serve the interests of the powerful. After all, its founder died on a cross because of what he said and did. He isn't remembered because of his opinion poll ratings."[2]

Today, Catholic bishops are seen primarily as enforcers of Church doctrine, particularly on abortion and contraception. If a poll were taken, they would be far less popular than the Catholic nuns who have been mostly silent on those issues while working unheralded among the poor, who are most in need of social justice. Now, as then, Bishop Sullivan would be an anomaly among his peers, only more so.

Unfortunately, some of the people closest to Bishop Sullivan died before they could be interviewed. One of them was his close friend Monsignor James McGrath. In going through a pile of letters, I found a note from McGrath to a mutual friend of the bishop.[3]

My dear Charles,

My novitiate time for meditating on the biography of Bishop Sullivan has expired and as we had agreed I would let you know my conclusions. . . . Biographical information must always stem from the start of an individual's life. Let that be the starting point. . . . It will build as it moves along. No one wants to sit in an archival area and plow through paper accumulation containing so much that will not be used. People would be interested to know if the bishop played Tiddly Winks as a boy and only he can tell us that.

The biographer is most grateful for the late Monsignor McGrath's opinion, particularly since it coincides with her own.

Phyllis Theroux
Ashland, Virginia

Chapter One

A Bishop's Beginnings

In 1953 Walter Francis Sullivan was twenty-five years old. In the parlance of the Catholic Church, he was a "lifer," someone who went straight from the eighth grade into the seminary and emerged eleven years later ready for the sacrament of Holy Orders. But there was something about Walter Sullivan that didn't sit quite right with the Sulpician fathers who oversaw his priestly formation. Twice before he graduated from St. Mary's Seminary in Baltimore, he was pulled aside and told they were going to delay his graduation.

Bishop Sullivan is a cheerful, self-effacing man. He rarely admits to having had a bad day, much less a bad year. When asked why the Sulpicians had their doubts about him, he smiles, makes a tent of his fingers, and bows his head over them. "I wasn't pious enough, I wasn't rebellious, and I always got good marks. But I never got an A in conduct. The seminary was such a regimented place, you stuck out if you didn't follow the rules. That's been the story of my life."

When he told his younger sister, Betty, that his graduation was being delayed, she burst into tears. It was not the first time that her brother had tripped over the church's threshold.

The Sullivans lived in a large brick house on Chevy Chase Parkway, NW, in a community full of big trees and big Catholic families, most of whom sent their children to the nearby newly constructed Shrine of the Blessed Sacrament parochial school. Walter and his three sisters, Patricia, Kathleen, and Betty, went there, too. "It was kind of a ritzy place," he said. "After my parents got married my mother had four children, all in a row. She was a very devout person, but not in a fanatical way." Their life revolved around the Church.

Catherine Vanderloo Sullivan was a nurse and member of the ladies' Sodality at Blessed Sacrament, responsible for washing and mending all the altar linens. "She believed in putting us to bed by 8:00 p.m. probably because she needed the time to herself," said Betty Sullivan Hughes. "We'd be up at 6:00 a.m., and she would say to us, 'Why don't you go up to the church?' So we got out bright and early and went up to the church playground."

When Walter Sullivan was four years old, his father and mother were divorced. In the heavily Catholic neighborhood of Chevy Chase, Maryland, being from a divorced family was a blight upon one's life. "You didn't use the word 'divorced,'" Betty Sullivan Hughes confirmed, "because it was so shameful. That was the philosophy in those days. It was the attitude of the people, but they got it from the Church."

"When our parents were divorced we weren't ostracized from the immediate neighborhood at all," said his sister. "But beyond that we weren't treated the same. One of my sisters was told by someone that because of our parents being divorced she couldn't wear white to get married, so she wore a blue suit. I didn't go along with that and neither did my other sister. We both wore white wedding dresses."

The Sullivans were close to their mother's brothers and sisters, who lived on Highland Place in Cleveland Park. They were some compensation for the absentee father and gave the children much-needed affirmation. But it was not an exact replacement. "I felt left out and different," said Bishop Sullivan. "I always felt that I had been deprived although what helped me a great deal was that my mother never said a negative word about my father."

The absent father (who promptly remarried), the lack of sufficient money to keep up with other, more comfortable friends, and the stigma of being from a "broken home" wrapped a cool cloak of disapproval around the Sullivan family. It had two noticeable effects upon Walter Sullivan's consciousness: it made him eager to be a success in life, and it sharpened his compassion for others who were different. Mrs. Sullivan was a good exemplar.

"My mother was very good to people," said Betty Sullivan Hughes. "One time I came home and opened up the basement door, and there was a lady down there. Her name was Miss Martin. She had a long white braid and was missing some teeth. Mother had found her on G Street and 14th Street, near St. Patrick's. She was homeless. The garbage man always got an egg and bacon sandwich on Saturday morning, and coffee—in a tin cup. She would not use good china for him. You wonder where Walter gets some of his compassion."

"We would sit on his lap, and I thought the world of him," said Bishop Sullivan. "We're all prejudiced, there's no doubt about that, but I grew up with an openness to people who are different because of my mother. She was a nurse, in contact with people of many cultures. The way my life has gone has a lot to do with my background."

The bishop's sister Betty is his best archivist. According to his Cub Scout membership card she has saved, when he was ten years old he weighed seventy pounds and vowed "to be square and obey the law of the cub pack." In photographs he is small and thin, with blonde hair and a wide grin. On the shy side, he kept his innermost feelings to himself.

"As a family," said Betty Sullivan Hughes, "we were very positive. We didn't talk about the negatives. Even though we were raised by a Dutch mother, she couldn't get the Irish out of us. We all have our ways. Walter is very quiet about his own thoughts. Even today I don't tread on them."

In the eighth grade, the future bishop had a thought that defined the rest of his life. "Our class received over twenty-five scholarships. I wasn't the brightest kid in the class, but I got a half scholarship to Gonzaga High School and a full scholarship to St. John's Military School in Washington. I didn't want to have anything to do with the military, the marching up and down, all that nonsense."

Then the vocational director of the Washington–Baltimore archdiocese paid a visit to his classroom and asked whether anybody was interested in being a priest. "I sat there silently, thinking about it, and then I raised my hand. The nun said, 'Sullivan, do you need to go to the bathroom?' And I said, 'No, I want to talk to the priest.' After I told him that I was interested, I was accepted on the spot. I think they were hard-up for vocations. Then I ran home and told my mother that I wanted to be a priest. I was her only son and the apple of her eye. She just looked at me and said, 'Be the best you can be.'"

While Sullivan was still in the eighth grade at Blessed Sacrament, he was on a bus going down to Gonzaga High School to play sports. "The announcement came over the bus of the bombing of Pearl Harbor. That was a shock. The next year I went into the seminary. Some of us were considered draft dodgers. If you skipped three months of school during that time you were drafted."

The cost of sending him to St. Charles minor seminary in Catonsville, Maryland, was beyond the family's reach. His mother took in boarders and did babysitting and sewing on the side to make ends meet. His father, who sent the family a small family stipend, could not be counted upon. But the women's Sodality at Blessed Sacrament stepped forward to pay his way.

In retrospect, Bishop Sullivan thinks that minor seminaries are a bad idea. "We all slept in a dormitory in high school. It looked like the Richmond jail. We were hothouse plants. There were no newspapers except for the sports pages, no radios, nothing to tell us about what was going on in the world. You don't get a full view of life. Thankfully, I grew up with three sisters."

When he was about to graduate from St. Charles, the rector came to him and told him that he could not be a priest in the Archdiocese of Washington–Baltimore. Until then, Walter Sullivan had not known that a priest with divorced parents was forbidden to serve in his home diocese because it might give scandal (i.e., encourage divorce) to parishioners who knew the family background. Archbishop Michael Curley from Baltimore had given Walter Sullivan the sacraments of Baptism and Holy Communion, but he was not prepared to give him Holy Orders.

"The rector told me that I was 'unattached.' That meant that unless I could find another diocese that was willing to finance me through the rest of my schooling, my education was over. Fortunately, the chancellor and vocation director of the Richmond diocese happened to be visiting St. Charles and heard that I was available. I was accepted in one day. I guess Richmond didn't have many vocations and so they weren't so particular."

In a rare lapse from good humor, Bishop Sullivan acknowledges that even now the pain of that unanticipated rejection is still fresh. "This is part of my life that I have always kept secret because I felt it was an embarrassment. It wasn't publicly known that my parents were divorced, unlike today, when there's almost something wrong with you if you're not. I have to talk about it now because it's part of my life and it would be wrong to leave it out."

A week before he was to be ordained, the Washington–Baltimore diocese had second thoughts and asked him to come back and be ordained there. He consulted the bishop in Richmond, who had supported him in his schooling, and Bishop Ireton said that it was his decision but to remember who had been faithful to him. He did.

On May 5, 1953, Walter Sullivan was ordained in the Cathedral of the Sacred Heart in Richmond, Virginia. His first priestly act was to marry his sister, Betty, to Fabian Hughes, a former seminarian classmate. Then he packed his bag and drove to his first assignment as an assistant pastor at St. Andrew's Church in Roanoke.

The assignment was not an accident. When Bishop Ireton agreed to sponsor Walter Sullivan, he made it contingent upon receiving permission from Archbishop Patrick O'Boyle, who headed up the Washington–Baltimore diocese. O'Boyle said that it would be all right, provided that Walter Sullivan's first two assignments were more than two hundred miles away from the Washington–Baltimore diocese. Roanoke met the test.

"They used to call him a renegade up here in Washington," said Betty Sullivan Hughes, "and we were so grateful that he didn't come back here. He couldn't have been himself. But those early hurts developed him into who he became."

Chapter Two

A New Priest

Except for the detonation of the first H-bomb in a Nevada desert, 1953 was quiet. There was an old pope (Pius XII), a young queen (Elizabeth), and a new president (Eisenhower). The Korean War ended in 1953. Stalin died. Jonas Salk announced a promising new vaccine against polio. Senator John F. Kennedy and Rev. Martin Luther King both were married, and the first bus boycott took place in Baton Rouge, Louisiana. Like many firsts, it went unnoticed. But in the Deep South, the civil rights movement had begun to stir.

The Catholic Church was still a mission Church, serving descendants of an immigrant population that had not yet been fully assimilated into the American Protestant culture. Nor did the Church wish to dilute its own influence. The rhythms of First Fridays, Saturday confession, and Mass on Sundays and Holy Days of Obligation regulated every parish congregation. The *Baltimore Catechism* was the book of moral questions and answers that every Catholic child had to memorize. The seven gifts of the Holy Spirit, the eight Beatitudes, the Ten Commandments: there was a soothing, numerical exactitude to the lists and lessons that made them easy to learn and difficult to forget.

Outside the Church, there were cracks in the cultural wall. In 1953 Aldous Huxley took LSD and wrote about it, the first issue of *Playboy* and the second edition of *The Kinsey Report* went on the stands. But the Catholic Church's Legion

13

of Decency could still make or break a movie's chances at the box office. Monsignor Fulton J. Sheen's *Life Is Worth Living* TV show was immensely popular with Catholics and non-Catholics alike, who tuned in every week to watch the witty, silver-voiced Sheen scribble "JMJ" ("Jesus, Mary, Joseph") on the blackboard before he faced the camera and brought everything he touched—from the Holy Trinity to the evils of Communism—to vivid life. In 1953 the first color television went on the market. It brought out the scarlet color of Sheen's cape and sash.

The lead story in the May 8, 1953, issue of the *Catholic Virginian* was about the six priests, including Walter Sullivan, who were ordained that week in the Cathedral of the Sacred Heart in Richmond. The other story above the fold was about a sixty-six-year-old Kentucky woman who was named Catholic Mother of the Year for "giving" five of her six children to religious life. Two nuns and three priests, plus one married son, flank her and her husband in a solemn, sitting portrait.

Inside is a piece about a Norfolk, Virginia, Catholic high school fashion show, inspired by a modest apparel movement. There is a photo of four pretty high school girls wearing sheath skirts and sweaters in front of a poster that reads "To show Him we care by what we wear."

The *Catholic Hour*, dramatizing the Glorious Mysteries of the Rosary (with Gene Lockhart and Ruth Hussey), is airing on NBC, in cooperation with the Catholic Daughters of America and the Family Rosary Crusade.

Readers of *The Time of Your Life* advice column are urged to "put the 'r' back in May," which is the month of Mary, and to remember that "all honest work is decent and can be a means of chopping off a chunk of purgatory if you are thoughtful enough to offer it up."

"I was part of those days," said Bishop Sullivan. "The Church was very measured, very ordered. I didn't challenge the system. I didn't follow it lock, stock, and barrel, either. But the Church is my home, my life. I believe in the Church, in the truth of it."

In July 1953 the newly ordained Walter Sullivan reported for duty to Pastor John Igoe at St. Andrew's Church in Roanoke. Until he received his assignment from the bishop, he didn't even know where Roanoke was.

In 1889 William Ginther, a devout Roman Catholic architect from Akron, Ohio, took his first and only recorded trip to Europe. He was clearly impressed by what he saw. After traveling to all the major artistic centers on the continent, he returned to Akron, left his old firm to open up a practice of his own, and spent the rest of his life designing schools, rectories, and—his hallmark—massive, Gothic-style Catholic churches. St. Andrew's in Roanoke, Virginia, is one of them.

Completed in 1902 St. Andrew's sits on a hill overlooking downtown Roanoke like Chartres Cathedral. But Roanoke is not Chartres. Once dominated by the old Norfolk & Southern Railroad, American Viscose fabrics, GE, tobacco, and meat packers, it is a blue-collar town that continues to be economically depressed. Nearly all of the funds for the lavishly appointed cathedral with its imported Italian marble altars and German stained-glass windows were raised by the parishioners themselves.

"There were no Catholic people with money in Roanoke," said Bonnie Neuhoff, who was a sophomore at Roanoke Catholic High School in 1953. "The money came from the German and Irish immigrants who came to work for the railroads. And they built the church close to the tracks, because that was where they lived, and most of them didn't have cars and had to walk to church."

Charlie Schwallemberg, whom Father Sullivan coached on the basketball team, would walk from his home downtown across the Norfolk & Southern Railroad tracks and up the hill to Roanoke Catholic High School. When the gates across the tracks were down, he took the overpass above the tracks, and when the steam engines passed beneath him, he would be enveloped in thick white fog. "We'd disappear for a while. It was beautiful."

A genial man with a salesman's gift of gab, Schwallemberg was part of a gang of boys, now in their seventies, who felt Sullivan's influence deeply. "He was probably no more than seven or eight years older than we were and he was very vital, full of 'ginger,' a hands-on type of priest, active in the community. When the class of '55 had our reunion a few years back, he was invited. I don't know that any of the other priests were. And he was still bishop so he had a full schedule, but he said he'd try to rearrange things to be there. And he came."

"Everybody loved him," said Bonnie Neuhoff, whose future husband's family frequently had Sullivan over for dinner. "The school was small in those days and, remember this, it was run by nuns. And the pastor, Father Igoe, was an older man. Father Sullivan was a different type of person in our environment. He laughed a lot. He made us feel like he was somebody we could talk to. What I liked about him is that he always listened. I think that some bishops don't listen."

Sullivan discounts the compliment. "I was the baby priest, the youngest by fourteen years. I think there was a natural attraction among kids toward someone who was younger."

Walter Sullivan slipped into the life of the St. Andrew's parish as easily as if he had lived there his whole life. For the next three years he rose at six, said the early 7:00 a.m. Mass at St. Andrew's, and, presaging the way he would operate for the rest of his life, moved like a rocket through the rest of the day.

In those days, the Catholic Church was an all-inclusive institution, reaching deep into the lives of the parish, which included a population of boys from troubled homes who lived at St. Vincent's Home nearby and went to the parish schools. Father Sullivan was a frequent visitor. He also coached the girls' and boys' basketball teams, coached the boys' football team, and ran both the Cub Scouts and Boy Scouts, until he collapsed from weariness.

"It got to be with the Scouts that I finally had to ask for help. I made a plea from the Sunday pulpit saying that I didn't see why I should care about their boys more than their own fathers. Thirty-five fathers stepped forward."

Other demands on his time involved counseling potential candidates for the priesthood. He sent several boys to the seminary. In addition, he separately instructed and brought twenty-four candidates into the Catholic Church. "In those days, it was a one-on-one proposition."

To assuage his loneliness and create deeper connections in the parish, he made friends with the Maronite community in Roanoke. "It was one of the joys of my ministry. They were wonderful people, mostly from Lebanon, and most of them went to St. Andrew's. They celebrated an ancient rite that had a unique liturgy." He was a regular at many family dinner tables.

St. Andrew's parish was close-knit. "The priests lived in a rectory," said Bonnie Neuhoff, "and whenever the Roanoke football team scored an out-of-town victory, when we got home we would ring the church bell to let the priests know we had won the game. If it was a big game we would ring and ring. If we didn't win, the bells would be silent."

"Bonnie was a cheerleader," said Bishop Sullivan. "I used to drive the cheerleaders to the games because that was when I'd get all the scuttlebutt as to what was going on in the school."

"He was the first priest who would get out in a scrimmage with us," said Tommy Mellenkamp, a retired state trooper. "He's left-handed and a real good basketball player. He kind of made me look bad."

"I remember one time we were all horsing around on the bus after a game and Father Sullivan told us to sit down. There was this one smart-aleck kid who wouldn't do it and said to him, 'Kiss my ass!' Father Sullivan had a bit of a temper. He grabbed that kid by the shoulders and bounced him up and down so hard that I thought his head was going to hit the top of the bus. 'Kiss my what?' he yelled. 'Kiss my what?' I think it takes courage to do something like that, and we all admired him even more after that."

Off the bus, Sullivan was frequently the court of last resort for nuns who would march their students down to the rectory and ask him to help them out. "In my senior year," said Tommy Mellenkamp, "I got into a fight in the classroom with my best friend. The nuns were like drill instructors for the Marine Corps on Parris Island, and I went there later so I know, and when she came across us fighting, she took us over to Father Sullivan to straighten us out. That was a break for us. He asked us what we were doing there and we told him and he said, 'Well, your punishment is to wash my car.' It was below freezing outside and the soapy water froze on the car."

"I couldn't even get the doors open," said Sullivan, whose history with Mellenkamp and his car had more than one chapter. One time he lent his car to him to go to the prom. "It was a new Ford sedan, robin's-egg blue on the top and dark blue on the bottom. I tore the whole side of it off, and I had to knock on his door and tell him what happened. He could have shot me right there and I would have deserved it."

Then suddenly, in 1956, Sullivan's assignment at St. Andrew's was terminated. "It came out of the blue. I was told that I was going to be moved."

He traced the decision back to a diocesan women's event in Richmond at which the parish women from St. Andrew's were praising Sullivan to the diocesan chancellor, Monsignor Justin McClunn. "Well," McClunn reportedly told the women, "we'll see what we can do about that." Shortly thereafter, he was told that he was being transferred.

To this day, Bishop Sullivan doesn't understand the reason. "Perhaps it was jealousy. Perhaps I was a little too popular. Honestly, I don't know, but I was very upset. My pastor was very upset."

To make matters worse, Sullivan's new assignment was to St. Mary's Star of the Sea on the military base of Fort Monroe. "I had seen Fort Monroe once before and I thought to myself then that this was the last place in the world I would want to be assigned. It was very structured. I just couldn't believe I was being sent there."

Fort Monroe sits on the southern tip of the Virginia peninsula in Hampton, Virginia. Completed in 1834 to guard the channel to Hampton Roads where three major rivers flow into the Chesapeake Bay, it was the only military installation in Virginia to remain in Union hands during the Civil War, a safe haven for slaves before Lincoln's Emancipation Proclamation. After the war, former Confederate President Jefferson Davis was held in prison there for several years. St. Mary's Star of the Sea is the only diocesan church in the United States that sits on military land.

Bishop Sullivan's days as a "peace bishop" lay ahead of him but temperamentally the regimented, military life did not appeal. Piling his belongings into an old station wagon, he drove from Roanoke to his new assignment in a depressed state of mind. "I was kind of boo-hooing, feeling very sorry for myself, but on that long drive I realized something—that I had to grow up. By the time I got there I had convinced myself that I would enjoy being at Fort Monroe."

Against the odds, he did.

His pastor was Father Julius Schmidhauser, whose forte was finances and construction. For most people his peculiarities outweighed his charms. For one thing, he talked with a lisp. For another, he could rarely remember anybody's name, and when he gave an order to a subordinate priest, he frequently rescinded it a moment later. "He would say to me, 'You celebrate the Mass, I'll preach.' Then at the last minute he would say, 'No, you preach,' and I would have nothing prepared."

Schmidhauser's demeanor in church could be unsettling. "One of my jobs was to do the Holy Saturday liturgy at St. Mary's," said Sullivan. "The whole time, Schmidhauser would never stop talking, making comments. When I sprinkled water over the congregation, he would comment, 'Father Sullivan's making water for Langley Air Force Base.'"

On another occasion, Schmidhauser came back from a trip to Europe with some pictures of the Blessed Mother. "After Mass, he would bring them out one by one from the sacristy, explain their meaning, and then invite everybody to come forward and kiss the picture. Then he would go back into the sacristy and get another one and repeat the whole thing. I remember there was one colonel in the back pew who yelled out, 'Hey, honey, give me a kiss. I've kissed everything else in this church today!' "

Sullivan held Schmidhauser in high, humorous regard. "He was a very eccentric person and tight-fisted with money. Every Saturday he would go to the hospital to pick up flowers from people's rooms for Sunday Mass. He would ask permission, but still it was odd."

Then Schmidhauser became mortally ill, but illness did not diminish the old priest's insistence upon liturgical correctness. "When he was dying," said Sullivan, "I went to see him in the hospital. I entered his room with a prayer. He said, 'Oh, Father Sullivan, you've got to do that *before* you come in.' I couldn't believe it. Here the man was dying and he was correcting my form. So I went out and did it over again his way. Finally, I took the water and sprinkled it over his face. 'Don't overdo it,' he whispered."

One of the young parishioners at St. Mary's Star of the Sea was Donald Riley, a research engineer at Langley. He and his wife, Agnes, who worked at the Air Force base at Langley, had four young children. When Bishop Sullivan moved into the rectory, Schmidhauser sent him over to their house to introduce himself.

"On our street there was us with four kids and the Shannons with six kids across the street. Father Sullivan would come for a visit whenever he felt down in the dumps. He would sit at the kitchen table drinking milk from a Mickey Mouse glass with a straw, and the kids would just mob him. He loved it, but when he shook them off to leave he would laugh and say, 'Thank God for the priesthood.' "

Sullivan's talent for friendship foreshortened his stay. He became good friends with the military chaplain, who was a very good friend of the diocesan chancellor, McClunn, who had formerly moved Sullivan out of Roanoke to Fort Monroe. Now McClunn was looking for someone to study canon law and take over as head of the Marriage Tribunal in Richmond. Once again Sullivan was abruptly transferred.

In 1958 he left Fort Monroe to study canon law at Catholic University in Washington, D.C. But Bishop Sullivan is famous for never severing a friendship, except by death. More than fifty years later, in 2010, St. Mary's Star of the Sea celebrated its 150th anniversary. Bishop Sullivan was there with Donald and Agnes Riley, now great-grandparents, beside him.

When it came time for him to speak, he confessed that being sent to Fort Monroe was "a providential assignment. . . . It was at Fort Monroe that I first came to truly understand and love the military. After all, we are in the same business. We are both working for peace."[4]

Chapter Three

Bishop Boot Camp

In retirement Bishop Sullivan's command post is his living room, where he sits surrounded by a large, uncurated collection of knick-knacks acquired over a lifetime. On a table by his chair is the Divine Office Liturgy of the Hours, the *Richmond Times-Dispatch* sports section, and a wicker basket full of correspondence. A look-alike figure of a bespectacled, white-haired bishop in a rocking chair, a kind of ecclesiastical Mr. Rogers, smiles down at him from the top of a bookcase. Filling up five shelves to the left of the fireplace is a large collection of ceramic houses from a generic Alpine village, swathed in a tangle of electric cords he usually forgets to plug in to illuminate them.

Sullivan collects a lot of things: miniature houses, U.S. stamps, coins, photographs, CDs, and Schnauzers which he started to acquire when he became rector of the cathedral. One of them usually sits on his lap when he's reading. Then there are his books, mostly history and psychology, some of them still encased in plastic, probably gifts he never opened. Getting up from his chair, he walks over and takes down a thick volume from a shelf. In 1958, when Sullivan was sent to Catholic University to study canon law, this was the book he used. The text is in Latin.

Its official name is the *Codex Juris Canonici.* The edition in Sullivan's hand is the 1917 revision (there has since been another), which gathers together ten thousand different

Church laws and regulations and distributes them between seven books. Each book deals with one large aspect of Church concern: the general norms (i.e., ways in which the code is to be applied throughout the book), the "people of God" and organizational structure above them, the means (i.e., schools, universities, missions) for dissemination of the faith, the sacraments, the way "temporal goods" are bought and sold, Church sanctions, and, finally, the Church's internal legal system. A casual glance at the Codex, which one can find in English on the Web, is like ripping open the backside of a pre-microchip-era computer and examining the intricate circuitry that makes the whole thing work.

"The Church is a business," explained Bishop Sullivan. "They need a way of doing things, and the Codex contains the general norms and rules they follow. This gives you a broader picture of the Church as a whole." Between 1958 and 1960, Sullivan happily reimmersed himself in the "broader picture" as a full-time scholar at Catholic University. "I was ready for it. It was an honor to be asked. And," he added, "I had a pretty good resume."

A degree in canon law is not a prerequisite for becoming a bishop. Most bishops, in fact, don't have one. "They don't need it," said Sullivan. "Nearly all of their responsibilities involve finances and the buying and selling of properties." But in Sullivan's case, he did. To run the Richmond Marriage Tribunal he needed a thorough understanding of Title VII, Chapter IX, Articles 1 and 2 of the Canon. One dealt with dissolutions of marriage; the other with annulments.

If on some level, Sullivan knew that by joining the chancery staff he was on the fast track for higher office, he is too canny to acknowledge it now. "It's all a matter of being in the right place at the right time," he is fond of saying. But it is also a matter of other people being in the wrong place as well. At that time there were certain power vacuums and personality disconnects that gave him opportunities to advance that might otherwise have been denied him.

There was, for instance, the temperament of Bishop Peter Ireton, who had ordained Sullivan in 1953. Ireton was, in Sullivan's words, "from a different era," routinely spending three months in the winter in Florida and three months in the summer in the Poconos. Important papers and letters would be sent to him. In the last years of his tenure, he was also in poor health, and long before his death in 1958, the diocesan chancellor, Monsignor Justin McClunn, had been the de facto head of the diocese.

"McClunn was very knowledgeable," said Sullivan, "but he had his prejudices. The majority of priests didn't like him because they didn't think he treated them all equally well."

When Ireton died, the new bishop, John Russell, moved McClunn to northern Virginia ("to get him out of his hair," said Sullivan) and created another auxiliary bishop who had been the head of the Marriage Tribunal to assist him. This left a space open on the chancery chess board. In 1960 twenty-nine-year-old Walter Sullivan arrived from Catholic University with his new degree in canon law to fill it.

Much of the Marriage Tribunal's business was done by mail, which sorted itself out into three main piles: the Privilege of the Faith cases (where the marriage between two unbaptized persons dissolves and one of them converts to Catholicism and wishes to be married in the Church), the Pauline Privilege cases (where only one of the divorced parties was a baptized Catholic at the time of the marriage), and annulments, where the two parties are baptized Catholics but there was something wrong with one or both of the parties with the marriage *ab initio* (from the beginning).

For a petitioner to pass through the eye of the tribunal process successfully the priest in charge had to know how to thread the needle. "There was a new emphasis upon the incapacity on the part of an individual to enter into the fullness of marriage," said Sullivan. "I would interview petitioners or advise priests in the diocese who had parishioners who wanted to dissolve their marriages. I enjoyed what I was doing and got a lot of personal satisfaction helping people and allowing them to remarry or get back into the Church."

But in fact Sullivan also spent a great deal of his time working on a fourth pile of petitions: from priests who wanted to be laicized. "Most of them were from northern Virginia," he said. "They had gotten jobs with the government and wanted to get married. I didn't have any problem with that. If the person sees where the Lord is guiding him, then that's what he needs to do. I must have handled at least ninety cases."

It was far easier for a priest to get permission to be released from his vows when Paul VI was pope. "Under Paul VI," Sullivan said, "all the priest had to do was write a petition, give his story, and provide two witnesses to confirm it. I would give my vota and that would be that. With Pope John Paul II there was a noticeable change. You almost had to prove that he should never have been a priest in the first place. This was very demeaning, and it was very upsetting to me."

Sullivan had one other job as well, as assistant to Monsignor Leo Ryan, the longtime rector of the cathedral. "Ryan didn't get along with anyone," said the bishop. "He had this idea about the priesthood being a glamorous profession. He never did any work." Rather than live with Ryan in the rectory, he moved into the bishop's house across the street from the cathedral where his new boss, Bishop John Russell, was ensconced.

Walter Sullivan's biological father left the family early and never had any place of significance in his life. With Bishop Russell he finally had a mentor, someone to whom he could look for guidance and confirmation. It was a relationship that was one of respect, trust, and mutual dependence.

Like his predecessor, Bishop Ireton, Bishop Russell came from Baltimore. He was in Sullivan's eyes a wonderful, balanced man. "He was dignified, the perfect bishop, very proper. And he also had a wonderful sense of humor. He was very alert and had a real sense of his priests. He tended to be forgetful at times and some people misunderstood him. But I felt it was my job to make sure that he always looked his best in public. I had his complete confidence, and when he discussed things he planned to do, he took my opinions seriously."

When the Second Vatican Council formally opened on October 11, 1962, all the princes of the Church, including Bishop Russell, went to Rome, and what was happening in Rome was extraordinary, beginning with the fact that it was happening at all.

Pope John XXIII was nearly eighty when he was elevated to the papacy in 1958. His predecessor, Pius XII, had come from an aristocratic Roman family that was part of the Vatican inner circle. Withdrawn and sepulchral looking, Pius had, in the words of one historian, "a supernaturally aloof personality," preferring to be carried in a papal chair when he went out in public. By contrast, John XXIII came from a family of sharecroppers in Lombardy. He had a wide girth and a wide perspective, loved to walk among the people, and was in every way an approachable pope with a common touch that instantly made him a beloved figure.

Given his advanced age, it was assumed that John XXIII would be, at best, a sanguine caretaker. But he had not been pope more than a few months before he announced his intention to hold a new Vatican Council. It would be an *aggiornamento*, an updating, a new beginning, an invitation to all the bishops and, by implication, all the faithful, to come together to reexamine, reaffirm, and usher the Holy Roman Catholic Church into the modern world. The Church would fling open the windows, bring itself up to date, renew its commitment to the Gospel, and invite leaders of other Christian denominations, their "separated brethren," to attend the sessions, thus widening the road between Rome and the rest of the world.

The way in which the pope decided to announce the council is significant. On January 25, 1959, he invited eighteen cardinals from the Curia, the chief governing organ of the Catholic Church, to accompany him to the Basilica of St. Paul Outside the Walls to be present for an announcement. It was not considered an important occasion and some of the Curia declined. While the pope knelt in prayer, only he knew that the contents of the announcement he was about to make when he got up from his knees had already been released to the media. The Curia had been bypassed.

"What they heard," wrote London reporter Desmond Fisher, "stunned them. The new pope . . . told them he intended to summon an ecumenical council and would they please give him their views about it. . . . They looked at the pope, first in amazement and then in horror."

Pope John remembers that day differently. He claimed that while he had expected the cardinals to clap their hands with approval, there was, instead, "a devout and impressive silence." Later, he embellished the moment further. On the opening day of the Second Vatican Council, he spoke of how the idea came to him and how it was received. "[It] came to us in the first instance in a sudden flash of inspiration." The

Curia's response "was immediate. It was as though some ray of supernatural light had entered the minds of all present. It was reflected in their faces; it shone from their eyes."[5]

In fact, the Curia thought a new Vatican Council was an ill-founded, ill-conceived, and unnecessary idea. Councils mean change. Councils imply that the bishop of Rome wants his brother bishops to be part of the governing process. In the long history of the Catholic Church there had been only one other Vatican Council (1868–70), which had been cut short by the Franco-Prussian War, but not before one important order of business had been taken care of: ratifying the doctrine of papal infallibility. Speaking *ex cathedra* on matters of faith and morals, the pope cannot err. Given this now settled doctrine, the Curia assumed, another Vatican Council was unnecessary.

Not having been consulted beforehand, the Curia tried in every way possible to derail the Council, and when that proved impossible they tried to take control. They were not successful there, either, but as Hans Küng, the young theologian who would one day be stripped of his teaching powers, said in an interview, "The Council was constantly hindered, corrected, and sometimes even obstructed by the Curia."

Nevertheless, it happened. As one Church historian wrote, "Within days it became clear that a majority of the Council was in favor of real reform in the Church."[6] From 1962 through 1965, more than two thousand bishops from around the world descended upon Rome to contemplate what that reform would be. The decisions they made—on the liturgy, ecumenism, and the way in which the Church rechristened "The People of God"—were radical in their intent and consequences.

Latin was to be replaced by the vernacular language of the Mass celebrants. The laity was encouraged to come forward and assume roles of responsibility within the Church itself. Catholics were urged to engage in dialogue with other Christian denominations. And most wide-reaching of all, the Church was to become an instrument of social justice. As historian Giuseppe Alberigo noted, "The statement [by John XXIII] that found the widest and deepest response in public opinion was that the Church must present itself to under-developed countries as what it really is and wants to be: the Church of all, particularly of the poor."[7]

Unfortunately, time moved more swiftly for Pope John XXIII than it did for the Council itself. He died in 1963, less than a year after Vatican II had been convened. But his successor, Paul VI, was a like-minded pontiff, a pastoral pope dedicated to the vision of his predecessor. When Bishop Sullivan paid his first visit to the pontiff as the head of the Richmond diocese, he was profoundly moved by the new pope's fraternal hospitality. Looking him in the eye, the pope extended his hand and said to him, "We are brothers." It was a statement that Sullivan recalls frequently, perhaps to offset other less pleasant memories of the Vatican after Pope Paul died.

With Russell away in Rome for long periods of time between 1962 and 1965, it fell to Sullivan to keep the diocese going. "Priests aren't trained in administration," said Sullivan. "They are trained in the mind of the Church. And you have to be with the mind of the Church. That's obvious. A bishop represents the Church, even if you stand out as bizarre." For the duration of Vatican II, Sullivan was in bishop boot camp. "I practically ran the place," he conceded. He also had a guiding hand in making Richmond one of the first dioceses in the country to update the way the Church related to its priests, its people, and the rest of the world.

In 1963 a commission on ecumenical affairs in Richmond was established. In 1966 a diocesan council of priests was formed. "That was Walter's idea," said Monsignor Bill Pitt, who was vicar general. "The idea was for the priests' council to be an advisory body to the bishop, to provide an opportunity for priests to talk about what was needed in the diocese. And that was only one of the consultative bodies Walter created. Before Vatican II, to have the bishop consult with anybody wasn't done. Nobody consulted."

One of the smaller and more amusing ramifications of Vatican II in the Richmond diocese was brought about when the Council approved cremation for Catholics. This prompted Bishop Russell to reverse one of his own previous regulations, which required Catholics to be buried in a Church-approved cemetery. Neil Doherty, the owner of Calvary Memorial Park Catholic Cemetery in Fairfax, was alarmed and called Russell to ask why he had not been consulted.

"Russell replied that there was no need for discussion," said Doherty. " 'I just made up my mind,' he said." Always one to consider both sides of the issue, Doherty replied, "Well then it seems to me it works both ways. I want to start burying non-Catholics." Russell replied that Doherty's idea made sense.[8] The ecumenical mingling had begun in the graveyard. Could the living be far behind?

Between 1965, when Russell returned from Rome for good, and 1970, Sullivan was elevated five times. In 1965 Russell named him chancellor of the diocese. In 1966 the title of "Monsignor" was added to his name, an honorific that carries no specific duties but is intended to be a mark of approbation, an unofficial sign to Rome that a priest is a candidate for even higher office. In 1967 Sullivan was appointed rector of Sacred Heart Cathedral. At last he was able to have a dog. "Before that, the priests who lived with me said they'd move out if I had one. Finally I got a priest who liked them."

Sullivan hung onto old jobs like old suitcases. When he was named rector, he continued to operate as the chancellor, and when, in 1970, Russell appointed him auxiliary bishop, he tried, for a while, to hold down all three positions. "I collected jobs. I couldn't seem to get rid of any of them," he confessed. But as auxiliary bishop with the power to administer the sacrament of Confirmation, he had to travel constantly around the diocese, and he had to let his old jobs go.

Then in 1973 Bishop Russell decided to retire. Just before Russell made his decision public, Sullivan got a call from the apostolic nuncio, Luigi Raimondi, in Washington, D.C., asking him to come up and see him. Sullivan was on vacation when he called.

"I was sitting on the beach under an umbrella reading a book when Raimondi said he needed to see me. I had to get out my black clothes, hop a plane in Norfolk, and take a cab to the papal legation. When I got there, Raimondi asked me, 'Does Bishop Russell really want to retire?' I said, 'Did you drag me all the way up here to ask me that? You could have used the phone.'" Sullivan confirmed that this was Russell's wish.

"He used to say to me," said Sullivan, "that it isn't fun anymore. In his experience, bishops were on a pedestal and their actions were never questioned. But after Vatican II, things changed. The windows were flung open and bishops were expected to be much more collegial and responsive." By then Russell was an old man and found it difficult to adapt.

Between April 1973, when Russell retired, and July 1974, when he was installed as bishop of the Richmond diocese, Walter Sullivan was the interim bishop, or apostolic administrator. During that same period, Luigi Raimondi retired as apostolic delegate and Archbishop Jean Jadot arrived to take his place. It was a fortuitous change in personnel. Both Jadot and Sullivan were committed to the Vatican II ideals of a pastoral Church, and both would pay a high price for it. Nationally, Jadot later incurred the wrath of the conservative hierarchy and laity. Sullivan would be the target of angry Catholics within the Richmond diocese who kept Rome busy reading their letters of complaint about him. But while Jadot was in Washington, Sullivan had an empathetic ally.

Among the upper echelon of the Catholic elite, Jadot was an unusually spiritual man. A devout, aristocratic Belgian, from a wealthy family whose engineer father tried in vain to persuade him to become a businessman, Jadot was set upon being a priest. His ascent to higher office was fairly swift. After serving as chaplain to troops in the then Belgian Congo, he was ordained a bishop, and was, successively, papal delegate to Thailand, Cameroon, Gabon, and Equatorial Guinea. Then in 1973 Pope Paul VI summoned him to Rome to offer him the Church's most prestigious nuncio post, Washington, D.C.

Jadot knew the offer to go to Washington was coming and had prayed over what he should do. He was not strong physically, and his health had declined in the tropical climate of his last two posts. But two months before Pope Paul asked him to be the apostolic nuncio, Jadot had read a passage from the Gospel of St. John ("It is not you who have chosen me but I have chosen you . . . ") and decided that it was not his place to refuse. In Rome to receive his instructions, Jadot was told by Pope Paul that he had been expressly selected because he was not linked or susceptible to Curia influence.

"Paul VI was very much aware of the fact that previous apostolic delegates had been pawns in the hands of powerful kingmaker American cardinals," wrote Jadot's biographer, John Dick. "Nor did Paul like the fact that most American bishops were, in his opinion, more big businessmen than they were pastors. . . . The new apostolic delegate would have to be a healer and a bridge-builder, someone who could establish 'bonds of affection.' "⁹

Jadot decided to let the American Catholic Church know, obliquely, that he was his own man. New York's powerful Cardinal Cooke had written to say that he would be pleased to greet him when he set foot on New York soil. In his memoir, Jadot recalls, "I wrote Cardinal Cooke to thank him for his kind intentions but told him that since there was a direct flight to Philadelphia, which then went on to Washington, I would take this flight. It would be faster and I would not have to change planes."¹⁰

Cardinal Cooke was furious, but Jadot went on with his plans and was greeted by a large group of important churchmen at Dulles Airport. Walter Sullivan, a tennis-playing friend of Jadot, whom he met during one of his trips to Rome, was one of them.

"Because I was the apostolic administrator of the Virginia diocese I was there when Jadot landed. He gets off the plane and there are all these cardinals and archbishops and he sees me and comes running over. Cardinal Krol [a conservative bishop from Philadelphia, who later sought to have Jadot recalled] was taken aback."

"How do you know him?" Krol asked.

Sullivan smiled. "I get around."

Less than two months later, on July 19, 1974, Walter Sullivan was installed as the eleventh bishop of the Richmond diocese. This time it was Jean Jadot's turn to make the trip to see him.

Sitting in the front row of the cathedral on the morning of July 19 was Bishop Sullivan's younger sister, Betty, who had driven down that morning from Maryland with her husband, Fabian Hughes, and their seven children.

"We only had this one car, and so I made the boys take off their shoes and shirts and we put them along with the girls' good dresses in the trunk of the car so they wouldn't get dirty on the ride down. Then about three blocks away from the cathedral we parked the car, got out, and started getting dressed on the sidewalk. People on their way to the ordination, all dressed up, looked at me handing out shoes and shirts from the back of the car. Then, once everyone was properly dressed, we walked into the cathedral to see him ordained."

Sacred Heart Cathedral was full of well-wishers. Irving Stubbs, a Presbyterian minister and friend of Bishop Sullivan, was one of them and surprised himself by becoming very emotional. In the late 1960s and early 1970s, Stubbs had worked with him in several ecumenical urban housing ministries and been struck by how genuinely humble he was, and how much backing and credibility his presence gave to all their ventures. When Stubbs caught a glimpse of Bishop Sullivan being escorted to the Bishop's Chair, Jadot on one side and Bishop Borders on the other, he was overwhelmed. "When I saw him coming down the aisle I shed tears. Now, I thought, he has even greater opportunities to use his goodness for the glory of God."

Traditionally, after a bishop's installation, the immediate family and the various cardinals, bishops, and dignitaries who were part of the ceremony are asked to an invitation-only formal sit-down dinner at the Hotel John Marshall downtown. But Bishop Sullivan said that he wanted to celebrate with a big picnic of hamburgers and hot dogs across the street from the cathedral in Monroe Park.

"When Walter announced his picnic plans," said Monsignor Pitt, "people said, 'Do you know the kind of people who will come? People who are hungry and there for the food.' And

Walter said, 'Well, isn't that a good thing, to feed people who are hungry?' "

"The people loved it," said his sister Betty. "Everybody piled out of the church into the park and they never saw anything like it."

In his gold and white vestments, ceremonial shepherd's crook in hand, the new bishop of Richmond happily strolled arm in arm with Jadot around Monroe Park, greeting well-wishers. The sun was bright, the air smelled of frankfurters, and before long the cathedral crowd and the denizens of Monroe Park were intermingled. Some of Sullivan's fellow bishops joined them. Others did not.

Chapter Four

Coming into the Kingdom

The ten bishops who preceded Walter Sullivan to the Bishop's Chair were not equal in stature. Some collapsed, others forged ahead, a few treated the post as a sinecure. But the Diocese of Richmond itself was jump-started by a rebellion.

In 1794, nine years after Jefferson's Act for Religious Freedom, newly liberated Catholic worshipers in Norfolk, Virginia, revolted against their pastor, claiming that they had the right to decide who their pastor should be. This so alarmed the Vatican that it decided to ensconce a residential bishop "to suppress the 'Norfolk Schism,'" although Rome did not exactly rush to the scene.

It wasn't until 1821 that forty-year-old Father Patrick Kelly, a former seminary president from County Kilkenney, Ireland, was sent to Norfolk to assume the post. But the Catholic population was so sparse and spread out and their financial condition so poor that Kelly was forced to operate a school to pay for his own keep. In 1822, he threw up his hands and went back to Ireland. In the words of one nineteenth-century Church historian, "The field seemed not ready for cultivation."[11]

After that false start, Richmond remained for twenty years under the aegis of the Baltimore diocese, which was the power center of the Catholic Church in America. Then in 1841 Pope Gregory XVI restored the Richmond diocese, and Father Richard Whelan from Baltimore became the second bishop of Richmond. When he arrived there were only six priests in the entire state. He called upon the Society for the Propagation of the Faith in Europe to send more priests, was instrumental in starting a seminary college, and eventually requested Rome to create a new diocese in West Virginia.

In 1850, Whelan left Richmond to become the bishop of Wheeling, West Virginia, and Bishop John McGill replaced him. McGill's service was long (over twenty-two years) and difficult: cholera and yellow fever epidemics, the Civil War (McGill was a Confederate supporter), and the rise of the virulently anti-Catholic Know-Nothing Party.

This line of relatively undistinguished prelates was broken by the fourth bishop of Richmond, who was destined to become a prince of the Church. James Cardinal Gibbons was only thirty-four (he was jokingly referred to as "the boy bishop") when he was consecrated in 1861. His six years in Richmond (1872–78) were not notable. But when he died he was arguably the best-known Catholic in America. After leaving Richmond, he was named coadjutor archbishop of Baltimore, and in 1886 he became the second American to attain the rank of cardinal.

Gibbons helped found Catholic University, championed the unions, was a staunch believer in the separation of church and state, and was the author of a widely read apologetical book on Catholicism, *The Faith of Our Fathers*.[12] He was known for his wide, ecumenical circle of friends, which included U.S. presidents, who sought his counsel. Theodore Roosevelt called him the "the most venerated, respected, and useful citizen in America,"[13] and even the notoriously anticlerical writer H. L. Mencken approved of him. When Gibbons died in 1921, Mencken wrote, "There is no record that he ever led the Church into a bog or up a blind alley. He had Rome against him often, but he always won in the end, for he was always right."

Following Gibbons in 1878 was Bishop John J. Keene, who, despite opposition, brought the Josephite Fathers to the diocese to serve the black community, and became the first president of Catholic University. In 1888 he was succeeded by Bishop Augustine Van de Vyver, a Belgian who was distinguished for founding a dozen new parishes and overseeing the construction of the Cathedral of the Sacred Heart in Richmond.

The seventh bishop of Richmond was Denis O'Connell, who came to Richmond in 1912. About his life there does not seem to be much of a record. "He was a priest for over 49 years and a bishop for over 18," said one reference source. O'Connell finally resigned, for reasons of ill health, in 1926. The eighth bishop of Richmond, Andrew J. Brennan, has a similarly accomplishment-free record, perhaps due to a series of strokes in the 1930s that incapacitated him until his retirement in 1935.

The ninth bishop of Richmond was Peter Ireton, who ran the diocese as interim and then diocesan bishop from 1935 until his death twenty-two years later. During his tenure, the diocese expanded greatly, both in population and parishes, which may not be due to Ireton (who suffered from undisclosed mental deficiencies) but to Monsignor Justin McClunn, his chancellor. "Whenever McClunn wanted to do something," according to Monsignor Pitt, he would say, "It is the mind of the bishop," to which somebody once replied, "The bishop has no mind."

When Ireton died in 1958, he was succeeded by Walter Sullivan's mentor, Bishop John Joyce Russell, who, along with his then auxiliary bishop, Walter Sullivan, successfully guided the Richmond diocese through the momentous period of change brought on by the Second Vatican Council.

Two facts of record distinguish Bishop Sullivan's tenure from the others: he remained in office longer than any other bishop to date, and he was the only bishop who did not come from another diocese to take the job. By the time he was done, he had redefined it. But two weeks after he took office, it was the diocese itself that was redefined.

The same day that Pope Paul VI announced that Bishop Sullivan would be the eleventh bishop of Richmond he also announced that the boundaries of the Richmond diocese were going to be redrawn. A new bishop would be named for a new Diocese of Arlington. According to Monsignor William Pitt, who served Sullivan as his chancellor, the impetus for the split came from the priests in the northern part of the diocese, led by the same Monsignor McClunn who had been transferred to northern Virginia by Bishop Russell. "They didn't like Russell and they didn't like Walter and they wanted to be free of them."

Bishop Sullivan corroborates Pitt's version. "There was a restlessness up there among the priests who felt they were stuck with Richmond, even though everything they were involved in was directed toward Washington. Some of them were mouthing off. I met with them and told them I felt certain the diocesan split was going to happen, but they had to pipe down. I didn't want the diocese to look like bedlam to the apostolic delegate, who was just across the Potomac."

Monsignor Justin McClunn was in the meeting. "He asked by what authority was I speaking to them. What were my faculties?" Sullivan had anticipated that power play and had his response in his hip pocket.

After Russell retired, Sullivan was made the interim bishop and apostolic administrator/residential bishop. The latter office carried more weight. "All the interim bishop can do is hold the fort down," explained Sullivan, "but a residential bishop is fully empowered to do whatever he wants. I had never spelled out to the priests what kind of powers I held, but when McClunn challenged me I was prepared."

" 'Well,' I said, 'now that you've asked me' . . . and I took out the orders I had been given from Rome and read them aloud. When I was done reading I said that if anybody opens their mouth publicly from this moment on I will transfer them to southern Virginia. All was quiet on the Western front after that."

The decision to break the diocese in two very unequal halves was akin to splitting up a family, with most of the rich relatives living on one side of town and the poor relatives on the other. The new, smaller Arlington diocese, known as "the Gold Coast," contained 136,000 Catholics in the wealthiest, most densely populated part of the state. The Diocese of Richmond's population dropped from 250,000 to 113,000, while acquiring most of the eastern shore, which had a very poor, very small Catholic population with a lot of migrants, and part of western Virginia, including Appalachia. The scenery was better but the economic floor was worse.

"By dividing up the diocese," said Bishop Sullivan, "we became a much more impoverished one. We were four times the size, seventy-four counties as opposed to twenty-one, but Arlington had two-thirds of the money. I received a letter from Rome telling me that I had to divide the money equally. I was mad as hops. We had various trusts and a large permanent bequest for six million dollars that was primarily for St. Mary's Hospital in Richmond. I went over to Rome to argue that these funds shouldn't be divided."

Bishop Sullivan had an appointment in Rome with the highest-ranking American in the Curia, Cardinal John Wright, the Vatican prefect for the Congregation for the Clergy. But Sullivan never saw him because Wright delegated a Spanish monsignor, who didn't speak English, to meet with him instead.

"I'll never forget that meeting. He didn't speak English. I didn't speak Spanish. What do you do if you don't know the language? You shout. I was shouting, he was shouting, and finally he threw up his hands and told me to go home and settle it. So I returned to Virginia and the bishop of Arlington [Thomas Welsh] and I got a mediator to help. Everything flunked out during our first session. People were saying we might as well give up. But I argued for that bequest tooth and nail and asked for a second session. Welsh was kind of propped up by some of the 'Let's don't help Sullivan' priests in the diocese. But at the second session, darned if Welsh didn't finally say, 'Oh, go ahead and keep it.' "

Marilyn Lewis was the bishop's secretary at that time. "The bishop was excellent with money," she said. "But Rome had to approve the arrangements. Canon lawyers were involved. It was a tug of war between Arlington and Richmond for some time. But now most of the people who were involved in the fight have either died or moved on and the tension is gone."

Once the split was a fait accompli, all that remained to be sorted out were the priests themselves, who could go to their bishop and tell him in which diocese they wanted to be.

"It was kind of a slave trade between bishops, but it wasn't formally announced," said Pitt. "And sometimes, it was a happy request, from the bishop's point of view. Father Tom Quinlan [whose legendary frankness and flamboyance got on some parishioners' nerves] said that when he asked the bishop of Arlington if he could transfer to Richmond the audience lasted ten seconds."

Monsignor William Carr, the current pastor of St. Bridget Catholic Church in Richmond, was tempted to go the other way. "I thought about it because my family lived in Arlington, and I grew up there. But I was a very young priest and somehow I knew that Walter Sullivan's vision would be exciting and inclusive. So I opted to stay in Richmond, and I have never looked back."

The Bishop's Men

Bishop Sullivan was at the center of many circles, and he moved easily back and forth between them. But within the diocese, the priests who became part of his inner support system, the knights at his round table, were attracted to the Diocese of Richmond for one of two reasons: they had heard there was a dynamic young bishop there whose Vatican II ideas coincided with their own, or they didn't like the political climate of another diocese where, as seminarians, they had trained for the priesthood.

"Walter has a knack for gathering people," said Monsignor William Pitt, now seventy-six, who was one of the first priests in the diocese to be recruited by the bishop to help him run it. Wry, soft-spoken, and astute, he is a natural storyteller with a prodigiously accurate memory. Like the bishop, he loves the Church. Unlike the bishop, he is candid about what that love does not include.

Born in Portsmouth, Virginia, Pitt was educated at St. Charles and St. Mary's in Baltimore, before going on to get a master's in Greek and Latin at Catholic University, picking up Education credits at the University of Richmond. For most of his priesthood he has been an educator, retiring in 2005 as principal of Norfolk Catholic High School, where a scholarship has been established in his honor.

"When Walter became auxiliary bishop in 1971 the times were full of life and hope," said Pitt, who was teaching Latin at St. John Vianney Seminary in Goochland when he met Sullivan. Pitt was a popular teacher who encouraged his students to make connections beyond the page. "We'd be studying the Gallic Wars and I would say, 'See the pattern? Caesar inflates all the numbers, the same thing that is going on in Vietnam.'"

In the 1970s, those kinds of subversive analogies, in a seminary that was already a lightning rod in the diocese for being too liberal and too liturgically innovative, made the head of the seminary uncomfortable. While retaining his teaching workload, Pitt was physically moved out of the seminary. "Bishop Russell told me I needed more *pastoral* experience," Pitt said sarcastically. Ironically, he was sent to a parish that had no pastor.

"The pastor had been sent away to an alcoholic rehab. I didn't know this until I arrived. I called [the auxiliary bishop] and said, 'I thought you'd like to know that the pastor is not here.' All he said to me was, 'Keep the home fires burning.' It was a huge parish and I had been ordained for only two years."

Between 1973 and 1985, Pitt came to work for Bishop Sullivan as the chancellor and then vicar general of the diocese. "As chancellor I was the CEO of the diocese. I did a lot of work in my car putting out fires in various parishes. Most of the problems revolved around people not liking their priest. But as vicar general I represented the bishop on anything and everything. I used to say, jokingly, that he kept me on in the job so long because he was too proud to admit he'd made a mistake."

When Pitt left the chancery and returned to his teaching career, he remained a good friend of the bishop, one of the "Sullivanistas," as they call themselves, who frequently saw Sullivan when he vacationed at his beach house in Sandbridge.

The bishop has asked him to speak at his funeral. Pitt has a story in his hip pocket.

"We took a trip a few years ago to Lucerne, Switzerland, where we went up to the top of Mount Pilatus, which involved taking a couple of finiculas to get there. When we arrived at the summit it was snowing a bit with ice on the ground, which made it slippery. The view was exciting, but Walter insisted on going to the edge of the summit, which was surrounded only by a small guard rail to see how far he could see in any direction. He seemed oblivious to the danger, and when I cautioned him to be careful, he said, 'But we won't be able to see if we don't get close to the edge.'"

"That's the way he is about life. And that was always a potential problem with people and with the Church. It was challenging for those of us who were on the journey with him. But Walter had a vision, and he thought he was taking enough care that nothing would happen. It seems like a metaphor for his life."

Father Tom Quinlan was Bishop Sullivan's brilliant problem priest, whom Sullivan defended until the day of his death, which fortunately did not occur until Quinlan had been interviewed several times for purposes of this biography. At the end of his life, he was a skeletal reflection of who he had been, a tall, naturally gaunt man, with a wide smile, a manic laugh, and a pair of eyes, neither of which worked. ("I can't see. What are you going to do?") Quinlan's mind made up for them.

Born in Springfield, Massachusetts, he went two years to Holy Cross College, and then order-hopped between the Passionists, the Trappists, and finally the priests of La Salette. He left them, too, because he didn't believe in the "fake vision," as he called it, where Our Lady allegedly appeared before two shepherd children in France. "In Portugal [where Our Lady of Fatima appeared] there's a book that claims that the kids went to the movies and that's where they got their ideas."

Originally, Quinlan had wanted to be a priest-missionary in Burma, but eventually he wound up following two other former La Salette priests to the Richmond diocese, where he was ordained in 1958. "The bishop [Ireton] who was to ordain me died the Monday before the ceremony. All my white-trash relatives were already in town. The legend grew that he died because he didn't want to ordain me. He was the best bishop I never knew. Ha!"

After ordination Quinlan started calling his mother by her first name. " 'Marie,' I said. 'I'm a priest. I'm important.' And she would laugh her ass off. I was the oldest of ten children. I've buried four. It's so sad."

Quinlan rattles off his spiritual provenance. "My greatest single influences were Søren Kierkegaard and St. Benedict Joseph Labre. He never did any work. I was a workaholic—and an alcoholic, for thirty years, but I never missed Mass. Walter sent me to five 'finishing schools.' He got hundreds of letters about me but he was a wonderful bishop. I wouldn't have survived in any diocese but this one."

His first assignment in 1970 was to Good Shepherd Church in Arlington. "It was a big northern Virginia church that was full of people in the military or lawyers. Once you convert the middle class," he said, "you have it made." It was there, on Palm Sunday, that Quinlan came up with the idea of reenacting Jesus' triumphal procession on a donkey through Jerusalem by driving a Volkswagen bug—the 1970 donkey equivalent— up the main aisle of the church. Phones were ringing in the bishop's office before nightfall. The bishop defended him.

Later, when he was pastor of St. Mary's, a black church in Norfolk that Bishop Sullivan reconsecrated as a basilica, Quinlan led the congregation through the reenactment of the trial of Nat Turner, who led a slave rebellion in the 1800s, on Good Friday. Again, phones rang and letters were sent to Rome. Again, the bishop was his advocate, not without reason. Beneath the flamboyance and the banter was an original thinker, a scripture scholar, and a controversial but immensely popular pastor whose Golden Jubilee celebration was attended by so many that they had to hold it in a tent.

"Quinlan was a hard worker. I watched him work his butt off," said The Reverend Mike Schmeid, who served under him when he was a deacon, "but he never stopped talking at a level that was both profound and profane. He had people read and think, and nobody, not even the bishop, was off the hook with him."

He was quoted by *Time* magazine as calling his parishioners "spiritual white trash who merely drop by church to fill up at God's gas pump" and once commented that people came out of church with the blank expression of someone coming out of a rest room. But Quinlan was a radical Christian, along the lines of St. Francis of Assisi, who loved the Church—for what it could be. "To me it's all real. If the Church would change it could change the world."

"We don't know how to wrestle with evil," he contends. "Original sin and the devil are disguises. People say, 'The devil made me do it.' 'No,' I say, 'You did it.' Getting rid of Original Sin would give me a positive outlook on my own sexuality."

About the current sexual abuse crisis he admits that he had been unaware of it. "I had no inkling, and yet it was my age group that's mostly guilty." But the cover-up, he believes, is shameful. "People know what's going on. The Church is lying to them. It's a power game of white males."

On Quinlan's bedroom wall is a poster, created to celebrate his fiftieth anniversary as a priest. There are lots of Pho-
toshopped young people in St. Peter's Square holding signs,
like "Kill Clericalism," "Chuck Celibacy," "Mary Never Left
Heaven," and "The Pope Is the Vicar of Peter."

The Vicar of Peter? "Yes, it's a clerical error to call him 'The
Holy Father.' To be a father implies children. I tell people to
stop calling me 'father.' I'm not your father. The Second Vatican Council articulated that paternalism."

Quinlan praised Bishop Sullivan for being a good cele-
brant of the liturgy. "You can't rattle off the prayers. The Mass
is a straight-on dialogue." He admires the way he mingles with
the people. "Sully hated the crozier and the miter. He was not
clerically aloof. He was not a good scriptural preacher. But he
got better, especially at Confirmations. Recently we went to a
funeral for a priest where Walter preached the homily, and I
told him later, 'You're a terrible preacher but at least you didn't
preach about his goddamn assignments.' That's what preach-
ers who don't have anything to say do."

Reflecting upon his long friendship with the bishop, Quinlan admits that it took a lot for the bishop to maintain his end,
sending Quinlan to all those alcohol rehab centers, dealing with
all those letters of complaint to Rome, writing on Quinlan's
behalf to the papal nuncio in Washington. But he knew he was
of value to Sullivan, that their friendship meant something.

"Walter is a year older than I am and our relationship is
very unusual. He is very diplomatic and really quite gen-
teel. Now that we're both retired we have become very good
friends. But I was a burden around his neck. Me and his dogs.
We were his kids."

In 2005 Quinlan retired, but was permitted to say Mass
when needed in the Virginia Beach area where he lived.

Shortly thereafter, he sealed his fate by referring in a Christmas Eve homily to the Virgin Mary's birth canal. Actually, he used the word "vagina." He defended the reference by saying he wanted to emphasize Jesus' humanity. But the damage had been done.

Parishioners who had complained before of Quinlan's outrageous remarks complained again. Bishop DiLorenzo responded by issuing a statement saying that Quinlan was forbidden to say Mass publicly because he had "engendered anxiety and emotional upset which interferes with an individual's religious experience." It was a blow from which Quinlan, who wrote a letter to Bishop DiLorenzo begging him to reconsider, did not recover. After suffering a fall, his health began to fail.

In the last months of his life, Quinlan was confined to his bed. He was surrounded, more or less continually, by his close friends, including Bill Pitt, who visited him at least once a day. He called himself spoiled. "Oh, yeah, so many people love me. I say don't tell me that. You just love people. How can you not?"

Father Tom Quinlan died on April 24, 2012. His defender, Walter Sullivan, delivered the eulogy at the Church of the Holy Family in Virginia Beach. All of Quinlan's remaining "white-trash relatives" were in attendance. As expected, the church was packed. So many people loved him. How could they not?

Father Pasquale (Pat) Apuzzo came to Richmond from the Archdiocese of Hartford (Connecticut). He almost didn't get in because of his connection with Tom Quinlan. "When I was in school at Catholic University I went to Good Shepherd Church in Arlington to help TQ. He asked me to get a youth ministry program going and I wound up taking a leave of absence from CU and staying on for a year and a half. That's how I got to know the people in Richmond. Bishop Sullivan was still the auxiliary bishop, and the diocese had not yet been split in two."

When it came time for him to choose a diocese, he asked to be transferred out of the Archdiocese of Hartford and be incardinated into Richmond. To do this, Apuzzo had to go to Richmond, only the second time he had been there, and appear before an admissions board. His association at Good Shepherd and Tom Quinlan played against him. "You've heard the story of the Volkswagen going up the aisle on Palm Sunday?" he asked. "I drove it."

"It wasn't an easy interview," said Apuzzo, "because of having worked with TQ [Quinlan]. Most of the questions were about Tom, not me. In the end, they rejected my application. I said I don't accept that. You weren't interviewing me, you were asking questions about Quinlan. I'm going to appeal."

"That was a new idea. I was told there had never been an appeal of their decision." A few weeks later, Apuzzo got a call from the vocational director telling him that he didn't have to go through the appeals process.

"I thought that meant that there was no hope. But instead they said that Bishop Sullivan had overridden the decision of the panel. I said, 'Who is Bishop Sullivan?' That's how much I knew about anything. I was told that the bishop had instructed the vocational director to disregard the admissions board and to let me know that I was welcome in his diocese, and he emphasized the word 'his.' "

Apuzzo's first parish assignment was cancelled before he got there. "The phone rang and somebody said that Bishop Sullivan wanted me to be his secretary. He probably saw trouble and wanted to keep me nearby. So now I'm reporting for work at the cathedral where two of the four priests who had recommended my rejection were the rector of the cathedral and the chancellor of the diocese!

"To be the bishop's secretary was to be his driver and master of ceremonies, pure and simple," he said. Apuzzo drove Sullivan all over the state, with the bishop using his car like a mobile office, dictating letters into a tape recorder, sorting through the mail, and, occasionally, looking up to pick Apuzzo's brain on a particular issue.

For fifteen years Apuzzo was by the bishop's side. He accompanied him on his prison visits, drove him to parish meetings, helped him with his speeches, and watched the way he used his office to bring attention to the issues he thought important. It was a prime spot for a young priest to learn, on a day-by-day basis, who Walter Sullivan was and what being the bishop of Richmond entailed.

"Critics of the bishop accused him of playing to the crowd," said Apuzzo, "of doing things like going into the prisons just for the effect. And it is true that the bishop had a great understanding of the power of symbols, and he used them to get across a message. He got things to change that way. For example, those who took issue with our peacemaking stand painted the Church as unpatriotic. The bishop would counter that by putting a bumper sticker of an American flag on his car. He'd say, 'We have to take back our symbols before the fanatics ruin them.'"

Frequently, the bishop was invited to officiate at a parish event of some kind. "When he got there," Apuzzo said, "the pastor or liturgical director would hand him a script of what was going to happen. In those days, the music was oftentimes a separate show, just for itself instead of supporting the particular event, like a Confirmation service. The bishop would take a look at the order of the program and say, 'No, we're not doing that.' And he would change everything around the way he wanted it. And the way he wanted it was the way it should have been in the first place."

Once Apuzzo asked the bishop, "If the liturgy is so bad when they know you're coming to a parish, what must it be like when you're *not* coming?" The bishop thought that was a good question. "The next thing I knew I was made the director of worship."

"When Sullivan was ordained the climate for him was difficult," said Apuzzo. "He was a priest from the diocese, not somebody brought in from another part of the country. What I saw from the inside was how he had to deal with other priests who might have been jealous that he was elevated, and they were not—a who-do-you-think-you-are kind of attitude. It may explain why he was reluctant to name some priests monsignor, thinking that if he elevated one priest it might do something to the others who weren't elevated."

Now the pastor at St. Gabriel's Church in Chesterfield, Virginia, Apuzzo sees the bishop regularly for dinner, either in Richmond or at Sullivan's beach house in Sandbridge. Like all of Sullivan's friends, he treats him tenderly, with a combination of affection and respect in perfect balance. When asked for personal anecdotes he shakes his head. "I don't have any grand visionary stories about him. We've known each other for so long that it's not that kind of a relationship. What he is is an amazing bishop because he is a non-amazing person, without any pretense at all."

Monsignor Robert Perkins comes from a blue-collar family on the south side of Chicago. He cherishes his background and attended the Benedictine order's St. Procopious College in Lisle, Illinois, where he majored in history and pre-law. Then in his senior year, 1967, he decided to enter the seminary.

"A couple of experiences with some happy, fulfilled priests, the personal witness of their lives," were what spurred him to do it. He chose the Joliet diocese in which to be ordained. "I didn't want to get stuck in an old-timey Chicago parish." But in hindsight, he thinks this wasn't the best decision. He was not in tune with the bishop of Joliet. "If you bracket a mentality, i.e., where change is going to happen or not, the Joliet diocese wasn't the place."

Perkins was not exactly a finished product when he chose the seminary he wanted to attend. Given a choice of six, he picked the one where he could play ice hockey: Denver. "Instead, they sent me to St. Mary's in Baltimore, which wasn't even on the list. But I managed to play hockey anyway. I just hid my equipment and snuck out."

He did so well at St. Mary's that they asked him to stay on as a member of the faculty. He stayed there for two years as the pastoral education director. In 1971 he was ordained. Two years later, he returned to Joliet. But his aversion to the bishop of Joliet was so intense that after five years he knew he had to make a decision. "Either I look for a new bishop or leave the priesthood." Perkins came to the Richmond diocese because of two factors: Walter Sullivan was bishop, and he knew two priests ahead of him at St. Mary's who were already there.

"There were so many aspects of Walter's time as bishop that were huge: his creation of housing for the elderly, his outreach to the Jews, his ecumenical connections, his opposition to the death penalty, his commitment to peace and justice. At a conscious and innate level, Walter Sullivan was a Vatican II spirit." Perkins considers himself part of that same tradition, although he speculates that the reason the two of them worked so well together was because they were temperamentally very different.

"On the Myers-Briggs scale, we were complete opposites. Walter is a high-thinking extrovert. He has feelings, but he doesn't do the touchy-feely thing. He's more Dutch than Irish in this regard. He processes his thoughts by going outside of himself to others. I am a high-feeling introvert. I process them from within."

Perkins worked on and off for Walter Sullivan from the time he arrived in 1980, becoming vicar for the clergy in 1995, when the previous vicar left the clergy. During those years, the bishop had to broker the disconnects between Rome and various priests who had been emboldened by Vatican II to speak out on issues that had never been addressed by the clergy—like peace, celibacy, and women's ordination. Perkins was actively involved in helping Sullivan deal with the papal investigation that came in the early 1980s, and when multiple sexual abuse accusations surfaced in the early 1990s, he worked alongside Pat Apuzzo to help the bishop meet them.

Now the pastor of Immaculate Conception parish in Hampton, Virginia, Perkins is clear as to why he continues to wear the Roman collar. "I wouldn't be a priest if it weren't for the open heart that Walter Sullivan had for the priesthood and for this diocese." For a "high-feeling introvert" that is saying a great deal.

Jim Griffin was ordained in 1982. "I was a kid who loved the Church. My memories are of riding my bicycle to the church and getting $5 for being an altar boy on Sunday. I thought it would be wonderful to be a priest." His first assignment after ordination was to be Bishop Sullivan's driver. "I took Pat Apuzzo's place when he left."

Griffin was a Vatican II priest attracted to the social ministry that was promulgated by the Council. "Pope Paul VI said give me some pastoral bishops. You don't become bishop unless you have certain traits that allow you to climb up through the ranks, but Walter never lost his ability to relate to people. His personality was one that accepted other faiths, accepted women, empowered the laity. For the first time in my life I had a hero to believe in, who spoke the truth."

"Walter loved being bishop. It's fun being bishop. You know the gossip, who's up, who's not, all the politics. But to be a good bishop you have to act as if you care about the diocese. You must be seen among the laity. And you must be a good liturgist, both traditional but trusting in the *aggiornamento*, which means 'always new.' And you also have to be honest. He was not bishop for himself. It was because of Christ."

A few years back, Griffin was in Haiti with some college students, up late one night and "feeling a little fire under me." One of the students asked him a question. "Father, I know what you believe, but is it real, or is it like Greek mythology?" "I remember it vividly," said Griffin. "I said to them that faith was like the story of the poor orphan kid pitching pennies in Philadelphia. A priest took him in, fed him, washed him up, and then released him back onto the streets. The other kids made fun of him, saying, 'Oh, that priest just used you and then threw you out.' But all I know is that I'm going to live my life as if my faith is true. I have seen power—sometimes power for the bad—and miracles. And perhaps the most heart-rending moment is when an inmate on death row who is going to die goes to confession. The only way you know that could happen is if there is a Christ. You have to believe, first of all, that He is the savior of the world."

Clearly, Griffin loves being a priest. But he just as clearly admits to the loneliness that is part of a priest's vocation. "In this life," he said, "when you get bitched at you go home and you're by yourself. Or you are loved, and you go home and you're by yourself. Either way, there's no one to share the good or the bad."

At the end of the day, the priest returns to his own version of solitary confinement, which may be why Griffin was drawn to prison ministry. As a young priest driving Bishop Sullivan around the diocese, he was exposed to the inmates on death row, which was part of the bishop's congregation. For many years, Griffin made it his business to visit death row inmates, including being there with them when they were put to death. "It's my niche ministry," he said. "Otherwise, you're just an administrator, pumping hands."

Griffin is currently the pastor of St. Mark's Catholic Church in Virginia Beach. It is a medium-sized parish, with over fourteen hundred registered families. The minutes of the parish council reflect the questions and concerns of a large community: new chairs are needed for the Great Hall, new ways are needed to get people to read the parish bulletin, there is a Taizé prayer group meeting, an upcoming mission trip to Haiti. As Griffin ushers a visitor into his office, he waves to some women in the parish kitchen who are making hot suppers for the homeless.

The priests closest to Bishop Sullivan all seem to be highly articulate communicators. But Griffin is perhaps the most poignant and open-hearted. Now that Bishop Sullivan has retired, he lacks a mentor with whom he can be as candid. "As a priest," Griffin admits, "there is presently no place in the institutional Church to go where you can tell someone who you are."

Chapter Five

The Least among Us

Less than a month before Walter Sullivan was installed as bishop of the Richmond diocese, he wrote a letter to the editor of the *Richmond News Leader.*

> To the Editor
> *Richmond News Leader*
> 333 East Grace Street
> Richmond, Virginia
>
> As of this date (June 13, 1974) I have no editorial to respond to. In fact, both of our papers have been strangely silent over Governor Godwin's recent appointment of Mr. Jack Davis as the Director of Corrections.
>
> I was both astounded and dismayed over the insensitivity of Governor Godwin to the needs of Virginia. I have nothing against Mr. Davis as a person. He himself admits his own lack of qualifications for the position.
>
> Who suffers from this appointment—the people in our communities who beg for an end to violence on our streets—the members of the State legislature who saw the need to overhaul an antiquated and unjust penal system—prisoners themselves who have a right to rehabilitation rather than become dehumanized in the correctional process.
>
> The Virginia penal system is a learning haven for crime and violence. By no accident our prisoners have

a high rate of recidivism. As a State we have propor-
tionately more citizens behind bars than any other
State in the country. Governor Godwin then proceeds
to appoint a corrections board from former members
of the assembly and other friends of the system. Such
action smacks of cronyism in its worst form. Why must
politics continue to stand in the way of the needs of
people? Have we learned nothing from the tragic reve-
lations of Watergate?

> (signed)
> Walter F. Sullivan
> Bishop
> Diocese of Richmond

The bishop knew what he was doing. In the racially and economically segregated town of Richmond, Virginia, the *News
Leader* was the archconservative voice of the establishment.
Its views consistently ran counter to advocates of prison
reform and the abolition of the death penalty, both of which
were deeply held commitments with Sullivan. By expressing mock surprise that the editorial page did not take exception to Governor Godwin's choice to run the penal system, he
obliquely drew attention to the governor's attitude toward the
prisons themselves.

Bishop Sullivan's relationship with Governor Godwin
began two years before the infamous Jack Davis appointment.
In 1972 the Supreme Court ruled that the death penalty was
unconstitutional, "as practiced at that time." All the states were
invited to reexamine the practice. Sullivan was part of a group
of laymen, ministers, and rabbis who met informally once a
month to discuss how to influence the General Assembly on
issues like prison reform and capital punishment.

"I remember one snowy night three of us went down to the Assembly to speak against capital punishment and because of our witness I believe the committee voted not to reinstate it. That's when Governor Godwin got involved."

In 1973 Governor Godwin created a legislative study committee that would report back to him with their conclusions. Bishop Sullivan was one of the members. "There were twenty-four people on the committee," he said. "Sixteen were Commonwealth attorneys or lawyers from various firms around the Commonwealth, and then a small handful of do-gooders."

In the first meeting, it was immediately proposed that a vote be taken. Sixteen voted for reinstatement of the death penalty and eight were opposed. Sullivan was shocked and raised his hand to say so. "I thought we were supposed to be studying the issue, not voting upon it." The committee backtracked, withdrew their vote, and for an entire year it met together every month to discuss the issue.

"The big question," said Sullivan, "was, did capital punishment deter crime? For all who were in favor of reinstatement, that was their underlying belief, that it did. The committee brought in psychiatrists and other experts who said that it did not deter crime. At the end of the year when we took another vote. Sixteen voted against reinstating capital punishment and eight voted in favor."

The committee then presented its majority and minority report to the governor, who chose the minority report. "I was hopping mad," said the bishop. "Mills Godwin had the General Assembly reinstate capital punishment! It was all political."

Shortly thereafter, Godwin appointed Davis, a former aide and ex-newspaperman, to run the Department of Corrections. Bishop Sullivan made a copy of his letter to the *Richmond News Leader* and sent it to his sister and brother-in-law.

Scribbled in pen across the top he wrote, "Betty—Fabe—I am back on the attack against the Richmond establishment. Will explain. Wally."

The *Richmond News Leader* ignored Sullivan's letter. But the bishop had taken the precaution of sending copies to other smaller newspapers around the state, and they did not ignore it. Most people had never heard of Bishop Walter Sullivan but now they were asking who he was. Godwin finally responded. Citing the inclusion of an Episcopal bishop on the corrections board, which should "take care of the concerns voiced by Bishop Sullivan," he added condescendingly, "I would think that the good bishop would wait until he could observe the performance of the new director of corrections and the Board of Corrections before he voices such criticism."

The clergy rushed to Sullivan's defense.

Future Episcopal bishop Jack Spong, then the rector of St. Paul's Episcopal Church in Richmond, wrote an open letter to Bishop Sullivan. "I particularly regret that he chose to suggest that the Episcopal bishop he had appointed to the board might be able to enlighten you. Be assured that this tactic of playing one religious group against another is doomed to failure in this ecumenical age."

Father James Groppi, a prominent Catholic civil rights leader, sent words of support that clearly mirrored his own struggles. "I know that you will receive enough negative reaction. The fight for social change can be a very lonely one. It is encouraging for me as a priest to see a bishop taking the lead to end some unnecessary and very painful human suffering."

Advocates of prison reform came forward as well: "I share wholeheartedly the belief that the Church . . . must speak out clearly and forcefully about the inhumane and unjust conditions that continue to characterize our 'correctional systems,' " wrote Kay Harris from the American Bar's Commission on Correctional Facilities & Services.

In a move to put Bishop Sullivan back where he belonged, the new director of corrections, Jack Davis, piled on by saying, "I have no comment to make about it, but if the Catholic diocese wants to help us, we need twelve color television sets in the penitentiary."

That was all Sullivan needed to act. He promptly wrote an open letter to Godwin saying how wholeheartedly he concurred with the governor's desire for "positive action rather than negative criticism for any realistic reform of the prison system."

"I am confident," he continued, "that the purchase of television sets is not considered as the important priority in the reform of the prison system. At the same time, I am sure that every improvement, no matter how insignificant, is most welcome, particularly to the prisoners." Attached to his letter was a check for $2,000, which the bishop took from a small trust fund given to him by his aunt.

"That went out like a rocket," said Sullivan. "The Catholic Church went from being a non-entity in the community to all of a sudden being thrust in the limelight. Then, when the TVs got delivered, the controversy erupted again. When people asked me what I was doing, I said that I was just following the suggestion of the head of corrections."

There were a few grumblers. The gift of the TVs prompted some inmates in the women's prison to ask for washing machines. The *Catholic Virginian* heard from one disgruntled Catholic woman who said that she was a struggling Catholic mother with three children, and she wished that the diocese would give her a color TV, too. But all in all it was a public relations coup.

"Va. Prison Reform Dispute Score: Bishop, 2, Governor, 0," trumpeted the *Tablet*, a diocesan newspaper from Brooklyn, N.Y. "Bishop of Richmond takes a Stand on 'Life Issues,'" ran the headline in a *Washington Post* article. But the small *Clarkesville Times* in Virginia drew the broadest conclusions:

"Both Godwin and Davis are, unfortunately, under the impression that religious figures have no place in a discussion of corrections.... This is the legacy of our religious institutions, which speak in broad moral terms each Sunday and then close their eyes to specific immorality, whether it be prejudice, neglect of our elderly citizens, or the destruction of those we consign to prisons."

Before the dust settled, the bishop received a letter from Jack Davis saying how much he appreciated his interest in "the state's correctional situation." Later Davis had to smile for the camera when the bishop came down to the Spring Street prison to present the television sets to the prisoners. It was, however, only one battle in an ongoing war.

In 1976 the Supreme Court reinstated the death penalty. On February 14, 1977 (Valentine's Day), Governor Godwin signed the bill that reinstated its use in Virginia. Since that time, 109 people have been executed, most by lethal injection.

When Bishop Sullivan first began speaking out against the death penalty, it was a surprise to him to realize that Catholic people were more in favor of it than anybody else. "They were very upset with me," he said. "They wrote to the governor saying that at least they had the choice of voting for him. They had no choice with me."

The bishop made two piles of letters. The largest stack was from Catholics who supported the death penalty. The other pile was from the ecumenical community that supported him. The bishop was out of tune with his own people.

"One of the things I realized is that we had Catholics in positions of political power in the Commonwealth, but they had sort of submerged their faith in the public arena. I remember when the former mayor of Richmond, Phil Bagley, who was a Catholic, came to see me. He shut the door of my office and said to me, 'You are a disgrace to the Catholic Church!' I asked him why, and he said, 'You are embarrassing us. Everybody's talking about us.' So we were in a conversation that was not a very happy one, and then he said, 'You should be more like Monsignor Ryan.' " (Monsignor Leo Ryan was the former rector of the cathedral.)

"That infuriated me," said the bishop. "I disliked the guy and I said to Bagley that of all the things he could have said to me, that was the greatest insult, and I threw him out of the office. 'Your time is up!' I said. 'Get out of here!' "

The Richmond diocese had never known a bishop quite so outspoken or unafraid to speak truth to power. ("St. Thomas Aquinas said that 'anger is the first step to courage,' " observed the bishop.) Nor was it used to a prelate who spent quite so much time with prisoners, or with other clergymen and social justice workers lobbying for prisoner rights.

One time the new director of the state penitentiary had a general lock-down of all the prisons. "The prison was worried that there might be a riot," said Bishop Sullivan, "so I went over to the state pen and found a group of thirty or forty people waiting to see members of their family in jail. The warden recognized me and said, 'Bishop, you can go in right away.' But I said that I wouldn't go in until these people who are ahead of me could go first. One of the men in the group came up to me and thanked me. He told me he had to see it to believe it. His name was Louis Farrakhan." (Farrakhan was the head of the Nation of Islam.)

"It was a huge hassle to get into the jail," confirmed Father Pat Apuzzo, who used to drive Sullivan around, "and all I could think is, if they're doing that to a bishop and a priest, how much worse are they treating other people trying to visit?"

Sullivan's initial interest in prisons grew out of his proximity to the Spring Street State Penitentiary, which was only five blocks away from Sacred Heart Cathedral. At first he was merely curious. Then he became a frequent visitor, often in the company of other clergymen, rabbis, and social activists who wanted to see for themselves how the prisoners were being treated.

"The prison work was very important to Walter," said Eileen Dooley, who headed up the diocese's Peace and Justice Commission. "He wanted hands-on involvement. Walter would always tell the inmates that Jesus knew what it was like to be in prison. He would bring the Eucharist and hear confessions.

"The first time I went with him to death row," said Dooley, "the prisoners were put in cages so they wouldn't intermingle. All of them were mentally slow but Walter treated them with such dignity and respect. One of the prisoners was not getting adequate health care. Walter would visit him and advocate for him. I wouldn't call him brave as much as I would call him pastoral."

Whenever an execution was scheduled at the Spring Street prison, Bishop Sullivan would lead a candlelight vigil procession from the cathedral or a church nearby the prison. In 1984, on the night of the execution of Linwood Briley, who had gone on a nine-day killing rampage in Richmond with his two brothers in 1979, the crowd outside the Spring Street Penitentiary was divided into those who were eager for his death and those who opposed it. Policemen on horseback patrolled between them.

Nancy Gowen, whose mother had been murdered by Briley, was with Bishop Sullivan. "He had led a procession from the cathedral where an ecumenical service had taken place because this was only the second execution that had taken place since the death penalty had been reinstated," said Gowen.

"On one side of the street were people shouting, 'Burn, nigger, burn,'" said Sullivan. "They came carrying coolers and were drinking. Then they began to be aggressive and started moving into Belvidere Street. The riot squad appeared."

"Our group was smaller and silent, holding candles," said Sullivan. "The interesting part was what happened when a reporter covering the execution came over to Nancy, who was standing next to me. He very flippantly asked, 'Why are you here, girlie?' And she looked him in the eye and said, 'Because he killed my mother.' The reporter was in shock."

The reporter looked at Gowan and demanded, "What would your mother say if she could see you?"

"I am not my mother," she replied.

Gowan was herself imprisoned for civil disobedience for demonstrating in Fort Benning, Georgia, at the School of the Americas, which trained Latin American soldiers, many of whom have been accused of committing human rights abuses in their countries. Bishop Sullivan drove four hours to Alderson Federal Prison in West Virginia to visit her.

"After they were searched," said Gowan, "we were led into a private room and when no one was looking the bishop dug into his inside pocket and produced a host. 'I was afraid they would find it when they searched me,' he said. Then he divided the host into three pieces; we held hands and said the Lord's Prayer."

If the condemned prisoner was a Catholic, Bishop Sullivan would visit him beforehand. Moving from the general population cells toward the death chamber put the emotional gears of the prison in reverse. "The deeper you got into the prison, the more humane the guards became," said Father Pat Apuzzo. "Usually there was only one person on death row at any one time. It would be just the prisoner and the guard. And when we went into the cell to see the prisoner, to anoint him and give communion, it wasn't a remarkable kind of event. Nothing big happened between us. But there was a sense of peace because the two of us were there. You could cut it with a knife."

One of the condemned prisoners Sullivan visited was Joe Giarratano, who had been convicted of a double murder of two sisters in Norfolk, Virginia, in 1979. With less than thirty-six hours until his execution, his conviction was commuted to life imprisonment by Governor Douglas Wilder, but to this day he remains in prison, despite overwhelming evidence of his innocence. When Giarratano met the man he calls "Bishop" he was on death row.

"It was a very bad time for me," Giarratano writes. "I had foregone my appeals, I was mentally ill, I was being force fed (injected) with painful anti-psychotic drugs. I was convinced that I was evil and that I deserved to die. Volunteer lawyers were attempting to convince me to appeal my case and were not having much success. Bishop, late one afternoon, came to the prison unannounced and asked if he could speak with me. Initially, I told the prison officials 'no.' The captain of the guard replied 'but that's the bishop. You can't refuse to see him!' I refused."

"Bishop came again the following day. This time he sent a message. I don't recall the exact words but it was something to the effect, 'I'm not trying to change your mind,' and said something about the last rites. I agreed to see him, and he was brought to the basement. We spoke. I asked him if he believed I was committing suicide. (One of my lawyers, an Episcopalian, believed I was.) Bishop said that he didn't think so but he had not really given it much thought. I was looking for ammunition to rebut the lawyer: 'I'm Catholic, you're Episcopalian, Catholic Bishop says I'm not,' etc.

"My first visit with Bishop was not very eventful, but I was a bit impressed. I sensed a genuine kindness in him. He was not pretentious. He made his distaste of the basement known to the guards/death squad, but did so in a way that respected their humanity. He had a real sense of humor. . . . Thereafter, every few months, Bishop would return. Whenever he came he had a hug for all of us. He was always relaxed, funny, never in a hurry to leave (often to the consternation of the local priest and the person traveling with the bishop)."

Sullivan wasn't the only member of the clergy who visited Giarratano. "I recall one really funny incident," Giarratano said. "I was a bit aggravated with the Church's official position on capital punishment. I would often discuss it with the local priest who was a really nice guy, but a stuffy priest. He would get very condescending on the issue. So I decided to write a paper on the topic, 'Capital Punishment and the Scriptures.' I shared it with Marie Deans, who thought it was quite good.[14] So I sent it directly to the Vatican addressed to Pope John Paul. About a month later I received a letter from the papal nuncio in D.C. with a message from the pope sent via diplomatic pouch thanking me for the essay, which raised many valid points, and that I would hear more in the near future. When I showed the letter to Father Prinelli during his next visit he got all bent out of shape, saying that I should have cleared my correspondence with him first, and that the bishop was not going to be pleased.

I wrote Bishop and sort of apologized and he replied that I should feel free to write the pope at any time. He asked me to say hello for him."

Giarratano tells the story of another prisoner, Manuel Quintana, a Cuban refugee who spoke no English and who suffered a massive heart attack. The prison didn't want to waste money on a death row inmate by giving him an operation and it was only after Giarratano and the bishop, among others, exerted moral pressure on the authorities that they relented. But before they could take steps to transport him to the hospital, Quintana suffered another attack and died. Various churches were asked if they would bury Quintana. "All hesitated and/or hem-hawed about it," said Giarratano.

Then the bishop was contacted, and he said he would take care of it. A funeral mass for Manuel Quintana was held at the Sacred Heart Cathedral with Bishop Sullivan officiating.

"It doesn't matter to me whether he believes in the Gospel or Jesus, or doesn't," wrote Giarratano. "My experience with the bishop is that he lives the heart of the message." Giarratano, a lapsed Catholic, attempts to do the same.

Since being released from death row, he has distinguished himself in many ways, including writing a legal brief for a mentally retarded inmate on death row, Earl Washington, which resulted in Washington's being exonerated and released from prison altogether. In 1992 he worked with writer Colman McCarthy and his Center for Teaching Peace and with Murder Victims' Families for Reconciliation founded by Marie Deans.

"Colman provided us with start-up funds. In short order we were able to obtain 501c3 status. I wrote to Bishop to see if the Church could help. Folks from the Office of Justice and Peace came to meet with us. We were awarded a sizable grant.

Bishop was very supportive of the program, generally, and of me personally."

Giarratano is currently incarcerated at Wallens Ridge Penitentiary in Big Stone Gap, Virginia, acting as a mentor and program facilitator in a prison ward dedicated to inmates with mental illness or the inability to function well in the general population. It is a new assignment that is already attracting attention from administrators in other prisons who have come to learn how Giarratano proceeds.

"Growing old in prison is hardly a joyful experience," he admits, "but what I have gotten from Bishop in all my encounters with him over the years is that how I live my life is more important than anything I may or may not believe; that the most essential element in that equation is compassion."

Father Jim Griffin, who entered the seminary during the ground-swell of optimism that accompanied Vatican II as priests got involved in civil rights and other peace and justice work, was Bishop Sullivan's driver from 1982 to 1984.

While Sullivan went through his mail and dictated letters into a recorder on the passenger side of the car, Griffin took him from one appointment to the other, often hundreds of miles apart. Prisons were part of his itinerary, and by the time Griffin left to pursue priestly duties elsewhere, he had found a model for the kind of priest and ministry he wanted to follow.

Bishop Sullivan took Griffin to death row for the first time. "When we got there he went over to one row of prisoners and said to me, 'You go over and talk to Joe Giarratano.' So I struck up a relationship with him, and Giarratano asked me if I would do Christmas Mass. I said I would and Christmas Mass became something I did every year."

In 1992 Sullivan took Griffin to Greensville Prison in Jarratt, Virginia, for the last day of convicted murderer Timo-
thy Dale Bunch's life. The bishop had been asked by Bunch,
who was a Catholic from Richmond, if he would be with
him when they electrocuted him. The bishop said he would
do that.

The bishop is not an outwardly emotional man. His report
of the execution he witnessed is gruesome but straightforward. "Beforehand, in his cell, I gave him Holy Communion
and anointed him. The irony was that they gave him a steak
dinner, and he ate it. Then they electrocuted him. It is a gruesome death. They feel the initial shock, and then it melts their
insides. Smoke was coming out of his shoes."

"Walter asked me if I would go with him to witness the execution," said Griffin, "and I said no, I can't do that. It would be
like watching an abortion. So I waited for him while he went
inside, and when he came out he said, 'That wasn't so bad.'
I think that means that he was able to get through it. But his
example gave me the courage to walk that last corridor. To me,
absolutely the best display of being pro-life is when you minister to prisoners," said Griffin. "Nobody gives a crap about prisoners. Walter Sullivan does."

After he left Sullivan's employ, Griffin served for several
years as a prison chaplain at Mecklenburg Penitentiary, where
death row was then located. To date, he has witnessed somewhere between seven and nine executions. "I've lost count. But
you do it because the prisoner asks you to be with them. You
can't say no. As Walter said to me, 'Jim, we can leave tonight
and he can't.' That's the same rationale he has for helping all
people. But I've gotten two speeding tickets after watching an
execution. After it's over you're just trying to drive as fast as
you can away from what you've just seen."

Griffin's own life has had its share of personal crucifixions. He credits the experience of being a witness to so many executions as the reason why he has been able to weather them without cracking. "I would say to myself, okay, I can do this. It's nothing compared to what these men being executed had to endure."

Perhaps the highest-profile and most controversial of the bishop's friends in jail is Jens Soering, a German exchange student who was convicted, along with his girlfriend, Elizabeth Haysom, of murdering her parents in 1985 in their Charlottesville home. The bishop became interested in his case when he read some of Soering's books, including one called *The Convict Christ*. "We don't think of Christ that way," said Sullivan, "but in fact he lived outside the law much of the time."

Jens Soering has attracted many high-level, influential supporters who have lobbied for his return to Germany. Finally, he was granted extradition by Governor Tim Kaine, only to have it rescinded by his successor, Governor Bob McDonnell. "We're still working on that case," said Sullivan, who wrote a foreword to *The Convict Christ*, in which he called the justice system "bankrupt."

In the bishop's view, Soering (who converted to Catholicism in prison) has been given an especially difficult time, once being placed in solitary for several months. "I think it was because what he wrote nailed some of the prison people and the parole board was hopping mad," he said. "When I went to see him, he was brought out shackled, both arms and legs. There were at least ten or twelve guards around him. He was in a straitjacket. I gave him Holy Communion through the bars." Following Bishop Sullivan's visit, Soering was put back into the prison population.

Sullivan's prison friendships are not predicated upon the guilt or innocence of the prisoners, but in Soering's case, the bishop thinks the conviction was unjustified and that his guilt was never established.

It would be easy to assume from the thickness of the files containing the correspondence between Bishop Sullivan and the inmates that they entirely consumed his life. In fact, the prison ministry took up only a fraction of his time when he was bishop, but he was intensely involved in the inmates' well-being and was scrupulous about answering every letter he received. When asked, he would try to grant their requests.

To one prisoner in the prison infirmary he sends a tape cassette of Catholic hymns and reassures him that he would visit soon. For another, about to be paroled, he writes to a friend, "He is wheelchair bound and will need some help in the Roanoke area." There are numerous letters from prisoners telling him, sadly, that once again they have been denied parole.

"The whole thing is outrageous," writes Bishop Sullivan to a prisoner whose parole had just been denied—for the twentieth time. "Do you realize that 40 percent of those in prison were Vietnam veterans?"

The inmate wrote the bishop back. "I need to have some time to talk with you, pray with you, and share with you. We have been together since 1976 and I do not know what is around the corner for me. I care a lot about you and want to just talk with you."

The bishop unfailingly treats prisoners with the same courtesy and affection that any friend requires. In return, the inmates treat the bishop the same way. "Hello Bishop Sullivan

Beloved Divine Soul," wrote one inmate in large block letters. "Have you laid down with the dogs yet?"

On March 6, 2012, Bishop Sullivan climbed into a waiting car in Richmond and was driven to Greensville Correctional Center in rural Jarratt, Virginia. A level-3 medium-security prison with three separate pods, it sits on a treeless 125-acre "campus" surrounded by spirals of razor wire, link fencing, and guard towers. Greensville is where prisoners on death row (called "Hellsville" by the inmates) are executed, now that the old Spring Street prison has been torn down.

"When death row was in Richmond," said Fletcher Lowe, now eighty and retired from active ministry, "we would go in procession with the bishop down to the Spring Street jail whenever there was an execution scheduled. Then, when they moved the execution chamber to Greensville, we would meet in a field near the prison and keep a vigil until we saw the prison van carrying the body away from the prison. Another way we took part in the bishop's prison ministry was on Good Friday, when we would celebrate the Mass of the Presanctified in prison."

March 6 was Good Friday. Fletcher Lowe was the other clergyman in the car.

At Greensville, visitors must pass through an unsettling number of locked chambers before reaching the place where the prisoners themselves congregate. But the day was sunny, the mood of the family members who had come to participate in a graduation ceremony was cheerful, and the tables inside the main lobby were full of cookies, barbeque, and other food items for sale to visitors.

It was not a typical Good Friday at Greensville. Nor was it a typical Good Friday for Bishop Sullivan, who had gone to the emergency room the previous day for unchecked bleeding.

This was the third or fourth time the eighty-three-year-old bishop had been taken to the hospital in the past year, once because he had tripped over one of his dogs in the middle of the night and fractured his hip. But people who have known him for a long time know not to underestimate his powers of recuperation.

On Holy Thursday morning, his secretary, Marilyn Lewis, called me to say that the visit to Greensville had been cancelled. On Holy Thursday afternoon, the bishop called me from his hospital bed. "We're going," he said cheerfully. "I'll be out of here this evening."

Once inside the prison and outside the room where the service was being held, the bishop unpacked his traveling suitcase, put on his white robe, red stole and cape and stood quietly outside a makeshift chapel—someone had hung a plastic holy water font by a paper clip on a wall switch—waiting to greet the first group of men. As they filed into the cinderblock room full of plastic chairs, some shook hands, some embraced him, and one cupped the bishop's hand tenderly in his own like a bird, and kissed it. An older inmate hugged him, backed off, and looked Sullivan in the eyes. Thumping his chest he exclaimed, "This is the biggest godsend in the world, just to see your face!"

Most of the inmates were middle-aged or younger and while Greensville's population is overwhelmingly black, nearly all of the sixty-odd members of this once-a-year congregation were white or Hispanic. They sat peacefully in their chairs, like thoughtful children, with their Good Friday programs in their hands, waiting for the service to begin. When the guitar music started, Bishop Sullivan popped open his mitre, placed it on his head, and processed into the room with The Reverend Lowe and Deacon Tom Elliott at his side.

The opening hymn was "How Great Thou Art." Instantly, the room filled up with strong male voices. The men knew it. "O Lord, my God, when I in awesome wonder consider all the world Thy hand hath made." Rich imagery filled up the bare room. After several verses of starry nights, rolling thunder, sweet flowing brooks and birds, the hymn takes a dramatic turn. "And when I think that God his Son not sparing, sent him to die. I scarce can take it in."

It is the right hymn for this congregation, as was the Passion according to St. Matthew, which they read aloud as a play, with prisoners taking the role of the crowd. Then Bishop Sullivan steps to the middle of the makeshift platform.

"I have been to this prison to celebrate Christmas, and it's kind of a downer. But Good Friday touches us in prison because it is a sign of hope. We live in hope, knowing God is with us. There are three mysteries: the Trinity, the Incarnation, and the Redemption. This last mystery reveals that the Lord is the Lord of mercy and love and we have to experience that mystery. We must ask the Lord for his mercy. I believe that completely.

"All of us are on the same spiritual journey. By us coming here, you help us on our journey. The Bible talks about Jesus and how 'by his wounds you are healed.' All of us need healing, all of us want it, and Good Friday touches us in prison because it is a sign of hope. We live in hope, knowing God is with us."

The service continues with adoration of the cross. The men file up, one by one, to kiss the feet of Jesus on the crucifix held before them. Then comes communion. The bishop looks over at the guitarist and whispers, "Can you play something?" Once again, the men come up to the front of the room to receive the Host.

And then it is over. The bishop stands by the door as the men file past him, shaking hands, embracing, and, in one instance, stepping out of line to whisper to a visitor that he is a Catholic because of the bishop, who baptized him in 2011. "Guys who were at the Spring Street prison would tell me about him and how the bishop would go to 'the Walls' [the inmates' name for the jail] to see them. It wasn't that far from the cathedral. It was easy just to shoot down the street to get there."

The last person to shake the bishop's hand is a former inmate of the Spring Street Penitentiary, who credits Bishop Sullivan with the life he has today—as a Protestant chaplain whose work is in the same prison where he was incarcerated. With his dark skin, intense eyes, and precisely trimmed goatee, Hasan Zarif stands erect and sharply dressed in an immaculately pressed black suit and waistcoat, a far cry from the confused, angry young man who found himself looking into the eyes of a Catholic bishop in a room full of prisoners in 1974.

"I was wearing dirty work clothes, and he walked toward the front of the room in his white robes, and when he came to me he just stopped and turned to me and gave me the biggest hug you could give a person. A whisper went all around the room because the Catholics knew I was a Seventh-Day Adventist and to some of them I was what you call 'the least of my brethren,' and in his clean vestments he hugged me in my dirty work clothes. I think he wanted to prove a point, that although I was a Seventh-Day Adventist he was interested in me as a human being."

Zarif remained at Spring Street until 1985, becoming what's known as a warden's runner. "When they had a prison riot in 1985 after the Briley executions, my life was in danger and so I was moved to Powhatan, where I stayed a few months. Then Bishop Sullivan got me out of Powhatan, which was a maximum-security prison, and into James River. From 1985 until my discharge, he monitored my situation."

A letter from Bishop Sullivan to Governor Tim Kaine helped Zarif to receive a full pardon. "When I got a job he sent funds to the Virginia Cares organization to support what I was doing. He not only kept up with me but he fathered me. He took my case personally."

Sullivan is a rarity among bishops, few of whom ever visit the prisons in their diocese, much less death row. When asked why this is so, Sullivan has no definitive answer. "I think what happens," he said, "is that the people in their diocese might threaten them financially if they did some of these things. Also, our church is now very middle class, even upper-middle class. We're too busy. And," he added, "it's frightening."

Like meeting Christ could be frightening, or confusing. In Matthew's famous gospel passage, Jesus says, "I was in prison and you visited me." But in the dim light of a prisoner's cell on death row, the suffering is so intense that the distinction between who is visiting whom can get blurred.

Chapter Six

A Different Kind of Shepherd

Traditionally Catholic bishops are viewed as exemplary but remote administrators who appear before the faithful in full regalia when they ordain priests or administer the sacrament of Confirmation. The rest of their time is taken up with the ongoing business of the diocese: allocating funds, assigning and overseeing diocesan priests, buying and selling property, establishing schools, hospitals, retirement communities, writing the occasional letter to be inserted into the parish bulletin.

There are exceptions: James Gibbons, Francis Spellman, Richard Cushing, the Church's first media star, Fulton Sheen, prelates who by virtue of their powerful personalities or dioceses caught the attention of the wider world. But by and large bishops are bland, quasi-invisible figures who don't occupy much emotional space in the life of their parishioners. When he retired it was a shock to Bishop Sullivan's predecessor, Bishop Russell, to realize that most Catholics in the diocese did not even know what he looked like.

Sullivan was a different kind of shepherd. He wanted to know his flock on a first-name basis. It was a daunting goal. The Richmond diocese was a large "pasture," 33,000 square miles, with 125,000 Catholics, many of them thinly scattered in small, out-of-the-way communities. The first thing Bishop Sullivan did was to get in his car and drive all over the state to meet them. It was a highly unusual and highly visible way for a Catholic bishop to behave.

Sullivan didn't think so. It was a practical solution to a goal he had set for himself. "I was anxious to have a Catholic church in every county in Virginia," said Sullivan, "and I discovered that in every county there were at least twenty-five to fifty Catholics, mostly not practicing because they didn't have a church." As Monsignor Bill Sullivan would say, "The cost of a new parish is a potluck supper with the bishop." He went to a lot of them.

Monsignor Pitt accompanied the bishop when, two weeks after the diocese split in two, the bishop was on the road. "In the blazing July heat, we stood in our black suits and collars on the beaches on the eastern shore, which was new to the diocese, and 'planted the cross' where people had never seen a bishop before. Then we went west and spent two weeks driving over hill and dale and mountains of Appalachia, which was new territory as well."

In remote mountain hollows where Catholics had never had their own church, or seen a bishop, Bishop Sullivan would pull up in his battered Volvo, sit down to a covered-dish meal, and leave a check behind for a new building.

Eileen Dooley, who came to work for the Office of Social Justice in 1978, often accompanied him.

"Before one of his *ad limina* five-year visits to Rome, the bishop decided to visit all 147 parishes in the diocese. He brought staff along. The format was we would meet with the pastor, have a potluck supper, meet with the various committees on the parish council, and end the evening with thanks and feedback. It was a wonderful way to get to know the diocese. We saw the connection between our ministries and the parishes."

There was a method behind the bishop's modus operandi. Step one was for Catholics to get to know their bishop, to know they were valued by him. Step two was for Catholics to get to know each other. While he was still auxiliary bishop, Sullivan had begun to put the structural supports in place.

With Bishop Russell's blessing, he created a priests council and a pastoral council so clergy and laity could talk among themselves about what was needed in the diocese. After he became bishop of Richmond, he began to create various commissions, the equivalent of extra chairs, where different groups of Catholics who had never been singled out before could come in and sit down at the table.

Vatican II's *Lumen Gentium,* the 1964 Dogmatic Constitution on the Church, had offered a new name for the Church: "the people of God." It was a major shift in emphasis, away from the top-down, authoritarian "father knows best" style of governance toward a more collegial, listening kind of Church where priests are servants of the faithful, not men set apart from them. Everything Sullivan did was intended to bring that message home.

"Walter changed the way the diocese operated," said Monsignor Pitt. "All of this was a brand-new experience and it created some problems."

Priests, newly emboldened to explore off-limits topics like celibacy or women priests, began to speak freely. There were times when the bishop had to do damage control, to explain why a particular priest was coloring outside the lines. But the bishop was not threatened by contending opinions. He was invigorated by them. It meant that priests and laity in the diocese were wading into deeper water, where the deeper issues lay.

"There was an atmosphere when Walter was bishop," said Father Bob Perkins, who was vicar to the clergy. "You felt he was really looking to hear the input of his priests. There were times when he was much more progressive than they were, more willing to take a stand than we were. On the issue of nuclear war, for example, he was much bolder."

Eileen Dooley came to work for the diocese in 1978 as the assistant to Walt Grazier, then director of the Office of Social Ministry, which was later renamed the Office of Justice and Peace. It was, in effect, the bishop's think tank, where staff members prepped him when he was to make a public statement on something that was important to him and the Church.

"We dealt with housing, homelessness, prisons, poverty, racial injustice—all the issues that were current at the time," said Dooley. "He had key people whom he depended upon to help him with the work. He would have them do the leg work. He really trusted them. And he expected a lot from them."

The word "workaholic" is never directly applied to the bishop, but he fits the description of a furiously industrious prelate who would return from Scandinavia with his suitcase, spend one night at the chancery office, and fly out to Arizona the next morning with another bag, already packed. His staff was an intricate, well-oiled machine that the bishop put together to make the diocese function.

"Also," said Dooley, "he compartmentalizes, which is probably a great gift that keeps him from worrying, keeps him optimistic. He has different agendas for different people and he related to all of us in different ways based upon what our responsibilities were. I wouldn't know what was happening with the clergy, for instance. My role was legislative agenda and parish concerns."

Dooley saw the bishop change outwardly. "When I first knew him he was always in his black suit and collar. Probably after the "Unite for Justice" convocation he began to wear a sweater with his suit when he was traveling in the parishes. Much later, you would see him in his black shirt but without his white collar, and in a sweater. An outward sign of inward change."

Inwardly, he changed as well. "Particularly as he became more involved in peace and justice issues," said Dooley. "As he traveled internationally, it expanded his horizons." But closer up, Dooley observed his willingness to change as well.

"Somewhere in the 1980s there was a new Code of Canon Law introduced and the bishop had originally planned workshops around the diocese for the priests. I said that he should also include lay diocesan and parish staff. We were sitting around in a group with some priests and possibly a seminarian or two, and the bishop said that lay people wouldn't understand the language of canon law. He said, 'For instance, what is manumission?' and looked around for someone to define it. None of the priests or seminarians responded. I said, 'You mean as in the manumission of slaves?' He said, 'Yes, how did you know that?' What I didn't know was that he had written his canon law thesis on manumission. The bishop was as good as his word and opened the workshops to lay staff."

"It was exhilarating to work for him," said Steve Colecchi, who succeeded Eileen Dooley as the director of the Office of Peace and Justice. One of many lay people attracted to Richmond because of Sullivan's reputation, Colecchi had wanted to be a priest. He was well-qualified: a graduate of Holy Cross, with an M.A. from Yale and a Ph.D. from St. Mary's in Baltimore. Eventually Colecchi decided celibacy wasn't for him and got married. But after he got married he still wanted to work for the Church and decided upon Richmond. "A Jesuit friend of mine said that there was a very dynamic bishop there."

For ten years Colecchi worked as a director of religious education in various parishes and then, in 1988, went to work for Sullivan himself, eventually becoming his only special assistant. "There was always a project that the diocese would be involved in that was responding to a sign of the times. Not only was the bishop's door open for me to go in, but he'd call me in when he had something he wanted to pass on or question."

One of the hats Colecchi wore was chief lobbyist in the Virginia legislature for the Richmond diocese. "We had them so confused. Were we liberal or conservative? On some things, like the death penalty, we looked liberal; on abortion, conservative. But we were always consistent in our defense of human life and dignity." Today Colecchi is the director of the Office of International Justice and Peace at the U.S. Catholic Conference of Bishops in Washington, D.C.

Lighting the Fire

Beginning in 1975, a series of convocations was created to bring the diocese together. Part family reunion, part teaching opportunity, and part call to action, the convocations were designed to turn a disconnected group of parishes into a large and potentially powerful family that could do great things, particularly if everyone was talking to each other. The bishop invited different points of view.

"I don't have any trouble with people saying, 'I don't agree with you,' " he said in a 1984 *Richmond News Leader* article. "Why is there this mystical new thing that everybody should agree with what the bishop says? We are calling people to maturity of thought.[15]

"The parish is a gathering place," said Bishop Sullivan, "a place to celebrate life, share faith, be uplifted. It is a place to experience God. But it is not an end in itself. We have to be about the kingdom. . . . But you can't expect people to take risks for the kingdom unless you take them seriously."

Some observers would say that Sullivan took the laity more seriously than the Church intended him to do. But the fat was in the fire and in the Richmond diocese Catholics were beginning to realize that they had a bishop who wanted them to share and take responsibility for the kingdom he had been called to lead.

The first time Sullivan brought the diocese together was in the spring of 1975 when he invited all the parishes to come together in Richmond. The winter before, Monsignor Pitt had gone around to all the pastors and made sure they understood the importance of the invitation to send representatives to a Mass and celebration in the Richmond Coliseum to be held in May. They did. Over seven thousand people showed up, bearing gifts that were intended to reflect where they came from: carvings from the mountains, seashells from the eastern shore. The theme was "To Light a Fire," which was the title of a song written expressly for the occasion. It reflected what Bishop Sullivan was trying to do.

In 1980 came another invitation to a week-long "Unite for Justice" convocation. "Originally," said Bill Pitt, "we called it a 'Call to Action' after the national 'Call to Action' convocation in Detroit in 1976. But that sounded way too active for Rome. It was the death knell, so we changed it to 'Unite for Justice' and that took the activism out of the title."

The groundwork for this larger, more ambitious event had been five years in the laying. Long, detailed questionnaires, designed to elicit the most informative answers, were sent out to each parish. After they came back from the parishes, Dooley explained how they were assessed and tabulated.

"Brother Phil Doherty, the diocesan theologian, was a key asset to Sullivan for years. What he did was take about thirty-two hundred responses from parishes and consolidate them, categorize them, into about eight hundred recommendations across eight areas of concern (Church, family, ethnicity/race, humankind, nationhood, neighborhood, personhood, and work). And then, at the Unite for Justice assembly, each of those eight major groups was further broken down into smaller groups of about eight people who would dialogue with each other. It was a real listening process. It was parish-based and came out of the concerns of the parish. There was nothing manipulative. The final recommendations were read out and printed up and distributed to the whole assembly and then presented ceremonially to the bishop on Sunday morning."

"The goal," said Kathleen Kenney, who was on the bishop's staff, "was to figure out how you get into a parish to educate the parishioners on these issues." Kenny cites the document *Justice in the World*, put out by the synod of Catholic bishops in 1971, as one of their most powerful teaching tools.

"It said, let's go back to our roots and see who we were supposed to be—a community. Oh! We were to care for the poor. Oh! The Church is here to help us be a presence of Christ here. It's about the people. Oh!" At the Unite for Justice meeting, the focus was upon how to bring these moral imperatives about. "We were trying to get people to follow social justice teachings, not unjust systems," said Kenney.

But before the "Unite for Justice" convocation took place, an exchange of letters between an assistant to Archbishop Jerome Hamer, secretary to the Congregation for the Doctrine of the Faith, and Bishop Sullivan revealed just how nervous Rome felt over the preparation process itself.

October 1, 1979
Dear Bishop Sullivan

The Sacred Congregation for the Doctrine of the Faith has learned of the Richmond Diocese Call to Action program from *The Catholic Virginian*. . . . In studying the newspaper reports, it was noted that diverse recommendations were made at the Conference contrary to the doctrine of the Church. For instance, objections were raised to teachings on artificial contraception, divorce, ordination of women, celibacy, etc.

Archbishop Hamer has asked that you be advised of the Congregation's judgment that the procedure adopted in Richmond whereby well-known positions of the Church are left open to discussion under the responsibility of the Chancellor is inadequate. He further suggested that you be invited to find a way to rectify this incongruity. Finally, the Archbishop would appreciate receiving any recent information on the Richmond Call to Action program.

Assuring you of my best wishes and with kind personal regards, I remain,

Sincerely yours in Christ

Monsignor Clemente Facciani
Special Assistant

Within the week, Facciani had a reply from the bishop. His letter was an artful mix of reassurance (bordering on obsequiousness), facts, and flattery, with a combative tone running beneath the surface.

Dear Monsignor Facciani,

I was delighted to receive your letter informing me that Archbishop Hamer has recently inquired about the Call to Action program sponsored by the Catholic Diocese of Richmond. I will be very happy to respond to his concerns and want to give assurance that whatever is done in the diocese will be in perfect harmony with the doctrine of the Church.

There are some in the diocese who have made a great effort to distort our program which we now call "United for Justice." For two years the diocese has gone through a reflective process where people have had the opportunity to voice their individual concerns. All of these concerns were listed . . . so that our people could then reflect corporately on what had been suggested.

You will be happy to know that the concerns raised by Archbishop Hamer have been basically rejected or not accepted by our Catholic people. Our people by a large majority do not favor divorce, the ordination of women, optional celibacy for clergy, etc. Our people are concerned about ministry to the divorced, to the alienated, and to those estranged from the Church. . . . Let me assure you that the diocese will not adopt or accept any issue or position which would prove contrary to Church teaching. . . .

I find it interesting that certain people have wanted to discredit the "United for Justice" program in our diocese. They have not participated in any way in the program. They are basically attacking the efforts on the part of our diocese to respond to the needs of the poor, to work for the eradication of discrimination and racism, to promote disarmament and world peace, and to affirm human rights and equality for all people.

The bishop concludes his letter by saying how "really delighted" he is that the archbishop has shown his concern, how he "rejoices at the opportunity" to respond, and that he is in perfect accord with the Holy Father who spoke "so eloquently and clearly on matters of the Catholic faith" during his recent U.S. visit.

This is one of the first times that the bishop refers in a letter to some of the dissenters in the Richmond diocese who had begun to write letters to Rome and the papal nuncio in Washington, D.C., complaining of their bishop's social activism. In Sullivan's personal archives is a thick dossier of letters that he wrote during his ministry to reassure Rome that he was a loyal son of the Church. Those closest to him agree.

"When Walter got a directive on faith or morals, he wouldn't disobey. It wasn't in him," said the diocesan finance director, John Barrett. Eileen Dooley concurs. "He never disagrees with Church teachings. He can go to the edge but he's really very loyal. There were always limits, internal to himself." She adds one modifying statement. "The group of bishops appointed by Jadot—Sullivan, Bernardin, Hunthausen, Weakland, Gumbleton—were loyal men of the Church but their loyalty went hand in hand with their love of people."

It was at the 1980 "Unite for Justice" convocation that Sullivan displayed that love and a talent for dramatic gestures. Appearing at the opening session resplendent in his bishop's vestments, he electrified the crowd by taking off his mitre and laying it beside his crosier at the feet of the people.

"You obviously have a lot of faith in your people," remarked one reporter who had witnessed the act.

"If the Church is to grow," he replied, "it can't depend only on the clergy."[16]

Later, Sullivan revisited that action and said, "I wanted them to take the place of the bishop and really express themselves to me. The Spirit is throughout the Church. It isn't just in the bishop. So often at a meeting someone would come up with an insight that was wonderful."

Two years later, in 1982, the Diocesan Pastoral Council again invited each parish to send three representatives to set the agenda for a convocation called "Parish and the Kingdom." "The atmosphere," wrote reporter Carol Clark of *Today's Parish* magazine, "was one of hope and joy. These people knew good things had been happening and believed they would continue to happen. . . . People who had not met since the Unite for Justice Assembly in 1980 greeted each other as trusted associates. Everyone seemed eager to move beyond his or her small circle of acquaintances, to hear new viewpoints, to make new friends."[17]

In the largest, most dramatic convocation, "The Great Jubilee Year Celebration of 2000," some very large issues were on the table: debt relief for poor countries, ecumenism, human rights. Sullivan did not have a specific outcome in mind, other than allowing Catholics in their parishes to determine how and what they would do to bring their lives into closer alignment with the Gospel itself.

Eight thousand people filled the Robbins Center at the University of Richmond. The emphasis was upon forgiveness, simpler living, returning to the core of the Gospel's teachings.

These are not radical ideas but taken to their logical conclusions they could have radical results.

The diocesan paper, the *Catholic Virginian,* "played a very important role during this time period," said Dooley. "Charlie Mahon was a superb editor, very independent. It had responsibility to the diocese, but it was also a wonderful newspaper, both a Catholic vehicle and an independent voice, carrying critical letters to the editor. With the bishop it is always 'both/and,' never 'either/or.' He respected Mahon's independence."

Looking back, Dooley credits Vatican II with permanently altering the way the people related to their Church. "The changes that have happened have happened. We went from 'pray, pay, and obey' to having parish councils and religious education being conducted by lay people. You can't put the genie back in the bottle."

The Mind of the Bishop

In the mid-1980s all the priests in the diocese, including Bishop Sullivan, took the Myers-Briggs personality test. It made an indelible impression upon all of them and became a favorite shorthand way of comparing and contrasting themselves with each other. When those who took the test spoke about their relationship to Sullivan, they oftentimes referred to it.

"We all took the test, including the bishop," said Monsignor William Carr, who is pastor of St. Bridget Catholic Church in Richmond. "There is no good or bad, it's just how you get energized and how you make decisions. Everyone ended up with four markers indicating their personality. Each combination of four markers corresponded to a job one might enjoy with that kind of personality. Bishop Sullivan's results indicated that he would make a good field marshal. And that's what he was, a field marshal. And if you look at all the great field marshals, like Napoleon and Julius Caesar, they all have a huge vision. Walter had a vision. When he became bishop he said, 'I am going to bring the Church to you' and he did just that. He left no stone unturned, no city unvisited in his desire to preach the Gospel throughout his diocese. It was profound."

Carr often got calls from Bishop Sullivan when Carr was pastor at St. Bede's in Williamsburg. "He would telephone from I-64 and say, 'I'm coming to stay with you for a few hours. I don't need anything, just a quiet room, a cup of coffee, and a newspaper.' But he always ended up taking calls, doing his mail, having meetings. The man worked hard. He was driven. He wouldn't know how else to be."

"Working hard was the key to Walter's friendship," confirmed Monsignor Pitt, who was chancellor and vicar general of the diocese for the first twelve years of Sullivan's episcopacy.

"If I wanted a rest room break," said his longtime secretary, Marilyn Lewis, "the bishop would say 'take your typewriter with you.'"

"He was perfectly suited for the day-to-day management of the diocese," said Father Pat Apuzzo, "for interaction with all kinds of different people, and he avoided like the plague too much long-range planning. He was very flexible. Of course, people might say that the dark side of being flexible is that you don't know where you're going. But Bishop Sullivan was in control."

Apuzzo offers up one story as proof. "As someone chosen to be bishop from among his own priests, there was another struggle for Bishop Sullivan at the beginning. There was a race among certain priests to get his ear, to be the one to help set the agenda from that point on. I remember early on, when I was his driver, being with him at an informal gathering of priests. The conversation got pretty heated with each priest injecting his 'you ought to do this, you ought to do that' opinion, all of them arguing among themselves. I remember Bishop Sullivan sparring with them but never getting too dug into any of the arguments. He finally did raise his voice but only to say, 'Listen, guys. This ship is about to sail. You either get on board or you get left at the dock.' Then he got up off his chair, and it was over. He did that, whether it was in a meeting, or at a meal, or just a chat. I could read his body language after a while. When he started to fidget and push back his chair that would be it. He'd stand up, and it was over."

Sullivan seems to understand his own temperament pretty well. "I'm right on the border between extrovert and introvert and on the line between perceiving and judging. But I'm off the wall on thinking and intuition, although they say that your best work is done from the feeling or sensing level."

What this means is that the bishop is not particularly interested in what he wears and sometimes forgets to comb his hair. "My niece," he conceded, "is very sensation oriented but I don't pay attention to those things, which means I spill a lot. I should wear a bib." But what the bishop did pay attention to was money, and as long as he was bishop he never spilled a drop.

Part of the bishop's ability to handle money well was hereditary. His younger sister, Betty, whom he strongly resembles physically, with the same bright blue eyes and wide toothy smile, is also good with numbers. After retiring as the registrar at Kennedy High School in Silver Spring, Maryland, she became treasurer for the Rockville Senior Center. "I'm treasurer for the Center fundraiser. I help at the Bingo and dole out the money during the games on stage." Like her brother, she is a nonstop worker. "We're a working family," she concedes. "I have to be active. But mostly I stay with the money."

Growing up, the Sullivan family didn't have any regular source of money except what their mother earned as a nurse or taking in boarders, or what they earned for themselves as teenagers. But on his estranged father's side of the family, there was some wealth and there came a day when the bishop would have the opportunity to prove his ability to be a good steward.

"My Uncle Ned was a vice president of Woolworth," said Sullivan. "He was a big financial supporter of the Assumptionist Fathers in Wisconsin, and when he died the provincial of the order called up my Aunt Margaret and said, 'I hope he left something for us.' Aunt Margaret got so mad that she changed her will and left all her money to charity, with me as the executor."

When his aunt died, Bishop Sullivan came into a million dollars. By careful investing, the bishop doubled it to two million, which over the years he doled out to various people and causes. "It was strictly for charity," he said, "and it's all gone now."

A Thing for the Elderly

Bishop Sullivan was forty-six when he became bishop, still a young man who wasn't looking ahead to his later years. But he was aware of the numbers of old, isolated parishioners who needed a place to live if and when their families were unable or unwilling to assume the responsibility.

Sullivan had an understanding of where to find the money the diocese didn't have. "I could see we needed to develop some homes for the elderly. At first we went with HUD [Housing and Urban Development] money, and four homes were started with government funding. But I didn't like the restrictions and red tape, plus HUD was gradually cutting back on funds. So I said let's get into our own housing business. We formed our own housing business and applied for industrial bonds under the name of the Diocesan Housing Corporation. We created about fourteen homes."

The diocese's CFO, John Barrett, knew what kind of risk was involved. "They were basically junk bonds, and the bishop was the guarantor until we reached a level of twelve audited months of a positive cash flow position. The diocese did not have the assets to cover the total of the bond issues, other than the full faith of Walter Sullivan as the bishop of Richmond." That full faith turned out to be enough.

"He used to say," said Barrett, "that the Protestant churches are taking care of the wealthy, HUD is taking care of the poor, but nobody is taking care of the middle class who live in month-to-month rentals when they grow old. He wanted these homes to be built in an urban setting, near a parish church, preferably with a school nearby so the children could come and forge relationships with the elderly. It really worked."

In 1983 he announced the establishment of a Task Force on Older Adults, a diocesan Office for Ministry with Older Adults, and a Commission for the elderly.[18] "The meeting absorbed my attention by confronting me with the reality of my own mortality. Instead of becoming despondent, I was caught up in the excitement of the participants. It is more than altruism to say that one can be as young or as old as one wants. One's life view and ability to accept the present moment have a great effect upon how one views the future."

Sullivan was fifty-four when he wrote those words. At eighty-three, he pulled into the parking lot of St. Francis Home in Richmond, one of fifteen homes for the elderly that he either founded or remodeled while he was bishop.

St. Francis Home is a clean, cheerful place, with washed windows and modern, comfortable furniture. "Let's all welcome Walter and Kitty," reads a sign on the bulletin board in the lobby. Residents, some on crutches, using walkers, or in wheelchairs, hauling tanks of oxygen, move up and down the corridors. There are three residence wings, one of which is called "Sullivan's Place." A well-tended rose garden with wrought-iron tables and chairs around a grass rectangle is outside.

The bishop is late for the ten o'clock Mass he says for the residents once a month. But he seems unconcerned as he vests himself outside the chapel and then walks in, the soul of cheer. "Good morning," he sings out. "I introduce myself as 'the *late* Bishop Sullivan.' The landscaper came to the house, and I had to show him around."

The Mass begins. He ad libs as he walks down the aisle to the altar. "It's an interesting Gospel today. The Lord goes to the other side of the lake and the apostles are terrified. Then the Lord calms them down."

As the cup of communion wine is being handed around by the bishop, a latecomer, a burly younger man with dark glasses, comes into the chapel. When the cup is passed to him he appears to be drinking the whole thing. "No, no," exclaims the bishop. "You're taking it all." The man protests. "I just had a little sip." The bishop is silent but eyes the cup as the man passes it to the next communicant.

After Mass, the bishop folds his alb back into his black traveling case and explains the history of the home. "Originally this was a home for unwed mothers. Bishop Russell told his priests, 'Help me fill up the maternity home,' and the priests started to laugh. 'I didn't mean it that way,' said Russell."

Bishop Sullivan gazed around the lobby. "Before we had the St. Francis Home these people were in Fulton Bottom. It was a firetrap for the elderly and I said let's bring them out here. And so we did. Then the fire inspector came to check us out. He was all set to say we were in violation of the codes, and I said, 'You must be out of your mind. Do you know where these people came from?' And he ran out the door."

"I have a thing for the elderly," he said. "It started when I began receiving letters from families asking what am I going to do for their parents? 'Why are you asking me?' I replied. But I could see that we needed to do something for them. These are the poorest of the poor. They cannot pay. But the home is supported by the other homes for the elderly in the diocese."

This Land Is Home to Me

On any given day, Bishop Sullivan might be breaking ground for a school, saying Mass for a group of migrant workers on the eastern shore, having dinner with a group of Catholic state legislators at his home, or testifying at a public hearing on behalf of a new home for the elderly the diocese wanted to build. But when the diocese expanded to include Appalachia, he immediately went west to see it for himself. He was dazzled by the beauty of the landscape and horrified by the ways it was being destroyed. King Coal dominated the culture and King Coal did what it wanted.

"I went with him once to examine the result of mountain-top removal," said Stephen Colecchi. "The place looked like a moonscape. It was devastating." Sullivan was devastated, too. He hurriedly signed on to a 1975 pastoral letter, "This Land Is Home to You and Me," the last of twenty-four bishops from thirteen southern Appalachian states to do so. It was a lyrical love letter to the people and land of Appalachia as well as an angry, plain-speaking indictment of the corporate greed that scars the land and lives of the poor who live there.

Some may say "That's economics," but we say that economics is made by people. Its principles don't fall down from the sky and remain for all eternity. Those who claim they are prisoners of economics only testify that they are prisoners of the idol.[19]

The pastoral was remarkable on many levels, including the tenderness that suffused the conclusion:

Dear sisters and brothers, we urge all of you not to stop living, to be part of the rebirth of utopias, to recover and defend the struggling dream of Appalachia itself. For it is the weak things of this world which seem like folly, that the Spirit takes up and makes its own. The dream of the mountains' struggle, the dream of simplicity and of justice, like so many other repressed visions is, we believe, the voice of the Lord among us.

It was the first time a segment of U.S. Catholic bishops had acted independently from the larger body of American bishops, which did not take a position either way.

"The pastoral was sparked by the Glenmary fathers, in particular Father Les Schmidt," said Sullivan. "They should get top billing for putting the bishops' pastoral together. But it grew out of the grassroots people in Appalachia. And the Glenmary sisters."

Originally from Ohio, the Glenmary sisters were a renegade group of nuns who had been profoundly influenced by Vatican II and decided that the time for wearing religious habits was over. Then the archbishop of Cincinnati demanded that they go back to wearing them. "A whole group of them, around twenty, broke away and settled in southwest Virginia," said Bishop Sullivan. "The Glenmary sisters were a great influence."

"There were not too many diocesan priests in Appalachia," said Monsignor Pitt. "The Glenmary priests in Appalachia ran everything. It was all about them, very clerical. By contrast, the nuns came in droves to work with the poor, and they were very much in touch with the people."

Seeing Appalachia firsthand, meeting its people, galvanized Sullivan into action. When the unions boycotted J. P. Stevens, the second-largest textile manufacturer in the country, Sullivan joined five other bishops who endorsed the unions. It was not a popular decision among some southern Catholics who criticized the bishop for stepping away from the pulpit.

"Regrettable, ill-advised, and divisive," said Edward Dowd, a prominent Charlotte, North Carolina, Catholic. But The Reverend Ed Molloy of the Charlotte diocese peace and justice task force was supportive. "The principle of collective bargaining is part of the Church's teaching and should be honored." In 1980 a ruling was issued saying that J. P. Stevens had acted in bad faith at the bargaining table, and the union was granted the right to represent the workers.

Sullivan was not the impetus for the boycott, but he was squarely behind it, and likewise supported the notion that the Church should be working in the world for the principles it espouses in the pulpit. Characteristically, he wound up becoming close friends of another textile manufacturer from Big Stone Gap, Tony Trigiani, who was on J. P. Stevens's side.

"I'm going to come down there and unionize your sweat shop," Sullivan mock-threatened. It was one of the bishop's gifts to separate the ideas he opposed from the people who supported them. (Last year he spoke at Trigiani's funeral.) Another gift was his ability to listen.

"I quickly learned that one enters the Appalachia region not with ready answers or easy solutions, but I became enmeshed in the spirit of the mountains, to be one with the people as a listening presence, to stand with the people in their pursuit of justice, and to be a voice for the voiceless."

Ironically, the voiceless in Appalachia were Protestants, not Catholics, who migrated late to the South and tended to come from the middle-management class who followed companies seeking low-wage, non-union labor. Most of the Catholics had not heard about the pastoral letter, and those who had didn't like it. There was a disconnect between the Catholic activists, like the Glenmary sisters, and the Catholics in the pews, most of whom worked for the industries that tried to discourage the bishops from signing the pastoral.

Sullivan called the people who sought to take over Appalachia and ship its natural resources out, without thought for the people who live there, "architects of exploitation." He was not fooled by the token ways in which King Coal sought to cover up its giant claw marks on the land. They "will point to stories of reclamation," he wrote, "but these are basically cosmetic improvements. . . . The Land, the mountains, the people, God's gift to Appalachia will never be the same."

As long as he was bishop, Sullivan travelled back and forth between Richmond and the far western part of the diocese, lending support, both financial and moral, to a variety of groups and causes that worked toward greater equality in the region. The sums of money were not large but they were critical. Fourteen new parishes were established. In 2002 the Bishop Sullivan Peace and Justice Award was established in his honor. It is given every year by the Catholic Committee on Appalachia to someone who has worked for at least ten years for peace and justice in the field.

Going Further Afield

On March 24, 1980, Archbishop Oscar Romero of El Salvador was assassinated by marksmen carrying out orders of the military dictatorship that ruled the country. "I was invited to go to his funeral by the Bishops' Conference, but I got bumped by the bishop of New Orleans," said Sullivan, who began to focus his attention on the Church in Central America. "When Romero was killed," he said, "that's when I got concerned."

In 1982 he went to Nicaragua with Monsignor Pitt and Eileen Dooley. While studying political science in graduate school at the University of Chicago, Dooley had made friends with a Jesuit priest, Cesar Jerez, who had been an advisor to Romero and Father Rutilio Grande, a Jesuit priest whose murder by a right-wing death squad had been the catalyst for Romero's transformation into an advocate for Salvador's poor. Jerez returned to Central America and became the provincial of the Jesuits in Central America. ("We'll all stay," he told a reporter, "until we all are killed or expelled.")[20]

"When Jerez came back to the States," said Dooley, "I invited him to come to Richmond to meet Sullivan, and they immediately developed a very close bond. Jerez invited us to Nicaragua after the Sandinistas [who had wrenched control from the Somoza dictatorship in 1979] had taken power. It was a very peaceful time." They visited barrios, observed the nuns who were working with the poor, and were struck by how stark the living conditions were, how low the life expectancy was.

"In Nicaragua," said Monsignor Pitt, "it came home in a clear way how everything was connected. With no roads it is hard to bring in food, or water, or teachers. That's when Walter made his decision about Haiti. He said he wanted to put the diocese on an outreach thrust." It was primarily a decision based upon geography. Haiti is closer to Richmond than El Salvador or Nicaragua.

In 1983 Sullivan went to Haiti on a fact-finding mission as a board member of the Christian Children's Fund. There he found that Roman Catholic churches from the United States had already gotten involved with third-world parishes. "As always," said Dooley, "the focus is on the Church wherever he goes." The bishop decided that the Diocese of Richmond should have a Haitian ministry.

That same year, the bishop met with a group of ten people who had all participated in a retreat in Haiti sponsored by the National Center for Young Adult Ministry. Two years later, the Richmond diocesan Haiti ministry became a full-fledged reality. Since then, it has become a large and flourishing vineyard.

Sixty-six parishes or schools in the Diocese of Richmond are currently twinned with a parish, organization, or group in Haiti. There is a Haitian Education Fund, a Haitian Health Care Foundation, and a Maison Fortune Orphanage Foundation, as well as a partnership with the Xaverian Brothers to support their programs in Haiti. Three different funds held by the diocese support micro-credit and literacy programs, a school and community project, and a fund that subsidizes Haitian seminarians for the priesthood.

There is also a school, named after Bishop Sullivan. "I went down for the dedication," he said. "They're beautiful people, the Haitians." His visits paved the way for other clergymen to follow. "Sullivan would go to places, like Haiti, Nicaragua, and Salvador, that other bishops could care less about," said Father Jim Griffin, whose church has an outreach project in Haiti now.

Paul Amrhein, the director of Human Concerns Ministries at St. Bridget, is a member of the St. Bridget–Sacred Heart Cathedral committee that is twinned with St. Paul's, a mission church and school in Carissade, Haiti. "People at St. Bridget have been very generous toward Haiti," he said. "It has been a way for them to act on their compassion. And the people who have actually visited Haiti and been with the people come back really changed."

How so? "They develop a real love for the Haitian culture and people, and they want to accompany them in their struggles. But it's not just about struggle. There's the joy. You think of Haiti as a downtrodden place, but you go to Mass there, and it could be as hot as blazes, but the men are in their suits, the ladies have their hats, and the kids are singing and dancing."

Does it make the visiting St. Bridget parishioners want to change the way they worship back in Richmond? "Not yet," said Amrhein. "We haven't had enough go over."

Amrhein asks if I know the bishop. "He's a hero of mine," he volunteers. When asked why, he pauses. "I guess it's because he really loves Jesus. That just comes through with him, and it just doesn't come through with a lot of the newer ones the way it did with him."

Chapter Seven

Enlarging the Tent

At the same time that Bishop Sullivan was trying to bring the diocese closer together, he also was trying to push at the edges to make more room for two groups of Catholics whose voices had either been muted or disregarded: women, and gays and lesbians. The larger group, women, were honored indirectly through the Church's long tradition of devotion to the Blessed Mother. In the pews, they did not get the same respect. But Sullivan, who grew up being bossed and tossed around by three affectionate sisters, had numerous close relationships with women whom he encouraged, promoted, and related to as equals, in and out of the Church.

Once, at an ecumenical meeting in northern Virginia, the bishop was introduced to a Lutheran woman minister who was wearing a Roman collar. "Is this upsetting to you?" she asked.

The bishop grinned. "I didn't know there were any good-looking Lutheran ministers."

"He likes women," said his sister Betty. "Other priests are intimidated by them."

Like Sullivan's mother, who washed and ironed the altar linens but was not allowed on the altar itself except to remove the old cloths and replace them with freshly laundered ones, Catholic women have always been the workhorses in the Church. They send their children to the parochial schools, run the PTAs, crank out the bulletins, organize the fundraisers, and volunteer for most of the parish works of mercy, like staffing homeless shelters and serving in soup kitchens. But serving at the altar is another matter.

Sullivan would get irritated with Catholics who objected to the presence of girls on the altar. He saw through it to the larger irritant, of women aspiring to the priesthood. "I wish we could be as concerned with the poor as some are about a girl on the altar," he said in a 1984 *Richmond News Leader* interview. "I think the issue is women, not that girls do this. [The issue is] to get the women off the altar."[21]

The bishop absolutely believed that women were equal to men, if not superior to them, and in a 1976 conference paper ("A New View of Mission and Ministry") he tackled the issue of women priests head on.

> I was pleased to read just this past week that the Pontifical commission in Rome voted almost unanimously that scriptural grounds alone are not enough to exclude the possibility of ordaining women. They further agreed that if the Church were to open up the priesthood to women it would not be contradicting Christ's original intentions. . . . [The] Church in our day has the same obligation to be as open as Jesus was in calling women to share in its mission.

> Several speakers [at a recent conference in St. Louis] equated ordination with the women's liberation movement and accused women with being disenchanted with their own authentic ministry by wanting to be clericalized or masculinized with "the probable effeminizing of men within the priesthood." Such statements show blindness to the gifts and talents of women and are another way of saying, "Girls, we know what's best for you and we will call you when we need you."

But apparently, Rome *did* know what was best for women and did not back down from Paul VI's earlier apostolic letter *Ministeria Quaedam* (1973), which said women could not become priests "in accordance with the ancient tradition of the Church."

Sullivan could not change the pope's mind but he knew his own and he did not wait until he was bishop to make what changes he could. He was the first rector at Sacred Heart Cathedral to hire a woman as pastoral coordinator. In 1975 a ministries formation program was organized and forty candidates, men and women, were recruited. "We quickly knew [he wrote in the 1976 conference paper] it would be disastrous to promote just another male clerical group like a hierarchical layer cake."

Sullivan committed the diocese to equal employment hiring practices and gave women religious in the diocese the option of being on a stipend or receiving a salary. In parishes where there were no priests, he installed women as pastoral directors.

"Sullivan began naming women after a 1983 Vatican document that gave bishops the right to appoint lay women to leadership positions," wrote reporter Ken Baker in a *Daily Press* story about Sullivan.[22]

"People will look back and say that he was a prophet in our midst," said Sister Jean Ackerman, who was one of eleven pastoral coordinators whom Sullivan appointed.

Ackerman, who calls herself "an itinerant Dominican preacher," is now eighty-one and living with her order in Racine, Wisconsin. Sullivan sent her to Vincent de Paul's Catholic Church in downtown Newport News. "At first," she said, "I think the parishioners thought they were being overlooked because they didn't have a priest coming. But it was the beginning of bringing lay people into the leadership."

Having women take the place of parish priests was a practical solution, not a theological shift. Priests still administered the sacraments and said Mass, which was at the core of the Church's identity. But the daily presence of a trained administrator allowed a parish to cohere and function as a Church family when a priest was not available. In the mostly mission parishes where women stepped in to make up the difference there was no resistance.

"We were kind of paving the way for people to see women in leadership in the churches," said Ackerman. "That became beautifully evident to me the first time I preached. A gentleman came up to me and said, 'I had never heard a woman preach before, but you really connected the scriptures to my life.'"

In 1982 a women's commission was established in the Richmond diocese after the "Unite for Justice" convocation. "The first thing we did," said Eileen Dooley, who was the commission's director, "was to institute a forum called 'Women Listening to Women' in the parishes. We used the model that we used in both the 'Unite for Justice' and 'Parish: The Kingdom' convocations. We understood that the listening process was very important. Vatican II said that the laity needed to become part of the Church in new ways."

Women were asked to reflect upon their past, present, and future hopes. What emerged from these groups were several main themes: insufficient recognition of the gifts of the women in the Church and failure to appreciate what women were doing in the Church. Domestic violence was another key theme.

"These were women who were very active in the Church," said Dooley. "Contraception was not a concern. It was about the education of their children, getting into the work force, examining their own status in society."

During this time, the U.S. Conference of Catholic Bishops was thinking about producing a pastoral letter on women. A draft report from the USCCB's Ad Hoc Committee on the Role of Women in Society and the Church notes, "In a hierarchal church in which pastoral office is the basis of judicial and administrative authority, the exclusion from ordination is, by that very fact, an exclusion of women from all the key posts of authority in the Church."[23]

Dooley and the women's commission gathered up all their "Women Listening to Women" reportage and sent it to the bishops for their use. The bottom line was that they didn't use it.

In 1988 a draft pastoral was produced, which basically said that Mary was women's role model and that the Church should promote women to administrative positions. Eventually, given the weakness of the text, the bishops decided not to publish a pastoral on women at all. Some bishops went on record as saying that it would needlessly alienate women, just as Paul VI's *Humanae Vitae.* reinforcing the Church's ban on birth control, had alienated many women and lay people in 1968.

Sullivan became auxiliary bishop during what was labeled "the second wave of feminism." Women had the vote and marital rights with regard to children and property. But "the problem that has no name," as Betty Friedan called it in *The Feminine Mystique,* was still on the table: lack of opportunity for women to pursue a full life in whatever career fit their talents and aspirations. In 1982, when the Equal Rights Amendment was before the states for ratification, Sullivan was outspoken in his support of it.

He admitted in a "Tidings" column that he had been silent for many years but that he could no longer stand back.[24] He used Vatican II's document *The Church in the Modern World* as fuel ("with respect to the fundamental rights of the person, every type of discrimination based on sex is to be overcome and eradicated as contrary to God's intent").

Sullivan endorsed the ERA even though there were fears that it might further the cause of abortion. "I don't fear the consequences of ERA so much as I fear for the many women who will continue to suffer blatant injustices and oppression without ERA. . . . Therefore I say yes to ERA because it promotes equality over discrimination, giftedness over maleness, dignity over subservience, personhood over sex."[25]

These words reflected Sullivan's values and Vatican II's vision, which was to embrace the world and bring social justice to those who had suffered from the withholding of it. But when the Second Vatican Council ended in 1965 and the bishops returned for good to their dioceses, the solidarity and euphoria that had been palpable during their four years together dissipated. The Curia, which had tried to keep Vatican II from happening, was determined to regain control. In 1978 it did.

Paul VI, who was by no means a docile pope by Curia standards, died on August 6, 1978. There followed quickly the death of his successor, John Paul I, a few months later. But with the elevation of a Pole, Karol Wojtyla, to the papacy, the Curia finally got what they wanted. John Paul II was a charismatic, anti-Communist conservative of great moral courage who captured the imagination of the entire world and took control of the Church the way a skilled horse trainer takes control of a stallion that needs to be reminded who holds the reins.

"A Pole has become pope," said Poland's communist leader, Edward Gierek. "It is a great event for the Polish people and a great complication for us." The same thing could be said for Catholics and the Church. John Paul II had a thrilling—and a chilling—effect upon both.

Globally, John Paul II was a papal rock-star, jetting around the world, speaking to huge crowds of the faithful, preaching reform, dialogue, and a return to the Catholic truths that are the Church's bedrock. It was part of his signature style to disembark from his papal plane and kiss the ground of whatever country he was visiting. But internally, in the Church, itself, he was an authoritarian who made it clear that bishops, priests, and Church theologians who questioned pronouncements of the pope could expect trouble.

"He was an imperial pope. Let's face it," said Joseph Fahey, who teaches peace studies at Manhattan College and was a co-founder of the American branch of Pax Christi, an international Catholic peace organization. "The world revolved around his ego and his posters. As Augustine of Hippo said on the subject of original sin, 'Roma locuta est, causa finita est' (Rome has spoken, the case is closed)."

John Paul II was a complex and compelling man, whose personal piety and goodness were observed by many. He made sincere efforts to build new bridges between other Christian churches, and with the Jews, who had been so badly betrayed by the Church during events leading up to the Holocaust. But his position on such critical issues as artificial birth control and the ordination of women were large stumbling blocks to ecumenical unification with other Christian denominations— and to bringing Catholic women closer to the Church.

Like chalices at a Mass, women were simultaneously raised up by the pope (with praise) and then put down again (with edicts and encyclicals) right where they had been before. John Paul II reinforced the papal ban against artificial birth control and came out with a theory of "complementarity," which was an oblique way of saying that the bodily differences between the sexes make their roles in life different but not interchangeable. Then in 1994 he attempted to end the discussion about women priests by his encyclical *Ordinatio Sacerdotalis,* which expressly stated that women could not be priests because Jesus didn't have any female ministers.

American Catholics were of two minds about John Paul II. As one of the pope's trusted aides, Cardinal Robert Tucci, observed, "I have the impression they like the singer, but not the song."

Bishop Sullivan was ordained when Paul VI was pontiff. But most of his episcopacy was carried out during the papacy of John Paul II in a very different, more restrictive time. Bishops like Sullivan, Gumbleton of Detroit, and Bernardin of Chicago—who had been chosen for their pastoral qualities by pastoral-minded popes John XXIII and Paul VI—had to be careful to stay on John Paul II's good (or blind) side.

Sullivan did this by making sure that whatever actions he took or policies he pursued were always backed up, explicitly, by official proclamations of the Church itself. But he balanced prudence with fortitude and was characteristically unafraid to speak his mind among his peers.

During a 1978 meeting at the U.S. Conference of Catholic Bishops, for example, he complained that the bishops as a group projected the image of "being very institutional, rather than spiritual." In a *Washington Post* story Sullivan accused his fellow bishops of being lobbyists, wanting to trade their support on Carter's Panama Canal treaties for greater sensitivity to Catholic issues.[26] "I never knew we backed the Panama Canal treaties to help Carter," Sullivan subsequently wrote in the *Catholic Virginian.* "I thought we did it for justice reasons. I don't think Carter owes us any favors. We shouldn't be in anybody's camp."

But as importantly, at the bishops' conference, the *Washington Post* reported that they refused to enter into a dialogue with some women who had come before them to discuss the issue of women's ordination. The bishops voted to establish a subcommittee, which included Sullivan, to meet "but not enter into discussion with them." Sullivan was outraged.

"We dialogue with other religions and even unbelievers. It would be tragic if we couldn't meet with those with whom we share the Eucharist. If you don't talk, all you do is alienate people."[27]

That attitude attracted women like Kathleen Kenney to come to work for the bishop. A former nun, Kenney had entered the convent at eighteen in Kansas City, Missouri. "It was a Spanish order," she said. "The motherhouse was in Madrid. And when Vatican II took place, the order began to make some positive changes. But then the community started to regress."

Kenney left the order and moved between various jobs, finally being hired by Catholic Relief Services in Baltimore to teach young people how to apply principles of peace and justice in their life.

"It was an excellent program, but the Church gets scared when you start talking about social justice. So I saw that there was a job opening in Richmond working for the diocese. Finally I had found a place where I could work with integrity. Walter gets the Gospel, and that it's about bringing the full message to institutions and people."

Kenney's overall job was to promote parish involvement in various issues that Bishop Sullivan thought were important, which included women. "He was very encouraging about whatever the Women's Commission did and would come to the meetings when he was invited."

She recalled one woman, a convert to Catholicism, who would talk frequently to Bishop Sullivan, telling him how much she wanted to take the next step and study for the priesthood. "Walter listened to her anguish and expressed compassion for the pain she was going through. He was very encouraging, but she had to know he couldn't change things."

Another woman in campus ministry met her husband when he was a seminarian. She was, said Kenney, "very committed to serving people, sharing the Gospel, especially with young people." Sullivan appointed her chaplain at Lynchburg College, where she remained for many years. Graduates asked her to marry them, and she sometimes held prayer services with the breaking of the bread. "People complained," said Kenney, "but the bishop never stepped in."

As the years went by and Rome issued one declaration after another saying that it was not within the tradition of the Church to admit women to the priesthood, Sullivan finally fell silent on the subject. "It's not going to be in my lifetime," he conceded in an interview after he retired. "I'd be in favor of it if it happened tomorrow," but he was careful to point out that he was not challenging the current doctrine. "I'm a coward."

There were, however, certain issues where the bishop fell out of favor with most feminists: he opposed sterilization, *in vitro* fertilization, and, most importantly, abortion. He was consistent in his belief that life has its own rights, whether it is a fetus or a death row prisoner. It confused some people who were eager to claim (or declaim) Sullivan as being a "liberal," which he was on many other issues. But as far as abortion goes, he was, in fact, not liberal at all.

In 1973 in *Roe v. Wade*, when the Supreme Court granted women the right to have an abortion, Sullivan made the connection between the recent end of the killing in the Vietnam

War and the new "legally arranged" killing of fetuses, calling it a "new means for the killing of our youth."[28]

In 1981, when Senator Orrin Hatch (R-Utah) proposed a constitutional amendment that would permit Congress and the states to pass laws regulating or banning abortion, Bishop Sullivan was on board, calling it "a first step in trying to make sense of what is going on in our country."[29]

But rather than rest in the certitude of a position by simply being against something, Sullivan was also clear that the abortion issue would not be solved until there was an equally strong push to support women facing a problem pregnancy. "We're called to be pro-life. I am pro-life. But you can't just focus on abortion. The Church should not demand that a woman have her child if the Church, in fact, seems unwilling to help her during the crisis points of pregnancy and after childbirth. If a woman feels abandoned, with no place to turn for love and care, then the pressure for abortion becomes overwhelming."[30]

Fletcher Lowe, who worked with Bishop Sullivan in many interfaith settings, was aware of his position on abortion but never felt it was "big on his radar screen." In this, Lowe may have mistaken the bishop's diplomacy among those who did not support his views for not supporting the Church's position.

"I don't think you're going to turn back the clock on abortion," the bishop said in an interview, but he was clear about what side of the issue was the one he espoused. "You're killing an innocent person. . . . How can you say this is good?" What isn't good, he added, is the way the current U.S. Conference of Catholic Bishops has turned abortion into their main issue. "Abortion is an easy issue to oppose. It's very safe. You don't have to do anything but just be against it."

As for artificial birth control, Bishop Sullivan feels little other than the duty to pledge allegiance to the pope and change the subject. "People have to form their own conscience," he said. "I will never come out in favor of contraception, but it's a lesser evil than abortion. I have to uphold Catholic teachings. My role is to be a teacher of the doctrine of the Church but when 90 percent of your Catholics don't even believe in this, . . . it's not [a] major issue today."

Prior to 1968, the birth control issue had been quiescent for some time. Before attending Vatican II, very few bishops even mentioned it in the questionnaire they were asked to fill out beforehand, listing their major concerns. But in 1968 Paul VI declared in his encyclical *Humanae Vitae* that using any form of birth control other than the rhythm method was immoral.

According to numerous Church historians who were present at Vatican II, *Humanae Vitae* flew in the face of the recommendations of the pope's own specially appointed pontifical commission, which had been ordered to examine the issue of birth control and report back their findings. They did and three years later advised the pope that he should declare birth control permissible. It put Paul VI in a terrible bind.

The only significant work done during the First Vatican Council (1868–70) was to declare the pope to be infallible in matters of faith and morals. Subsequently, both Pope Pius XI and Pius XII declared birth control to be a mortal sin. Any change of position would cause the Church to look theologically inconsistent.

Writing for the *National Catholic Reporter*, journalist Robert Blair Kaiser commented, "If he dared change the not-so-ancient (1931) teaching, he would lose his moral authority. The ironic outcome: He didn't change the teaching and lost his moral authority. . . . Almost half of the Catholic bishops in the world issued statements that nuanced *Humanae Vitae* into nothing. In the next ten years of his reign, the pope never wrote another encyclical."[31]

In Washington, D.C., fifty-one priests signed a statement protesting the pope's position. Archbishop O'Boyle promptly suspended them all, which was a shock to the liberal Catholics in his diocese, as O'Boyle was known as a liberal when it came to other issues, like civil rights. Bishop Sullivan remembers that shortly after the O'Boyle incident was made public, Bishop Russell called him into his office and asked him who he was with, the pope or the dissidents, on *Humanae Vitae.*

"My answer was, 'Don't ask me'—and he never did."

The other group that had never been publicly welcomed into the Richmond diocese were gays and lesbians. Initially, they were not in Sullivan's line of vision. Then, in the early 1970s, he was invited by a Catholic gay group in Richmond called "Dignity" to meet with them at Virginia Commonwealth University. "One thing kind of led to another," he said, "because there were people involved."

"We were all a nervous wreck," he recalled. "We had never talked about it before, but when one Catholic lawyer in a big Richmond firm said that if the firm knew he was gay he would be fired, I was shocked. I never realized there was such prejudice. I just couldn't believe that people would do that!"

That meeting at V.C.U. was the beginning of the bishop's education and involvement with the gay community. "I remember one fellow saying, 'Bishop, why don't you wake up? There are more gay people who are married than not.' Over time I have found that to be true."

He began to visit people with AIDS who were living at home. "One of them was a woman who was skin and bones. I would bring them communion and there was a certain uneasiness at the beginning. One of the men I was sitting across from asked, 'Do I make you nervous?' There was no point in not being honest. 'Yes, I am nervous,' I said."

Gradually, the bishop began to realize that there was a sizable gay community in the Richmond diocese. In 1976 he directed the diocesan Office of Social Ministry to form a task force to examine their needs. In 1977 a human sexuality committee was established to implement the recommendations of the task force. In 1983 he changed the name to the Committee on Sexual Minorities, a diocesan body that reported directly to him.

Under "Services" of the Sexual Minorities Committee was included "providing assistance to the formation and promotion of local chapters of Dignity, an organization for gay and lesbian Christians. . . . Pastoral ministers are encouraged to contact local Dignity chapters and find out more about Dignity." He allowed Dignity members to hold their meetings on Church property.

In 1997 the Richmond diocese conducted its first Mass for gays and lesbians called "A Liturgy in Celebration of Gay and Lesbian Catholics." In his homily, Bishop Sullivan said, "You know you belong here. It's about time somebody said that to you. . . . This is your spiritual home."

The Mass became a yearly ritual. "The cathedral would be two-thirds full," said Sullivan. "I would make a point to say, 'Welcome, you belong here. This is your church, you are part of our family.' Sometimes they would cry."

Sullivan also met with the parents of gay children. "That's top secret, too, that their children are gay," he said. "They were wracked with guilt over whether they had somehow caused their sons and daughters to be homosexual and would wonder aloud whether it was something they had done that caused it. I told them they had nothing to do with it. It has to do with chromosomes. Homosexuality was *ab initio* [from the beginning]. There would be arguments that homosexuality was an acquired behavior but given the public disdain who in the heck wants to be gay?"

In 1992 an unsigned document from the Vatican was circulated among American bishops at their June meeting. It warned against "well-intentioned" support of antidiscrimination laws that could allow homosexuals to participate in areas like adoption, military service, and teaching and coaching. Sullivan was only one of two bishops who signed a statement along with fifteen hundred other Catholics protesting.

"This wasn't the pope," he said. "It came from some office in the Vatican. I don't know why more bishops didn't join with us. Maybe they were scared. Tom Gumbleton was the other bishop who signed. He had a gay brother who lived in Richmond."

Occasionally, the issue of homosexuality would get more personal. Robert Kline, who is one of the bishop's oldest friends, met him in the 1960s when he owned an ad agency in Richmond. The Kline family was Catholic and attended Mass at the cathedral. Their daughter, Jeanie, was very active in the life of the parish and came in frequent contact with the bishop.

"In 1987," said Kline, "when she was teaching at St. Gertrude's School, she outed herself as a gay lady. Until then I'm not sure she knew what she was, but somehow the word got out at St. Gertrude's and then the ultra-conservative Catholic newspaper, the *Wanderer*, wrote a story about Jeanne that said some terrible things about her. Walter Sullivan wrote us a letter, which we still have."

A week following Kline's interview, the letter Kline was referring to arrived in the mail.

March 31, 1987

Dear Bob and Jean,

I received a very thoughtful letter from Jeanie and I was very distressed to learn of the pain caused to you because of the articles that appeared in *The Wanderer*. I did not appreciate sufficiently the depth of hate in the articles until I realized that people are willing to be judgmental of others in a spirit of self-righteousness. I am contemplating writing a letter to the *Wanderer*, not in my own behalf but in behalf of those who have been deeply hurt by such malicious articles.

I have written to Jeanie because of my great admiration for her. She is a person of deep faith and deep convictions. She will always have my personal support.

Yours sincerely,
Walter F. Sullivan
Bishop of Richmond

"My wife nearly wept when she read the letter," said Kline, "as did I. It was very powerful."

On the issue of homosexuality, Sullivan walked an exquisitely straight line. There is no record that he ever wrote to the *Wanderer* but earlier that same month in his "Tidings" column, fully two-thirds of it was devoted to a sympathetic discussion of the pain and suffering that gay Catholics endure. The last third of his column stressed that he has never "promoted or condoned homosexuality" and that a recent letter from the Congregation of the Faithful now forbids the Church from supporting any organizations that undermine, are ambiguous, or are silent on the Church's teaching on the subject.

"In keeping with that directive, I, as bishop, will discontinue permission for the scheduling of religious services or the use of church buildings by the Dignity chapters." In a follow-up letter to "All Priests" in his diocese, Sullivan reaffirmed his decision to withdraw support from Dignity while adding "the Church mandates pastoral care to homosexuals. Under no circumstances should we lessen our commitment to those who are very alienated."[32]

Finally, in what must have been a coordinated action, Charles O'Keeffe, the head of the diocese's pastoral council, wrote a respectful, canonically precise letter to the apostolic nuncio, Pio Laghi, in Washington, D.C., which was designed to sweep the path clean of all opportunities for Rome to misinterpret Bishop Sullivan's words or action.

> Excellency, be assured that the foundation on which the Diocese of Richmond's ministry to homosexual persons is based, is rooted in the "To Live in Christ Jesus" pastoral letter which has its origins in *Persona Humana*, and is in context with the aforementioned instructions.[33]

O'Keeffe respectfully asked that the apostolic nuncio forward a copy of his letter to the Curia and to anyone writing to Rome or Laghi complaining, and that copies of their letters and Laghi's response be sent to the Richmond diocese.

In 1998 the U.S. Conference of Catholic Bishops came out with a pastoral letter called "Always Our Children." "The underlying message," said Father Pat Apuzzo, "was that parents have gay children and they do not disown them. They are still their children. Walter capitalized on that approach. For instance, with the Catholic gay and lesbian group Dignity, there was a big clamp-down from on high that the Church was to have no more to do with that organization. Sullivan complied and no longer allowed Dignity to convene on Church property. But he continued to have a sexual minority commission that was active in the diocese. Gay Catholics could meet there. What Walter learned was that the Church has a pastoral solution to most problems."

In other instances when the Vatican ordered him to do, or un-do, something he had already done, Bishop Sullivan was not adverse to citing the Church's best interests as a reason to leave well enough alone.

In 1984 a collection of scholarly articles on the Church and homosexuality called *A Challenge to Love* was published. "I didn't read it," said Sullivan, "but I wrote the introduction. Then I got the word from Rome that I had to remove it. I said that I would, out of obedience, and I did remove it. But I also told them that doing this would mean that many more books would be sold. And when the news came out that's exactly what happened."

The relationship of the Church to gay Catholics is a tangled one, made more so by the presence of gays in the priesthood, even though seminarians must attest that they "do not suffer from a disordered sexual orientation, i.e., do not consider oneself to be homosexual." These two sides of the issue came together for Bishop Sullivan when one of the most popular priests in his diocese asked to see him.

"He told me he had AIDS and then he asked, 'What are you going to do with me?' I'm a great believer in symbols. You set an example. I said, 'Why don't you come and live with me?' So he came to live near me, staying with Bishop Foley. But he ate every day at my table. AIDS is not poison ivy. You can't get sick by being near it."

The hardest thing Sullivan had to do was to convince the priest to go public. "Everybody suspected it but people were tiptoeing around the subject. I told him that we can't say anything until you give us your consent—and it took him awhile to get up his nerve. His mother did not want him to say anything. I told him to go back and ask her again. Finally, he gave permission and I put an announcement in the *Catholic Virginian*.

"There was this tremendous outpouring of love toward him. By going public, it allowed people to minister to him." Or almost everyone. The bishop remembers hearing from one angry reader who wrote in and said that the bishop never mentioned how he got AIDS. "I wrote back and said it's none of your business. I had no need to know."

When the priest died, Bishop Sullivan said a funeral Mass for him at the cathedral. The cathedral was packed.

Chapter Eight

To Unite All in Christ

In 1959, when Pope John XXIII first announced his decision to hold a Second Vatican Council, the Vatican's two major news organs, *l'Osservatore Romano* and *La Civiltà Cattolica,* ignored the news. Perhaps, thought the Curia, the pope's idea could still be derailed or neglected to death. But the rest of the world paid attention.

"The people," wrote Church historian Giuseppe Alberigo, "Catholics and non-Catholics, instinctively understood that the elderly pope's initiative was a highly significant act and saw in it a sign of hope."[34]

The ecumenical climate among Christians in the United States in the 1950s was not warm. Reinhold Niebuhr called the lack of connection between Protestants and Catholics in America "a scandal and an offense against Christian charity."[35] Protestants feared domination by a religion whose members swore allegiance to an infallible pope. Catholics feared contamination by exposure to religions that were, by definition, heretical and therefore full of error. When the term "ecumenism" was used by most Catholic theologians, it referred to heretics and schismatics returning to the Holy Roman Catholic Church.

The fullness of Vatican II would develop slowly, but Pope John XXIII knew at the outset what he wanted the Council to provide—an opportunity for the Church to refresh itself with the waters of the Gospel, to reexamine its roots, and, very significantly, to spread out its arms to the rest of the world. It was not an accident that he announced the Council for the first time on the last day of the Octave of Christian Unity. The Second Vatican Council, said the pope, was "an invitation to the separated communities in the quest for unity which joins so many souls from every quarter of the world."[36]

Toward that end, the Secretariat for Christian Unity was created, which would allow the participation of Catholic bishops and, most especially, Catholic theologians who were outside the Curia's orbit, even those who had been sanctioned by them. Vatican II was not simply or even primarily about reunification between the various Christian traditions. "Nevertheless," wrote Alberigo, "Pope John had repeatedly emphasized that the Council must signal a fundamental shift in the willingness of Catholics to participate in ecumenical efforts for unity among all the Christian Churches."

Bishop Sullivan was, by temperament and belief, a bridge-builder, someone who easily and instinctively reached out to other people. Whenever he saw the chance to join with other faith communities or, in one instance, to create a new one, he took it. And in the mid-1960s the ecumenical scene in Virginia was a nearly empty stage waiting for players.

With the exception of the Virginia Council of Churches, the Chaplain Service of the Churches of Virginia, and the Anti-Defamation League, there were very few watchdogs paying attention to what was going on in the city or surrounding areas. But that would change, largely because of Walter Sullivan and a small group of like-minded clergymen who were looking for each other.

In 1967 the Episcopal priest Fletcher Lowe fell in step alongside the bishop. A native of South Carolina, Lowe was deeply influenced by an African American woman who worked for his family. "It was Rachel," he said, "who planted the seeds of social justice within me." During the height of the civil rights movement in the mid-1960s, Lowe worked in two southern parishes where integration was a primary focus.

Then he came to Richmond as the Episcopal Diocese of Virginia's point man on matters of social justice. "I was director of the Department of Christian Social Relations. That meant I was the conduit on matters of race, the Vietnam War, and so forth. One of my gut principles was to work with other people of faith. I wanted to get out of the Episcopal box, and so I looked around to see who felt the same way. I was looking for a mentor and that's when I met Walter."

Jim Payne was another clergyman who found his way to Sullivan's side. A Presbyterian minister, he resisted the ordination call for a while. Finally, after serving in the Marine Corps during the Korean War ("I had seen all of war and killing that I ever wanted to see") he decided to enter the seminary. After two pastoral assignments, Payne got a call from the Presbyterian Synod in Richmond. "They told me we ain't cuttin' it."

In the Presbyterian Church it was a time when large issues were often being sabotaged by small concerns. "In 1968 the whole country was immersed in the issues of segregation and war," said Payne, "but some of our churches were threatening to withhold their contributions because beer was being allowed at Hampden-Sydney College! The Lynchburg Presbyterian Home was a segregated institution with a substantial endowment, but they were not moving significantly toward inclusiveness."

That April, Payne took the job as the executive secretary of the Presbyterian Synod of Virginia. "One of the first things I did, along with some other forward-thinking members of the Synod, was go down to the city manager of Richmond and ask how we could be helpful. I met Walter at a meeting of TRUST, which was a new interfaith group that wanted to get congregations involved with urban renewal. He was very much inclined toward ecumenical things."

Payne's first assessment of Sullivan was that he was bright and committed to cooperation but unaware of some of the nuances in the ecumenical community. But he had a tremendous ability to pick exceptional people for his staff. "Eileen Dooley was one of the most competent people you could ever find. Stephen Colecchi was another."

At that time the major ecumenical presence in Virginia was the Virginia Council of Churches. "It did a lot of policy analysis on faith and order. There were some pretty groundbreaking projects in the area of child welfare and migrant ministries. But Walter thought the council was too narrow in its scope, membership, and public policy involvement. He sent representatives to the meetings but let it be known that if the Catholic Church was to join, he wanted additional religious organizations to be included."

Eventually, both Lowe and Payne joined up with Walter Sullivan and others to create an informal group of religious leaders that called itself "The Tuesday Morning Breakfast Group." "We saw there was no presence of the faith community before the General Assembly," said Lowe, "and so a number of us began to meet, sometimes at Walter's house, sometimes at the downtown Y. We would invite the head of corrections in, or various senatorial candidates. We were a force but not organized."

In time, the Breakfast Group grew into the Ecumenical Social Concerns Alliance, which was led by a small but robust roster of interfaith leaders from the Richmond faith community: Father "Nick" Dombalis from the Greek Orthodox

Church, Rabbi Myron Berman from Temple Beth-el, The Reverend George Ricketts of the Virginia Chaplaincy Service, Eileen Dooley and Father Virgil Funk from the Catholic Diocese. They held brown-bag seminars, went on overnight retreats, visited prisons, and tried to stay on top of legislative issues being introduced in the General Assembly that were of concern to them, writing letters of concern or protest where needed.

The minutes of their meetings reflect a wide range of issues:

> Father Dombalis noted the problems faced by watermen who have lost their employment because of the closing of the James River due to Kepone poisoning.

> Boat People Ad: This advertisement, focusing on the needs of the Indo-Chinese Boat People, cost $163.68. Please send your contribution to the Jewish Federation.

> It was noted that there is currently an inmate on death row who is scheduled for execution in mid-June. After some discussion, it was suggested that Mr. Lowe request a stay of execution from the Governor.

> Heard briefings on: Strip Mining, Welfare, Housing, Aging, Energy.

> Capital Punishment Open Hearing October 25.

"Walter really wanted a public policy organization," said Payne. "He put one thousand dollars into a feasibility study. A very big helper was the director of the Anti-Defamation League, Norm Olshansky." In 1982 the Ecumenical Social Concerns Alliance joined with some of the denominational groups in the Virginia

Council of Churches to create the Virginia Interfaith Center for Public Policy. That same year, Payne became the Center's founding director.

"That's when we went out on a limb and stamped it," said Lowe. "We were no longer simply a group of volunteers. We formalized it.

"Walter was the charismatic leader," said Lowe, who would frequently accompany Bishop Sullivan to various prisons around the state. "If it was just a couple of Protestant clergymen, we weren't always successful in gaining entrance. But when the bishop was there, it was a different story. You had to take the bishop seriously. Walter opened doors, and we followed behind him."

"I remember," said Bishop Sullivan, "a bunch of us trudging down to the state capitol at midnight, and it was snowing and icy outside, to talk against capital punishment. I think they were impressed by the fact that we came that late at night. But there was one legislator there who was reading a newspaper while we testified. I said that I would appreciate it if he wouldn't read the paper while we were talking. That used to be called 'bad manners.' He put it down."

Charisma aside, there were practical reasons why Bishop Sullivan took the lead. Had any one of his Protestant or Jewish colleagues taken too prominent a position on an issue like opposing the death penalty, or promoting a nuclear freeze, they could have found themselves without a job. But a Catholic bishop is more insulated. Technically he serves at the pope's pleasure, but unless he is convicted of a felony or reaches retirement age, he is not usually removed. Then too, as a bishop, Sullivan's prominence gave everyone else the kind of cover that allowed them to take more profoundly Judeo-Christian stands.

As far as Christian unity was concerned, Sullivan was realistic about ecumenism, which had a honeymoon period that
ended right after Vatican II. Writing in his "Tidings" column
("On Christian Unity") Sullivan admitted that at first "most of
us believed that centuries of division and mistrust would disappear once sincere folk sat around a table together. . . . We
learned very quickly that ecumenism involves more than the
way we cozy up to one another."[37]

Sullivan was the first Catholic bishop to take part in the
annual ecumenical pilgrimage to St. Luke's Church in Smith-
field. He spoke often at various Protestant churches and Jewish synagogues on the need for unity. And when he preached
at a Reformation Day service for twelve Lutheran churches, he
charmed/stunned the congregation when he declared "Martin Luther was right. What do we do now?"

While he was still the rector of the cathedral in the late
1960s, Sullivan got together with a half dozen fellow clergymen from the Stuart Circle area of downtown and formed
what became known as the Stuart Circle Parish. They held
Lenten services, Palm Sunday processions, and later opened
up an adult day care center and a feeding program.

"For two or three decades, Bishop Sullivan was the voice of
the Christian Church in the Commonwealth of Virginia," said
The Reverand Jonathan Barton, director of the Virginia Council of Churches. "He had that level of relationship and respect
from everyone. When Walter rose to speak it was E. F. Hutton
time. He could articulate and read Christians in a way I have
not seen anyone else do."

Barton also knew the bishop the way a grieving parent
knows a comforter. "When an auto accident took my daughter
Katy's life, Walter offered to be part of the service and he came

in the full vestments of the Catholic Church. I was totally grateful for his presence.

"I don't know too many people who are as open, tolerant, and not threatened as Walter," said Barton. "Look at what he and Episcopal Bishop David Rose did at Holy Apostles. They just sat down and said, 'We can do this.'"

In 1975 Bishop Sullivan and Bishop Rose announced the formation of a committee to explore the possibility of bringing the Anglican and Roman Catholic churches under one roof in a religious community in Virginia Beach. Two years later the committee announced that they were ready to go forward in a "bold venture in faith, open to members from both the Roman Catholic and Episcopal communions."

The announcement did not go unnoticed in Rome. In October 1977, Bishop Sullivan received a letter from the Congregation of the Clergy. He wrote back and told them what he was doing. On November 13, the bishop got another letter saying that he was to withdraw the Church's participation. But it was too late. The bishop wrote back and told them that he had opened it already, on November 1, All Saints' Day.

"Rome asked me not to establish the joint Anglican and Roman Catholic parish basically because it had never been done before. We were very careful to only worship only where we were in agreement with each other," said Sullivan. "That way it was an authentic joining. I said I will withdraw our support, out of obedience, but I will tell people that I was ordered to do it. They said, well, maybe we'll see what happens."

That was thirty-five years ago. Today, the Church of the Holy Apostles is a small ecumenical showplace, the only one of its kind in the world. The congregation worships as one body until communion time. Then the Catholics receive communion at one altar and the Anglicans at the other, after which the community comes together again. "And here's the delightful thing," said the late Father Tom Quinlan, who was on the committee that set the congregation up. "Episcopalians now allow Lutheran ministers to substitute for Episcopalians, so now we've got the three of them together."[38]

The quest for reunification did not begin and end with one experiment. In 1983 Sullivan pursued the theme by signing a joint pastoral letter (along with Bishop Thomas Welsh of the Arlington diocese) and the three Episcopal bishops of Virginia asking for prayers for the reunion of the Anglican and Catholic traditions worldwide. The letter was read in all parishes later that month.

In a 2004 interview, theologian Hans Küng declared that ecumenism was at an impasse, particularly because of *Dominus Iesus,* the Vatican's statement of 2001 that specifically referred to other Christian denominations as "deficient" forms of religion. There is quite a lot of grassroots ecumenical activity, Küng said, but those in the hierarchy "do everything to hinder, for instance, Eucharistic communion. . . . They are very strong in words and gestures, they are always saying we are very ecumenical, but practically speaking, they are hindering it."[39]

Sullivan is widely considered to have been a liberal bishop in a conservative diocese. But as Monsignor William Carr observed, "Walter is conservative in certain important ways. There was an 'old priest' sense about him even when he was young. You find many priests who look like everybody's favorite uncle, but if you tread on their devotions, a different side emerges. Old priests have a deep devotion to the Eucharist."

John Barrett, the diocesan CFO while Sullivan was bishop, supplied a supporting anecdote. "The bishop was going to give communion to somebody when I was with him and he went to the cathedral to pick up the host. I said to him, 'So you're going to bring some bread to your friend?' And he said, 'Don't you ever call it "bread" in my presence again. You and I both know it's the Eucharist.'"

But Sullivan's reverence for the Eucharist and his understanding of who should receive it are not the same thing. When it came to giving out communion he could be disarmingly (or alarmingly, depending upon your point of view) informal. "Once," said his friend Bob Kline, "when I was coming up the aisle to receive, Bishop Sullivan saw me coming and whispered, after he had given me communion, 'Bob, let's have lunch.'"

On another occasion, when Bishop Sullivan was saying Mass in prison, one of the inmates who saw him give communion to his Episcopal colleague, Fletcher Lowe, turned stool pigeon and wrote a letter complaining about it. "I think I got a letter from the papal nuncio about it," said Sullivan. "I don't remember."

Virginia's Episcopal bishop Peter Lee has taken part in many ecumenical services with Bishop Sullivan. He learned the difference between northern and southern hospitality in Virginia when he attended the funeral for Bishop Keating in Arlington.

"The funeral was held at the Cathedral of St. Thomas More," said Lee. "It was a very conservative crowd. Justice Clarence Thomas and Justice Antonin Scalia were in the front row. Before the service there was a public announcement that 'only active Catholics' could receive communion. We knew that. But the message we all received was that we were not welcome. By contrast, when the Richmond diocese had its centennial service at the University of Richmond, the ecumenical crowd was seated to one side. When communion time came, Bishop Sullivan waved us all forward to the communion table."

That gesture of inclusion made a deep impression on Peter Lee. "Walter was and is so open. I think his innate kindness has won over so many hearts."

"There was a period when Walter was younger," said Monsignor Pitt, "when he knew the rules, whatever they were, about who could receive communion and under what circumstances. But later in life he was, how shall we say, more generous in his interpretation."

When Bishop Sullivan was asked how he, personally, felt about the giving of communion, he knew his own mind. "The altar rail should not be a battleground. Who knows the state of a person's soul?"

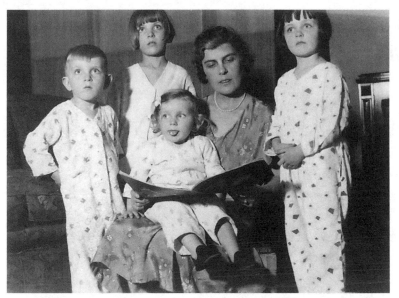

Walter Sullivan with his mother and three sisters, Patricia, Kathleen, and the youngest, Betty.

An altar boy.

A seminarian at St. Mary's in Baltimore.

A young priest.

Bishop Walter Sullivan's first "ad limina" visit to Rome in 1972. This was the moment when Sullivan recalled that Pope Paul VI grasped his hand, looked him in the eye and said, "You and I are brothers," to which Bishop Sullivan replied, "Aye, aye, Sir." To the pope's left is the future Cardinal Justin Rigali, who was serving in the Vatican's Congregation for the Clergy. He would later become the Archbishop of Philadelphia, where his resignation in 2011 occurred against a widening sex abuse scandal involving many priests in the archdiocese.

Celebrating Mass.

*Bishop Sullivan with Pope John Paul II during
a later ad limina visit to Rome.*

Bishop Sullivan giving a talk in the Cathedral of the Sacred heart in Richmond.

Bishop Sullivan and Bishop Raymond Hunthausen in Seattle, during the time they were both being investigated by the Vatican.

Walter Sullivan in a Brazilian favela during a trip with the Christian Children's Fund: "I went into the favela and there was this woman who might have had two or three children out of wedlock. That's how she survived, by her body. That poor woman, I thought. If there is a God, God is here!"

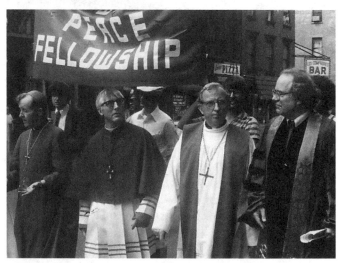

An anti-nuclear peace march in New York City, June 12, 1982. From left to right: Bishop Jack Snyder from St. Augustine, Florida, Auxiliary Bishop Thomas Gumbleton from Detroit, Bishop Sullivan, and the Rev. William Sloan Coffin, Presbyterian senior minister at Riverside Church in New York.

The bishop with his terriers, in retirement at Sandbridge, Virginia

Performing a home baptism, 1998.

Bishop Sullivan's last meeting with Pope John Paul II in Rome, shortly before the pope died.

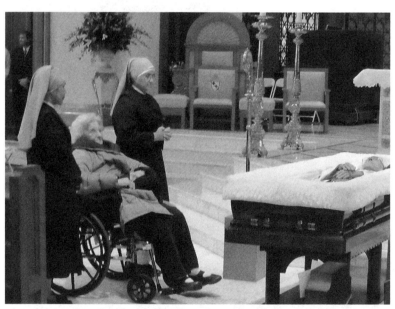

Mourners beside the bishop's casket in Sacred Heart Cathedral.

Chapter Nine

Journey for Peace

Walter Sullivan considered himself a political conservative, confiding to one friend that he had voted for Nixon
in the 1968 presidential race. He does not, to this day, consider
himself a pacifist. "I believe in the right to self-defense. We
have to protect the innocent. Passivity is not a way of life for
me." But until he personally experienced the anguish of the
Vietnam War, which was splitting the country apart, he was
passive enough.

The 1960s had been a bloody and demoralizing decade.
President John Kennedy, Martin Luther King, and Robert
Kennedy had all been assassinated. Defense Secretary Rob-
ert McNamara admitted that the massive carpet bombing of
North Vietnam had been ineffective. President Lyndon John-
son, defeated by huge anti-war rallies that had turned the
country against him, declined to run for a second term. The
Pentagon Papers, leaked by Daniel Ellsberg to the *New York
Times* in 1971, revealed that Johnson and his predecessors had
lied to the American public about the war.

Then in the early 1970s, Bishop Sullivan met with several
young draft resisters in the Richmond diocese who wanted to
go to Canada as conscientious objectors. "I said sure, I was all
for that. I realized the trauma they were going through, particularly with their families who didn't understand."

That experience affected him but did not pull him out of
his orbit. "Walter had been part of the peace movement in

an antiseptic way," said Monsignor Bill Pitt, who helped draft Bishop Russell's letters to the draft board for conscientious objectors. "But it was the Jesuit priest Dick McSorley who said, 'To work with the poor, to work for peace, you have to keep your hands dirty.'" Before 1971, Sullivan's hands had not yet come together on the subject. Today he admits that "unless something had not really moved me I might not have gotten so involved."

That "something" happened in the summer of 1971 when he received an invitation to speak at a large Knights of Columbus banquet in northern Virginia. The bishop had many friends in the Knights and for several years was their state chaplain. Had he spent a little time prior to his speech reviewing the history of the Knights themselves, he might have not been so shocked at the reception his speech received.

The Knights of Columbus was founded in New Haven, Connecticut, in 1882, to provide insurance benefits for Catholic immigrants who were denied access to labor unions and other benefit-giving fraternal organizations. Today it is the largest Catholic fraternal organization in the world with a credit rating that is higher than that of the United States government, or would be if the rating agencies had not refused to rate an American organization higher than its country of origin. It has given away billions of dollars to various charities and its founder, Father Michael McGivney, is now "the Venerable Michael McGivney," a candidate for sainthood.

The Knights' roots in the military history of this country run deep, beginning with several of the founding members who fought for the Union side in the Civil War. In 1916, the Knights set up service centers for General Pershing's troops during the Mexican Revolution. In both world wars, they provided places of recreation and spiritual refreshment for the troops. Knights chaplains worked alongside Catholic military chaplains. There is an ongoing commitment to provide scholarships, loans, and grants to military families and organizations related to the armed forces.

The weekend before he was scheduled to address the Knights, Bishop Sullivan spent time at his beach cottage in Sandbridge, turning over various ideas for his talk. Giving talks was part of his job description. "If you're a bishop you have to give a speech everywhere you go. It's expected. People say, 'Let's hear it from the bishop.' So I was looking around for something that was non-controversial and decided I would talk about how Jesus is our peace. Nobody could argue with that, right?" On the night of the banquet, the bishop got his answer.

It was a large banquet, with about four hundred Knights with their wives in attendance. When Sullivan started to talk about Jesus being our peace, the mood in the hall changed dramatically. "They got very hyper. I could see it on their faces. And that made me more hyper, and so I began to talk about the conscientious objectors I had counseled. After I had finished, all my friends came up to me and demanded to know how I could give such a talk."

It was a moment of shock and clarification for Sullivan, who had been unprepared for such instant hostility. "When I gave that speech, and others like it after that, I realized the deep hatred of the whole peace movement. Peace was a dirty word. It wasn't the military but the civilians, like the Knights, who were upset by the word. Just to challenge them was unbe-lievable. They canonized the Vietnam War!"

Had the story ended there, the bishop may not have returned home much different than how he had left it. But the evening was not over. "After all the haranguing, a man on the edge of the crowd, with a military haircut, came up to me. He identified himself as a retired Marine sergeant. 'I want to thank you,' he said. 'Tomorrow my son is going to Canada and I had been ready to disown him. Thank you for saving my son for me.' That had such an effect upon me that I began my journey for peace."

In 1971 the bishop was not traveling alone. He had the very real support of Pope Paul VI and small but growing group of other "peace bishops," many of whom the pope's papal nuncio, Jean Jadot, had recommended, at the pope's direction: Bishop Leroy Matthiesen of Amarillo, Archbishop Weakland of Minneapolis, Bishop Hunthausen of Seattle, Auxiliary Bishop Thomas Gumbleton of Detroit. They were called "Jadot's boys," and Sullivan was one of them.

The "peace bishops" never came close to holding the majority vote in the larger conference. At their most influential, they added up to less than 60 out of more than 250 colleagues. But the influence of Vatican II upon the Church, both in the United States and the world, was such that it tacitly or explicitly encouraged other like-minded Catholic organizations to come into being.

Pax Christi is an international Catholic peace group founded in Europe in 1945 to reconcile France and Germany after the war. In 1972, as the Vietnam War was winding down, Bishops Carroll Dozier of Memphis and Thomas J. Gumbleton of Detroit met at Dozier's home in Memphis with several others to discuss how to keep the momentum of the peace movement alive. They decided to create an American branch of Pax Christi.

"It got off to a rocky start," said Joseph Fahey, a former Maryknoll seminarian who taught peace studies at Manhattan College and was in on the organizing sessions. "We had our first national assembly in 1972 in Washington, D.C., but it fell apart because the priest who was running it turned out to be married. So we reconstituted ourselves two years later at Manhattan College. I became the general secretary. Thomas Gumbleton of Detroit and Carroll Dozier of Memphis were the first bishops to join."

In 1977 Archbishop William Borders of Baltimore agreed to host the first Bishops Mass for Peace in his diocese. "It was a way to get the bishops to do something public," said Fahey. "We linked it to the annual pope's World Day of Peace and in study sessions after the Mass a priest, Jack Lucal, and I gave off-the-record lectures on peace. The bishops admitted that they had never studied peace in the seminary and knew nothing about it."

Once again the Knights of Columbus came into view. "There were about twenty-five or thirty bishops and cardinals there," said Fahey, "and when Borders looks out into the congregation, there right in the middle of them was a group of Knights in their full regalia. In order for the bishops to get to their seats they had to walk under crossed swords—at a Peace Mass! Borders was furious. I said to him, 'Who cares?' All the other bishops laughed."

Walter Sullivan was present at the Mass. "There was nothing episcopal or clerical about him," said Fahey. "The next day, before the bishops went into a session, I happened to be walking with him and I said, 'Bishop Sullivan, I hope you'll consider joining Pax Christi.' And he looked at me and said, 'Joe, that's a great idea. I've been looking for a way to get involved in the peace movement for some time.' I said to him, 'This is it!'"

After the session was over, Sullivan came over to Fahey and said he was going to follow through with the invitation. "Then," said Fahey, "he started to come to the annual meetings. I said to Tom Gumbleton, 'Isn't it great we now have a third bishop?' and Gumbleton said something pretty profound. 'Joe, it's really not. We should have three hundred bishops.'"

The momentum for peace was building. A national nuclear freeze movement to stop the inexorable drift toward a nuclear showdown between superpowers was started in 1979. By 1980 the freeze had gained support from a broad spectrum of peace groups and was on the ballot (along with Republican candidate for president, Ronald Reagan) as an issue in the 1980 election in western Massachusetts. Fifty-nine of sixty-two towns voted in its favor.

That same month, Bishop Frank Murphy stood up at the U.S. Conference of Catholic Bishops meeting in Washington, D.C., and introduced what is known in the Church as "a varium," or "deviation" from the agenda. Signed by six bishops, including Sullivan, it called for a discussion on the threat of nuclear war and the arms race.

"This is what is different about the bishops' conference now," said Gumbleton in 2008. "We don't allow variums to come into our meetings any longer. You can't do anything spontaneous. We can't do anything that would relate to the concerns that are going on in the world around us when we're meeting and we're supposed to be the moral leaders of the Catholic Church."[40]

But in 1980 Archbishop John Roach, who was president of the Conference, made room for discussion. It went on for two or three hours, and after Gumbleton had had his turn and sat down something unusual happened. A few bishops began to clap and then it was picked up by some others, and then it went all around the room. It was decided that the bishops would work upon a pastoral letter addressing those issues. In the summer of 1981 a five-man committee, headed by Archbishop Joseph Bernardin of Chicago, was formed to produce a draft.

In retrospect, 1981 was a pivotal year, not only for the U.S. Conference of Catholic Bishops in general but for Bishop Sullivan in particular. To borrow from Bob Dylan, "the times, they were a-changing." But in Virginia, which one Washington pundit jokingly described as "a hotbed of social rest," change is usually paired with the phrase "resistance to."

Virginia is a particularly beautiful state, with an abundance of mountains, rivers, and majestic trees much older than the Declaration of Independence. If you ride west from Richmond to Charlottesville, the pristine fields and farms seen from a car window on Route 64 look about the way they looked to Thomas Jefferson as he traveled on horseback to Monticello. The James River winds around the city of Richmond, past old plantations-turned-tourist-attractions, before emptying into the Chesapeake Bay, joining the rivers Roanoke, York, and Rappahannock. But Virginia is not just a beautiful state. There are deep scars of battle beneath the grass. Of the 384 recorded battles during the Civil War, fully one-third of them took place on Old Dominion soil. Nor is its military history a thing of the past. Present-day Virginia is the most highly militarized state in the union.

"Texas and California are big defense states," said Steve Baggerly, who has been with the Catholic Worker in Norfolk since 1989. "And Connecticut also has a lot of military. But I don't think there is any state that is more militarized than Virginia." A quick trip to the Internet proved him right.

There are twenty-seven military bases in Virginia and over 14,000 defense contractors that in 2011 reported over $54 billion in revenue, up from $17 billion in 2000. ("War is our number-one business," said Baggerly. "Our entire economy is war-based.") The greatest concentration of bases and contractors are in the Tidewater area of Hampton, Newport News, and Virginia Beach, On one block in Suffolk, the "big five" companies of Raytheon, Boeing, Lockheed Martin, McDonnell Douglas, and Northrop Grumman all have their headquarters on one corner.

"Our nation is pretty much one vast armament factory and military base," said Baggerly matter-of-factly. "But the Hampton-Norfolk area, where I live, is the most militarized place in the western hemisphere."

Around the time that Bishop Sullivan was beginning to be active in the peace movement, there was a small but ardent group of peace proponents in the Richmond area that began meeting during the Vietnam War. Formed in 1979 after Rev. William Sloane Coffin was invited to speak at St. Paul's Episcopal Church in Richmond, it coalesced into what became known as the Richmond Peace Education Center. Two years later, Bishop Sullivan invited them to move, rent-free, to their present quarters on North Laurel Street across from the cathedral.

John Gallini was a member. An engineer with DuPont, he had moved with his young family to Richmond in the early 1970s. Settling into the Bon Air section of Richmond he became part of a "small community of inquiry" with four other couples at St. Edward's parish who were interested in connecting the Gospel to the issues of the day. One of those issues was what to do with the large influx of Vietnamese and Cambodian refugees who were pouring into the country after the war ended. The group decided to sponsor one of the families.

One of the women in the group, Phyllis Conklin, started it and began working with parishes to take on responsibility for a family. Bishop Sullivan, following her lead, established an office of refugee resettlement. "That grew to a point," said Eileen Dooley, "where it became an office with a large number of staff members. It had offices in Tidewater, Roanoke, and Richmond. The diocese was extraordinary in the number of resettled families they helped. It was an incredibly moving time."

One of the bishop's strengths was the ability to set aside what he thinks he knows and listen to other people. He was not an intellectual pushover, and he could be stubborn. In fact, stubbornness was another one of his traits. But Sullivan was collaborative by nature, and his ability to recognize a good idea enabled the people who had them to find their rightful place in the larger organization.

"None of us get there by ourselves," said Gallini, who helped draft a letter to Sullivan urging him to ban Selective Service from recruiting at Catholic schools. The bishop agreed to do it. In 1980, again with the bishop's support, they formed a local Pax Christi chapter.

"It was a totally different time then," said Gallini. "Priests who tended to think seriously about the Gospel had an excuse. The bishop saying these things gave them permission. We did things like inviting Bishop Tom Gumbleton and The Reverend Richard McSorley to speak at a retreat. Gumbleton and McSorley were heroes in the peace movement. The next year, Dan Berrigan came. A number of women religious led our retreats. Sullivan would almost always be there."

To be for peace in Virginia was easy. To be for peace and against war was complicated. Certainly Bishop Sullivan could not count upon editorial confirmation from the archconservative *Richmond Times-Dispatch.* Nor was there a very deep cushion of support in the Catholic diocese. Most Catholics in

Virginia were uncomfortable with a bishop who challenged the policies of a popular, albeit hawkish president (Ronald Reagan) whose "Peace through Strength" policies depended upon a nuclear build-up, not a nuclear freeze.

In 1980 the Richmond chapter of Pax Christi decided to try to get the parish councils to sign on to the national nuclear freeze statement to stop adding to our nuclear weapons. "We were able to get as many as a dozen parishes to sign on to it," said Gallini. "Then in 1981 Reagan came out and said he wasn't for it. We got all these calls saying that they wanted to take their names back."

Bob Quirin was a parish priest in the Richmond diocese from 1974 to 1981. A committed anti-war activist, he preached against the war from the pulpit and flew the American flag upside down—the universal sign of distress—outside his church on Moratorium Day in 1969, a day on which hundreds of thousands of protesters marched across the country. (His parish responded by putting him "on trial" for three months.) Quirin was part of an "early warning system" around Sullivan who nudged, tugged, and irritated him into greater awareness.

"In the early days Bob was much more active in the peace movement than I was," admitted Sullivan. "He refused to pay his taxes, even on his telephone. He sold his house, his car, anything the IRS could attach. You would think he didn't have a penny to his name."

One time a couple of IRS agents came into Sullivan's office and said that they were going to garnish Quirin's wages and if the bishop didn't want the Church to be embarrassed, he could pay the back taxes. Sullivan was outraged.

"I said, 'You can't come to me. I don't pay his salary. He's self-employed.' But they were fussing and fussing and finally

I stood up and said, 'Get out of here. Don't badger me! If you want to put him in jail, do it. But if you come back here again I'm going out on the steps of the cathedral to do an interview about your tactics.' "

The IRS agents never returned, but after they left, Bishop Sullivan called Quirin. "I said, 'Listen, Bob, this is taking up too much of my time. Pay the damn tax. It's only $13!'

Bill Pitt was another priest who nudged Sullivan along the peace path. He credits Vatican II with being the catalyst for social justice in the clergy. "The most important thing about Vatican II is that it thrust us out into the world," said Pitt, who quickly discovered that not all the clergy were on board. "I would preach on peace and racism in the pulpit and would be told by the pastor, 'Now, Billy, we don't need to preach on that anymore. We're losing some of our best people.' "

"Most priests were against the peace movement, saying that their people didn't like it. They encouraged them to sign a petition to get rid of me." But Pitt persisted anyway, celebrating World Peace Day in 1972 (which Pope Paul VI instructed the entire Church to observe) by having a performance of the play *The Trial of the Catonsville Nine* about anti-war activists, including Phil and Daniel Berrigan, who burned a shopping cart full of draft files in a parking lot in Maryland. "I invited the draft boards and the military chaplains," said Pitt, "but the chaplains wouldn't come."

Monsignor Carroll Dozier asked Pitt to give a talk on peace to two different diocesan groups, the Council of Catholic Women, in Arlington and the Council of Catholic Men in Roanoke. "I said, 'I would but I'm scared.' " He had reason to be. "The Catholic women were very enthusiastic and positive," said Pitt. "The Catholic men received the same talk very harshly. I barely got out alive."

Like Sullivan, Dozier was a progressive who gave support to draft resisters, opposed capital punishment, and was a vocal supporter of ecumenism and the rights of women. In 1970 he was appointed by Pope Paul to be the bishop of Memphis. A year later, he got an urgent call from Rome from Cardinal Wright, the Vatican prefect of the clergy for the Congregation and the highest-ranking American in the Curia.

"Wright told Dozier that they needed to get together for lunch," said Pitt. "Let's meet, Wright said, at Orly Airport outside of Paris. Dozier flew over, and during lunch Wright told him that Paul VI was very concerned that the bishops in the United States were not speaking out against the Vietnam War."

Then in 1973 Dozier asked Auxiliary Bishop Tom Gumbleton of Detroit to be a the first president of Pax Christi. He accepted the offer. By 1977 Sullivan had joined Pax Christi, too. (In 1991, he would be elected bishop-president.) Then in 1981 Sullivan decided to accept an invitation to speak about peace in the heart of the military-industrial complex of Virginia Beach.

If the "Jesus is our peace" talk in 1971 before the Knights of Columbus was Sullivan's baptism into the peace movement, then the talk he gave in Kempsville, Virginia, was when he was confirmed.

The Kempsville neighborhood of Virginia Beach is near the Oceana Naval Air Station where the F-18 fighter planes are maintained between deployments. Nearly all of the two hundred people at Ascension Church who listened to Bishop Sullivan on Sunday, September 13, 1981, were Catholics who were connected, one way or another, to the Navy. As he always did, Sullivan began by making clear to the audience that he was here before them to speak about peace from a faith perspective.

"I'm not here to argue military language. I'm here to share my faith with you. Our search for peace has to be centered in our faith experience. I don't care what's politically expedient."

He spoke about his experience as a member of Pax Christi and urged them to consider joining. He read from a report of Pope John Paul II's recent trip to Hiroshima, followed by a harrowingly graphic account of the bombing of that city on August 6, 1945. "I am absolutely convinced," he said, "that if nothing is done, we are going to see a nuclear holocaust. And the way we're going, we'll bring it on ourselves."

After going into some detail about the way the United States is stockpiling nuclear warheads, focusing upon first-strike capability and neutron warheads, as well as spending billions of dollars a year on nuclear and conventional arms programs, he posed the questions, "What are the values we wish to proclaim? Are these values rooted in the Gospel of Jesus or rooted in blind national self-interest disguised as patriotism?"

One of the best-kept secrets of Catholicism, continued Sullivan, is that the Catholic Church for years has condemned nuclear weapons. Then he dropped a bomb of his own. It is immoral, he declared, to be associated with the making or using of nuclear weapons. How many men and women in the audience were doing just that, nobody knows.

But the bishop wasn't finished. He spoke passionately about El Salvador, in the middle of a bloody civil war, where weapons supplied by the U.S. government to a right-wing military government were being used against its own people.

"We don't want to talk about this," said Sullivan. "We don't want to hear what is happening. Why are we afraid to answer these questions?"

"Are you suggesting," asked one member of the audience, "that we let leftists have all the weapons, and the people opposing them nothing?"

The bishop replied that the conflict in El Salvador is a matter of social justice, and that providing military assistance to the government that oppresses its own people makes matters worse, not better. On the contrary, the Reagan administration was using the notion of national security to justify "any decision, any aggression, any expenditure."

"What do we do?" asked one woman.

"You are the Church," replied the bishop, returning the question to the questioner. Again, the question was repeated by someone else. He answered, "Each person has to address this individually." As for himself, he confessed, "I cannot identify Jesus with the atomic bomb. They're totally incompatible, there's no room for both."[41]

Writer Ed Offley was present at Ascension Church for the speech and wrote about it in a subsequent newspaper column. "The implication of Bishop Sullivan's tough talk to his parishioners and, by extension, to all of us, is this. As the nuclear superpowers edge toward a final confrontation, the moral choices faced by each individual in dealing with the nightmare requires strength based on spiritual resources, not on the false confidence of the intellect, nor on the narrow world-view of each person's occupation."

Newspapers all over the state seized upon Sullivan's words the following week. "Bishop Upsets Military Crowd with Comments." "Handling Nukes Immoral, Bishop Says."

In the *Roanoke Times & World News* the lead paragraph was explicit: The bishop of the Roman Catholic Diocese of Richmond, upsetting many members of a largely military audience, said Sunday it is "immoral to be associated with the production or use" of nuclear weapons.[42]

In February 1982, Sullivan was at it again, this time before an overflow crowd at Blessed Sacrament Church in

Harrisonburg. ("Noisy Peace: A Bishop's Views Spur Heated Debate" was the *Daily News* headline.) Again, Sullivan stated that the production and use of nuclear weapons should be condemned. "I am not a pacifist," he declared, saying that he wasn't because if you are, "people write you off."

His views were angrily challenged by the audience, which included a former federal employee who said that U.S. policy would be too moral to target for destruction centers of innocent people. Sullivan replied that "hundreds of thousands of Japanese disappeared or were killed at Hiroshima and Nagasaki" when the U.S. dropped the bomb. We are "the greatest peddler of arms throughout the world. . . . We yell, we go berserk about the dictator in Poland," he said, and then support a dictator in El Salvador. Sullivan called the U.S. policy "absolutely contradictory."

Back in Richmond, Sullivan could not resist chiding Virginia's governor, Chuck Robb, in an open letter to the *Richmond Times-Dispatch* for the absurdity of the executive order he signed outlining the details of the state's emergency operations plan. "It is reassuring to know that all our lives are in good hands if the occasion should arise that we are asked to endure a nuclear holocaust [although] half a million people would be eliminated in a matter of seconds. . . . Can you imagine Richmonders calmly donning knapsacks and marching out of the city?"[43]

The *Richmond Times-Dispatch* retaliated by saying it was appalled to learn that Bishop Sullivan was refusing to allow schools in his diocese to be used as bomb shelters. But the bishop replied that cooperation with the Department of Defense "gives credence to the myth that our government can protect us at the time of nuclear holocaust or that nuclear war is winnable."

Readers jumped into the act:

"I was extremely pleased to read the editorials relating to the anti-nuclear stand of Bishop Walter F. Sullivan. Finally, a respectable institution has openly challenged the ridiculous views of the present bishop of Richmond."

As the shepherd of half the Catholics in Virginia, Bishop Sullivan should gently guide and protect them. He, however, has always driven many of his flock away from him due to his radical views. I for one support the logical stand of our president in relation to the nuclear arms race.

"Reagan was very headstrong," said Sullivan. "People liked that."

If one were to plot a graph of Bishop Sullivan's life, the 1980s would be the decade when it spiked with furious activity, as if the previous decades had been nothing but a warm-up exercise. In his early fifties, with seemingly boundless energy and enthusiasm, Sullivan seemed to be everywhere at once, attending large peace rallies, visiting draft resisters in prison, writing editorials, and giving interviews. As his sister Betty observed, "When Walter does something, he does it!"

The national news media began to pick up on the story. On October 30, 1982, Sullivan was interviewed along with another "peace bishop," Leroy Matthiesen from Amarillo, Texas, on the *McNeil-Lehrer Newshour*. The following March he testified, along with Episcopal bishop John Walker, in a congressional Armed Services hearing on "The Moral Implications of the Military Budget," where he described the proposed military budget as a "theft against the poor" and the United States as an arms dealer "spreading death around the world."[44]

"How can we mobilize the American people?" asked the chairman, Congressman Ron Dellums, who was clearly sympathetic. Sullivan replied, "The task of the Church is to raise the consciousness of the people," adding, "We have compartmentalized our lives, identified religion as 'church on Sunday.' At what point does our faith tell us we must act? I am told all the time: 'You are meddling in politics.' "

As he went around the country, Sullivan urged people to support those resisting war taxes, to counsel young men facing the draft and to reconsider the relationship between the Church and the military. "There should be chaplains to the military," he said, "but not military chaplains."

"Outspoken Bishop Won't Bend under Pressure" was the headline in the *Lynchburg Virginia News* of June 3, 1982, which details how Sullivan's speech in Kempsville had been criticized by other heavyweights in the Catholic Church.

Cardinal Terence Cooke of New York, who was in charge of the Catholic military chaplains, had recently issued a letter to be read aloud in the pulpit which claimed abhorrence of the nuclear arms build-up but defended a nation's right to protect itself "by proportionate means." (The cardinal's solution to war was to say the rosary during the month of May.)[45] Cooke supported both the possession of nuclear weapons and the "just war theory."

Bishop Sullivan has no use for just war theory. When a Jesuit academic wrote on the morality of nuclear war he sent a letter to the editor vehemently disagreeing with him. "The article fosters a theology of war at a time when the world needs a theology of peace. . . . The just war theory has rarely prevented war throughout history. In fact, it has been used to justify wars. It is on the basis of the just war theory that two countries can go to war in the Falkland/Malvinas Islands, each with the blessings, prayers, and approbation of their Catholic prelates."[46]

"That idea," declared Sullivan in an interview, "began with St. Augustine and the conversion of many converts in the military. Augustine gave them examples of what a just war consisted of. Now you have presidents using the just war theory. They should put it in a drawer and lock it up."

Bishop John O'Connor, the head of the military vicariate that ministers to Roman Catholics in the armed services, came behind Cooke in his condemnation of Sullivan's views, citing the same "just war" theory and saying, "In no instance that I recall has the Church stated categorically: 'All nuclear weapons are condemned.'"

Sullivan responded by saying that the two military bishops must believe that "unless the Church has officially condemned something—Church meaning pope—then none of us can express our own convictions." Then, referring to Cooke and O'Connor's connections to the military, he added, "And, of course, you don't bite the hand that feeds you."[47]

O'Connor and Sullivan had crossed swords before. "I was on the elevator in Washington at a bishops' meeting," said Sullivan, "and O'Connor got on. We were alone. He said, 'You and Tom Gumbleton are a disgrace to the Church!' I came right back at him although I don't recall what I said. I liked O'Connor. I used to call him 'Admiral' because he had been chaplain to the military."

In 1984 O'Connor succeeded Cardinal Cooke as archbishop of New York. A year later he was made a cardinal. Cardinal O'Connor was quoted in a *Wall Street Journal* article as saying about all the "peace bishops" he opposes that "when you try to give a rational presentation all you get back is the Gospel's manifestation of love. I think that's inadequate."[48]

In that same *Wall Street Journal* article, mention is made of the way in which several high-up Catholic members of the Reagan administration (notably Eugene Rostow and Alexander Haig) were trying, without success, to get the bishops to back off their position of being against nuclear war. It wasn't working. ("They thought the Church would be a pushover and it wasn't," said Monsignor Pitt.) National rallies in favor of a nuclear freeze were building up steam.

In 1982 some members of the Richmond peace community traveled by bus to New York City to join over 750,000 demonstrators who were in favor of a nuclear freeze. Bishop Sullivan was one of them. "We stayed at Regis High School. Everybody slept on the floor. I got the couch to sleep on."

"Few things annoy public men quite so much as vast public manifestations of disagreement with official policy," wrote *Washington Post* columnist Mary McGrory. "The sight of streets clotted with citizens saying no to stated wisdom is destabilizing. It is an implicit criticism of the way officials are doing their jobs."[49]

The noted Jesuit peace activist and writer John Dear was a just-ordained priest in 1993 when he almost immediately got himself arrested for hammering on an F-15 fighter plane in North Carolina, as part of a Plowshares demonstration (so-called, from the verse in Isaiah, "They shall beat their swords into plowshares"). Sullivan, who was by then the bishop-president of Pax Christi, visited Dear several times when he was in jail in North Carolina; when he was released in 1994 for a year of house arrest at a Jesuit community in Washington, D.C., Sullivan made it possible for Dear to attend a fiftieth anniversary of Pax Christi International in Italy.

"Ramsey Clark and some other lawyers went to federal court and got a judge to let me go—as long as I was under the care of Bishop Sullivan, who would face arrest if I didn't return. So we went, had a great experience in Assisi, and after that went to Rome to see Pope John Paul II. Once he met us, he was so overwhelmed he cancelled the rest of his afternoon and we all spent hours with him. Walter gave a little speech to the pope introducing us and explaining our hopes and work for peace. I remember Walter would not let me go in unless I was wearing a clerical shirt. Eventually I gave in."

When they were still in Assisi, Walter asked Dear if he would come to Richmond and replace the outgoing director of the Sacred Heart Center in south Richmond. "It was one of the great community centers in the country," said Dear, "serving four hundred African American women and children in the neighborhood of south Richmond, through a school and after-school programs for kids, tutoring classes for women, and an evening program for the men. We had fifty African American women on the staff and over a thousand people in the center at all times. The diocese owned the building, and the Jesuits ran it. Sullivan was president of the board."

Dear was one of the few Pax Christi members who knew Sullivan in both of his worlds. "He was the opposite of most priests and bishops," said Dear, "always laughing and telling stories. Of course I realize now what a great gift that was and how many gifts he had. There I was, a self-righteous young Jesuit, and now that I'm older I realize that's the whole point of the Gospel—to be humble, childlike, and peaceful, to enjoy life as you work on these serious issues. He was worlds ahead of me."

For a "peace bishop" Sullivan was highly combative. "I don't know if he ever got arrested," said Kathleen Kenney. "But in 2000, Pax Christi had a conference here in Richmond and they decided to block the entrance to a military facility in Yorktown. When they found out the bishop was coming, they just opened up another entrance." But rarely a day went by that Sullivan was not defending or responding to an attack upon an issue or value that, as the bishop of Richmond, he felt morally compelled to address. And for somebody who was genuinely nonjudgmental and anxious to make sure that he gives no injury to others, the bishop had no qualms about taking on the Richmond establishment.

After reading a *Richmond Times-Dispatch* editorial ("True Confessions") about a Jesuit priest in Guatemala who was tortured into confessing that he was part of a Marxist plot to undermine the government, Sullivan wrote: "Congratulations on beginning the new year with an attack on the Catholic Church. . . . You have accepted, carte blanche, the remarks of a man made under severe duress. . . . It is most unfortunate that the editorial failed to mention that Father Pellecer is still not a free man. . . . I would hope that future editorials would be more insightful in pursuing truth. Otherwise 1982 will be a trying year."[50]

Responding to another editorial about how the Sandinista revolution in Nicaragua was a failure, Sullivan fired off another open letter. "I have just returned from a ten-day visit to Nicaragua. After reading your editorial, I must have visited a different country with the same name."[51]

The *Times-Dispatch* could barely contain its disdain for Sullivan and the other peace bishops, warning that the views on disarmament of "Sullivan and his type" would lead to totalitarianism. "To the extent Polaris subs and MX systems stand between us and Dachau II, they are moral."[52]

This kind of editorial anger was mirrored by the reaction of many Catholics, not only in Virginia. Monsignor Pitt recalls being in Emporia, Virginia, where he was conducting a workshop on what Catholics might expect to find in the bishops' peace pastoral, which was still in draft form.

"The thing they reacted most violently to was the section where it stated that we needed to do penance for what we did in Nagasaki and Hiroshima. By violently, I mean they were yelling at me, shaking the papers that they had in their hands. That section didn't make it into the peace pastoral itself."

In early 1982, the eminent Washington, D.C., journalist William Greider came down to interview the bishop for *Rolling Stone*, a magazine that is not found on too many rectory coffee tables. Greider has the eye of a courtroom illustrator and he caught the essence of the bishop in a few deft lines, describing him as "a loose and shaggy man" whose "talk is cluttered with verbal mannerisms—'oh sure' and 'you know' and 'golly'— that suggest a fuzzy desire to be agreeable. A nice man, in other words, who may seem too nice to be dwelling on hardball politics." By the end of the evening, Greider had revised this view.

Sitting in the back of a hall at the Church of the Epiphany in a suburban subdivision of Richmond, Greider took notes while Sullivan spoke to about sixty affluent parishioners, "Catholics who had made it," Greider opined. For an hour, they listened politely as the bishop laid the philosophical foundations for his convictions that a "just war" in the nuclear age is a moral impossibility. Then he presented his conclusions.[53]

"We need to challenge the moral legitimacy of the strategy of deterrence. The U.S. has every intention to use its nuclear weapons, the so-called first-use policy. The intention to use the nuclear weapon is, of itself, immoral and must be condemned."

Just before he opened up the evening to questions, he said, "I am very hopeful. I'm sure the spirit of God is calling us to look at this problem in a new way."

"Most of the parishioners," wrote Greider, "had not yet heard that call. What followed was an extraordinary confrontation between a spiritual leader who preaches disturbing truths and followers who do not wish to hear them."

"If we don't build up our arms," a middle-aged man began, "wouldn't the other side go ahead with theirs?" This question was on everyone's mind. "Wouldn't that automatically bring on war?" the man went on. "The number one issue is what about the Russians?"

"You might as well hear this," Sullivan responded somberly. "Our image in the world is not the peacekeeper, as Ronald Reagan says. Our image is frightening."

"Russian propaganda!" an elderly man yelled.

"I don't think that's just Russian propaganda," the bishop shot back. "They've got plenty of reasons to be scared. I'm not soft on Communism or anything like that. . . . The Russians are human beings. They want to live. They don't want a nuclear holocaust. One of the mistakes we make is that we dehumanize the enemy; they're all idiots, crazy."

The bishop was embattled, surrounded by righteous challenges. A young man shouted that the pastoral letter was pointless unless endorsed by both the Russians and the Americans. "I don't want to be disrespectful, Bishop, but you still haven't answered this question." Others at the peace talk murmured their agreement.

"Let's stop talking about what the enemy will do and start talking about what we will do," Sullivan insisted. "I'm convinced we are headed toward a nuclear holocaust unless we do something to stop it."

An elderly man jumped in with a different line of attack: "I think the bishops have destroyed their credibility, their value. We look to them for our moral values, not for our national security. We have leaders to do that."

"Do you see the moral dimensions?" Sullivan replied.

"Absolutely. But it doesn't take priority over survival."

"The moral issue is what the bishops are addressing."

The dialogue turned hostile. The initial deference vanished, and the group was directing its resentment not at the Russians but at their own spiritual leader and the hierarchy of the Catholic Church. Sullivan invoked Pope John Paul II's pronouncements on the evil of the arms race. Somebody even asked if the pope is a military strategist.

Finally, a young parishioner charged that the peace movement is being manipulated by Soviet agents. It's true, another said, citing Reader's Digest *and Ronald Reagan as authorities.*

"I was with 850,000 at the peace march in New York, and I didn't find any Communists," Sullivan said. "You're saying that I'm being influenced by the Communists?" An uproar drowned him out.

"You don't even know you're being influenced!" an angry voice shouted.

The bishop stood his ground, remarkably calm. He challenged them all to read and study, as he had done, before they dismissed his teaching. "I don't think the bishops of the United States are a bunch of idiots," he observed dryly. "The nuclear arms race is morally debilitating right now because it destroys young people's faith in the future, because it raises up a false god of total mass destruction. People ask, 'Why don't young people get married and have children? Why don't they care? Well, folks, as far as they're concerned, there is no tomorrow."

Groans of disbelief from the audience.

"Russia wants a war!" one woman insisted.

"How do you know Russia wants a war?" the bishop replied evenly.

"Oh, come on, Bishop."

For a moment, the raised voices subsided in exhaustion. The earnest Catholics at the Church of the Epiphany had hurled every argument and accusation at their bishop, yet he stuck stubbornly to his moral challenge. At last a well-dressed businessman named Sam raised his hand to speak. Sam is a leading layman in the diocese, one who has worked closely with the bishop on many projects.

"I have trouble speaking," he said, "because you know I love you. But . . . "

"But," the bishop repeated, smiling. Everyone laughed.

"But the last couple of years I've been concerned about the direction you're going," Sam said. "You say you're speaking as an individual, but you are the bishop of Richmond. You say you're not for unilateral disarmament, yet the positions you take are leading in that direction. Do you really think that if we laid down all our arms, the Russians would somehow lay down theirs?"

Once more, the bishop patiently explained himself. He supports the idea of a nuclear freeze by both sides. But, he said, in the long history of the arms race, it is the U.S., not the Soviet Union, that has introduced each generation of new weaponry. Unless the U.S. is willing to change, there is no hope that the Soviets will.

"That's a military opinion," Sam snapped, his voice heating up. "You say they are catching up. Many people would say they're ahead. But I think it's out of your field for you to decide that."

"I'm not deciding anything," the bishop said softly.

"My government tells me—people who I think have a great deal more information than you do—that we're not on parity."

"And you believe them?" the bishop asked.

"I do. Why should I believe you?"

"That question," wrote Greider, "went to the heart of the matter: whom should Catholics believe—their Church or their government? These good Catholics have been raised to believe that God and country were united in a common struggle for good; now they felt betrayed. Their bishop was trying to tell them that true Christians must put themselves in opposition to their own government. A most subversive thought."

"I'm sorry," Sullivan said at last, "but I just cannot equate Jesus with a nuclear bomb."

"Nobody can," someone said.

"Well, then," the bishop said gravely, "we either follow the way of Christ or the U.S. government."

The audience exploded. So did Sam.

"Unfortunately, Bishop, much of what you've said in the last couple of years is just in that tone. The U.S. is a great country."

"And a Christian country!" a bald man chimed in.

"Do you really think America is a Christian nation?" the bishop asked, stoking their outrage. "A nation that sanctions three million abortions a year? That allows poverty and hunger amid affluence? That threatens world destruction as a strategy for national defense?"

More shouts. Another round of denials. The bishop seemed unperturbed, even pleased.

"I don't have any problem in saying that we see things differently," Sullivan concluded. "The important thing is to discuss it. What I have tried to share with you is the direction the Catholic Church is going."

Later, speaking with Greider, the bishop explained his understanding of the evening. "Catholics are superpatriots. It's their very upbringing. It comes out of the immigrant stage of having to identify with Americanism—the need to be accepted, not as a foreigner but as an American."

Greider came away from the evening realizing that the bishop of Richmond was "a tough character. . . . He refused to tell his flock what they desperately wanted to hear—that God is on America's side in the nuclear arms race."[54]

John Barrett, the diocese's chief financial officer for most of Sullivan's time as bishop, would agree that the bishop was, indeed, very tough. "He stood alone on many social issues and he didn't care if you agreed with him or not. If he felt his stance was the correct one, he took the stance and the adverse publicity that came with it."

Betty Sullivan Hughes provided a more homespun spin on her brother's leadership. "People would get angry with him and he would say, 'That's good. They're thinking.' He's not insecure and he won't stop."

Monsignor Michael Schmeid is the pastor of St. Augustine's Church in Richmond's southside. It is 40 percent Anglo and 60 percent Hispanic, mostly from El Salvador. The older members of the Salvadoran community came to the United States during the civil war of the 1980s when Romero was assassinated. They were fleeing for their lives. The younger Salvadorans have come because of the poverty. When they come to him to be married, their baptismal certificates often bear the names of priests who were murdered by the terrorist militia.

The walls of Schmeid's office are hung with drawings or photographs of his peace heroes: Archbishop Oscar Romero, Thomas Merton, Martin Luther King, Dorothy Day, Teilhard de Chardin, the four American churchwomen killed in El

Salvador. The same year Sullivan began his peace journey, 1971, Schmeid was ordained. Later, Sullivan made him the first vicar of a new Hispanic ministry in the diocese.

Schmeid witnessed Sullivan's efforts to educate the Richmond diocese about nuclear war and peace firsthand. "It would be too strong to say the military jumped on board," said Schmeid, "but as the bishop kept delivering a pretty consistent message, many military seeking ethical guidance—particularly after the horrors of Vietnam—became more open to his ideas."

Because of the changing political atmosphere in the United States, the bishops' peace pastoral was taken very seriously by the new Reagan administration, which tried in various ways to grab the wheel and steer the bishops toward their arms buildup, "Peace through Strength" policies before the peace pastoral was finalized.

"The Reagan hawks. . . . are right to be alarmed," wrote Greider. "What these bishops are really launching is a great national teach-in."[55]

The bishops went back and forth on the question of nuclear deterrence, which pivoted upon the dangerous possibility that possession and use of nuclear weapons are linked in the possessor's mind. Bishop Gumbleton raised that question with Caspar Weinberger, Reagan's secretary of defense. "I felt if anybody should know, he ought to know the policy of the United States. 'Is this simply a threat, or do we really intend to use them?'

"We were sitting in his office, a big office in the Pentagon, very comfortable, and he had been very gracious and very welcoming saying, 'Stay as long as you want. I got all afternoon if you want,' and so on. He was very accommodating, and he was a very soft-spoken person and seemed quite gentle in his demeanor. Yet when I asked that question, without hesitation, he said, 'Well of course, we don't want to use them, but when we have to, we will. Clearly we will use them.' "[56]

To write the peace pastoral, Bernardin chose one pacifist (Gumbleton), one hawk (O'Connor), and two moderate bishops to complete the five-man committee that he chaired. Joe Fahey sat in on many of the sessions.

"There was a real battle over what was going to come out. We were going over whether we could get the bishops to declare deterrence immoral, i.e., mass murder. We'd be given one set of ideas from Gumbleton and O'Connor would give another. At every point O'Connor was trying to get the bishops to justify nuclear weapons on the battlefield. Once you justify that you're no better than the Crusades."[57]

Eventually, John Paul II laid out the path.

In a 1982 visit to the United Nations, the pope said that while nuclear deterrence is not an "adequate strategy as a long-term basis for peace," it was a morally acceptable short-term plan as long as a plan was in place for all sides to move toward nuclear disarmament. "A small group was called to Rome," said Fahey. "The bishops wound up endorsing the just war theory, but they weakened it."

On May 3, 1983, the final draft of the bishops' peace pastoral was presented to the full conference for ratification. "When they took the vote in Chicago at the Parker House," said Fahey, "I was up in the gallery with reporters all around. This was momentous. The bishops had never issued a statement like this and the vote was 238-9. I was jubilant and went down to the floor, searching out our bishops. I happened to bump into Bishop [Bernard] Law, and he said to me, 'I bet you're happy.'

'Aren't you?' I asked. He replied, 'Certainly not. This is the first sign that the Church is selling out to the liberals.' "

In a letter published in Richmond's afternoon paper, former mayor Phil Bagley Jr. (whom Sullivan once threw out of his office) was angry about the bishops' vote:

> It should be remembered that most of the current bishops are products of the Liberal, Hippie, Jane Fonda, Berrigan Era, espousing the protest mentality of the 50s and 60s. In due time they will be replaced by seminary products attuned to conservative thinking, after having witnessed the failures, including the present naive action, of their predecessors.

> The bishops should remember they at best are just branch managers of the Catholic Church and that final decisions are made at the Vatican supreme headquarters in Rome.[58]

Bagley is not a Church historian, but his "in due time" prediction was eerily prescient. Today's U.S. Conference of Catholic Bishops is a far more conservative, less empowered group. As for Bagley's "branch manager" view of what a bishop is, Sullivan was very clear as to who he was, and was not.

"The Church comes across as a hierarchy, a dictator, all about law and order. But they're very respectful of the bishops," said Sullivan. "When I began my journey as bishop people always thought it was a branch office of Rome. It is not. When I first met Paul VI after becoming the bishop of Richmond, he took my hand and looked right in my eye and said, 'You and I are brothers.' " Bishop Sullivan has never met a pope he did not like on a personal level. But John Paul II was clearly not going to continue Pope Paul VI's "you and I are brothers" theme.

The pope's dazzling personal style made him a formidable actor on the world stage. It also had another, less obvious effect upon his brother bishops. They were, ipso facto, diminished by his presence, and there is no reason to believe that John Paul did not, in fact, intend to emphasize that difference.

Joe Fahey bumped into Sullivan when he and the other American bishops met with John Paul II in Chicago. "It was just the two of us," said Fahey, "and I asked him how it went. He said, 'Joe, he treated us like we were altar boys.'" Bishop Sullivan does not remember saying this but recalls that when he first met the new pontiff, Pope John Paul II seemed "kind of triumphant. [Father] Jim McGrath," he added, "thought he was a tyrant."

The U.S. bishops, who had been encouraged by John XXIII and Paul VI to come closer to the Vatican and lend it their counsel and support, were in the process of losing their short-lived position of privilege and collegiality. The political difference between the American bishops and the bishop of Rome was demonstrated in the text of the peace pastoral itself.

It was a strong statement that condemned nuclear war as a curse upon the world, labeled preemptive war immoral on its face, called for laws to protect the rights of conscientious objectors, and cast serious doubt upon the idea that a limited nuclear war was even possible. In many people's minds, the pope's insistence upon leaving in a caveat about deterrence (i.e., an arms buildup show of strength) being a morally acceptable short-term plan was a "virus" that fatally weakened the final product. But in January 1984, diplomatic relations between the Vatican and the United States, which had not sent a representative since 1867, were reinstated.

Bill Pitt is not alone in suspecting how and why that came about. "Consider the cast of characters. The pope was Polish, he was iron-fisted and there was no bending. The American bishops' pastoral got a big negative reaction in Rome—the bishops don't have this authority. I'm willing to bet that there was collusion between Reagan and Rome before the pastoral came out."

There is scholarly support for Pitt's suspicion. In *Catholics and Politics: The Dynamic Tension between Faith and Power,* Thomas Carty writes, "When the U.S. Catholic bishops continued to resist Reagan's foreign policy . . . the president changed tactics and pursued formal diplomacy with the supreme leader of global Catholicism, Pope John Paul II."[59]

What one Vatican II theologian called the age of "faithful dissent" was being replaced by what the conservative intellectual George Weigel called "the adventure of orthodoxy." Both phrases have a slightly oxymoronic ring to them. But in the Richmond diocese "the adventure of orthodoxy" had a darker side.

Days after the bishops' peace pastoral was released, Sullivan received a letter from the apostolic delegate in Washington, D.C., telling him that the Vatican had decided to investigate the Diocese of Richmond "to clarify objectively questions which have arisen concerning both doctrine and discipline."

The price for Bishop Sullivan's peace journey had come due.

Chapter Ten

The Investigation

To put the investigation in perspective, we should note that the last time the Holy See sent an apostolic examiner to scrutinize a bishop's kingdom in the United States was in the late 1800s, when Rome dispatched the archbishop of Baltimore to look into some complaints about the bishop of Cleveland. "[It] is surely not without precedent," admitted historian Monsignor John Tracy Ellis, but "I don't think there's any question but that this must be very awkward and uncomfortable for the bishops involved."[60]

Sullivan was not the only prelate under the microscope. The Vatican had also decided to investigate Bishop Raymond Hunthausen of Seattle at the same time. They were very similar kinds of bishop. Hunthausen had been outspoken in his calls for nuclear disarmament. In 1982 he had withheld half his income tax to protest the Trident missile program (which he called "the Auschwitz of Puget Sound") and the stockpiling of nuclear weapons. An ardent supporter of the Vatican II vision that the Church should serve the poor and the disenfranchised, Hunthausen, like Sullivan, was welcoming to women and homosexuals.

"I think the higher authorities in our leadership wanted us to be silenced for stands," said Bishop Sullivan. "It got political, and in my diocese the spark that lit the fuse was when a priest at St. Paul's Church in Richmond said that the Benedictine Military School in Richmond teaches boys to kill. I said no, no, that's not true, but it hit the fan. The priest became a lightning rod."

165

Even without the Benedictine incident, Bishop Sullivan had good reason to suspect that he was going to be called on the carpet. An ad hoc group of Catholics in the Richmond diocese had been waging a war of whispers and letters for some time. Sullivan did not know who signed the letters or what the specifics were of their complaints. But since 1978, which coincided with the beginning of the papacy of John Paul II, there had been a slow drip, drip, drip of letters from the apostolic delegation in Washington, D.C., to Bishop Sullivan asking him to explain, correct, or stop certain practices in the Richmond diocese.

The language was courtly but insistent. "Be advised of the Congregation's judgment. . . . " "[It is] further suggested that you be invited to find a way to rectify this incongruity." "May I draw your attention to certain statements. . . . " Most of the requests appeared to be triggered by a group that called themselves "The Roman Catholic Confraternity" that had taken it upon themselves to be a kind of Curial watchdog, searching for any example of doctrinal, liturgical, or clerical deviance that would put the bishop in a poor light. No example was too slight or too out of context to escape their eye.

How else would Rome know about a sexual education pamphlet mistakenly offered to a religious ed teacher that spoke of masturbation as normal? Someone had sent the apostolic delegate a diocesan questionnaire where, buried in the text, dialogue on the subject of women's ordination is mentioned. In one parish, the Eucharist was reportedly being stored in a tin that had previously been used to hold margarine; in another parish, one of the priests had reportedly said summer Mass in shorts. "At least he wore underwear," said Sullivan sarcastically.

"I had an old Irish priest who said to me once, 'If you want to beat a dog you can always find a stick to beat him with,'" said

Robert Quirin, a former priest in the diocese. "They couldn't complain about peace so they looked for other stuff—the liturgy, his use of general absolution.'"

For some time now, Bishop Sullivan had been putting out fires, some of them clearly the work of "arsonists" who were angry over the way Sullivan was running the diocese and were looking for evidence, real or imagined, to invalidate his ministry.

Then in 1981 another subject was introduced into the correspondence that created a separate, larger stream of mail. Bishop Sullivan asked Rome to grant him an auxiliary bishop.

At first, the new apostolic delegate, Pio Laghi, said that the Vatican was extremely reluctant to even consider it. ("The Sacred Congregation does not deem it opportune to ask the Holy Father . . . at this time.") Instead, episcopal vicars (priests with special duties) were suggested.

Sullivan rejected the Vatican's suggestion. ("Over half the parishes in the Richmond Diocese are staffed by one priest. Already priests are overworked. Priests serving as episcopal vicars could not fulfill expectations. . . . ") Then there was a slight break in the clouds, and it was agreed that the idea of an auxiliary bishop, pursuant to new guidelines issued by the Vatican, could at least be explored. ("Let me repeat," wrote Laghi, " . . . this response from the Holy See is not to be considered an affirmative response to your petition.")

For months, Sullivan and Laghi sparred back and forth with each other, the bishop offering names of candidates that were rejected, followed by Laghi suggesting others that Sullivan could not accept. "They were only nominating bishops from the Northeast," said Sullivan. "I said why do we have to go to Philadelphia, which, symbolically, is the most conservative part of the Church?" Conversely, the bishop's choices were drawn from the Richmond diocese with names that had been suggested by his Priests' Council. These were summarily rejected by Rome. "I think there was a stop on Walter creating any new bishops," said Monsignor Pitt, "because he might create one like himself."

The two lines of correspondence, complaints about Sullivan and Sullivan's pursuit of an auxiliary, ran parallel to each other. Then, on November 18, 1982, in a letter from Pio Laghi, they were joined.

> Dear Bishop Sullivan,
>
> I am writing today to confirm our conversation on November 16 concerning your request for an auxiliary. . . . [Y]ou may either present two more candidates for inquiry or accept a *terna,* which would include candidates from outside the diocese. To this you remarked that an auxiliary from outside the diocese would not be completely acceptable to the priests.
>
> I also mentioned to you that as a result of our inquiries, we have become aware of some serious difficulties in the diocese in a number of areas which might well result in certain decisions on the part of the Sacred Congregation.

"Certain decisions on the part of the Sacred Congregation"? Sullivan was alarmed. That sounded like a threat of papal investigation. He wrote Laghi back asking for a meeting. In the meantime, he conferred with some of his key advisors. One of them, Father Tom Caroluzza, took it upon himself, without asking Sullivan's permission, to write to Archbishop William Borders of Baltimore, asking for a meeting of his own.

January 21, 1983
Dear Archbishop Borders:

Yesterday Bishop Sullivan called a special meeting of his Diocesan Consultors. As you are aware, our diocese may come under canonical investigation in the near future. The very announcement of that news was a source of discouragement to all of us, since we have all worked so hard to implement the renewal called for by Vatican Council II. Unprompted by anyone, I have decided to write you this letter. . . . I would like to share my candid reflections with you on the condition of the Diocese of Richmond. . . . I am certain that a group of priest consultors (from Richmond) would also be happy to be there. I would like to assist in any way I am able in order that the good work of Church renewal under Bishop Sullivan's leadership is not reversed or disturbed, but encouraged.

Looking forward to hearing from you, I am

> Sincerely yours in Christ,

> Rev. Thomas J. Caroluzza, Pastor
> Our Lady of Nazareth Church
> Roanoke, Virginia

Father Bob Perkins was present at that meeting. "Six of us went up to Baltimore to meet with Archbishop Borders to support Bishop Sullivan. It was a meeting that very few people knew about. I remember that Tom Caroluzza and Ben McDermott were along. One of the interesting things that happened was when we were saying that part of this letter-writing campaign against the bishop had nothing to do with the issues being named but with the issues of war and peace. The archbishop asked us, 'Why do you think it's only laypeople who are writing letters?' Borders was a classic gentleman with a good pastoral heart, and I think he was saying, without being specific, that you've got priests who are writing letters too."

In early April, the bishop met with Pio Laghi in Washington, D.C. A page of scribbled notes in Sullivan's handwriting gives the reader a glimpse of what was discussed. "The Church of the Holy Apostles, letters dried up, informal investigation, *ad limina,* Richmond candidates not acceptable—ordination of women, celibacy."

Finally it happened. In a letter dated June 7, 1983, Pio Laghi informed Bishop Sullivan that the Holy See had decided to send an apostolic visitator to the Diocese of Richmond.

The actual physical visitation was a swift and relatively painless operation. By June 28, 1983, Archbishop John May had flown from his diocese in St. Louis to Richmond, conducted his interviews with perhaps three dozen people, including representatives of the Roman Catholic Confraternity, flown home, and submitted his report to Rome.

Bishop Sullivan had some reason to believe that May sympathized with his predicament. "You have the same crazies in your diocese that I have in mine," May told Sullivan, who took this to be a good sign. In a "Dear Walt" letter on June 29, 1983, Archbishop May told him the report had been sent to Rome and added, in his own handwriting on the bottom, "I hope this does it!"

Almost immediately after Archbishop May left Richmond, Bishop Sullivan flew to Rome for his five-year *ad limina* meeting with Pope John Paul II. He knew what issues were on the table: the ecumenical Holy Apostles Anglican–Roman Catholic Church in Virginia Beach, the use of general absolution, and the introduction he had written to *A Call to Love*—an anthology of essays on the Catholic Church and homosexuality.

The bishop's first appointment was with Pope John Paul II. He was not nervous. "I had nothing to apologize for." But in any event, it was a perfunctory visit. The pope waved him off, saying that he had to see Cardinal Ratzinger.

"Ratzinger couldn't have been nicer," said Bishop Sullivan. "He was a very soft-spoken, gentle person, which is why I would like to go back and see him. And he never brought up the peace issue. Never. But I think that peace was at the bottom of everything."

Present with Cardinal Ratzinger was Archbishop Hamer, who had figured in some of Laghi's correspondence to Sullivan, insisting that the bishop conform more rigorously to Church teachings. The bishop did not like him.

The first issue they dealt with was the Anglican–Roman Catholic Church of the Holy Apostles, at that time only one of four such ecumenical communities in the world. (Three of them have since dissolved.) The conversation revolved around how was it possible to have a joint liturgy of the word. "Hamer asked me what do you do for the lectionary? and I said we don't have to do anything. Catholics and Anglicans have the same one. Hamer said they don't. Ratzinger looked at Hamer and said, 'The bishop is right.' "

"Rome said you cannot do that, i.e., have a parish with Episcopalians and Catholics together," said Monsignor Pitt. "Walter said it's not a parish, it's a community."

Nevertheless, Ratzinger said he wanted the ecumenical experiment to be ended, and Sullivan knew this was a battle he could not win. Before going to Rome he had already notified the Catholic members of Holy Apostles that they could no longer participate in a joint liturgy although they could continue to worship in the same building. Sullivan's counterpart, Episcopal bishop Charles Vache, expressed disappointment, but said he did not see it as "the death knell for Holy Apostles." In the long run, it was not.

For the Anglican–Roman Catholic community to be officially dissolved, Rome needed to take one more official step which never happened. There are two versions as to why that step was never taken. "I told the Curia that I would do it out of obedience and they said well, maybe we'll see what happens. That was thirty years ago and the Church of the Holy Apostles is still going."

Monsignor Pitt supplied a back-up story. "John Cardinal Wright was an American in the Curia, a conservative, but an appointee of Paul VI. Wright didn't take the next step and the church was allowed to remain intact."

The second item concerned Bishop Sullivan's introduction in the book *A Challenge to Love,* which was a scholarly, well-reviewed collection of essays by Catholic thinkers on the subject of homosexuality and the Church. "They picked out one sentence in the whole book in which one of the writers justified a gay relationship," recounted Sullivan. "I asked them how did they like my introduction. They didn't answer. They just said we want you to take your name off the book. I told them that doing this would probably cause the book to sell more copies, but I said I would do it, out of obedience. I have no reason to do it otherwise, but I told Ratzinger I would like a letter from him instructing me to do it. Cardinal Ratzinger agreed that he would."

Finally came the practice of giving general absolution, in lieu of priests hearing individual confessions. This was a relatively recent addition to canon law (1973), making it permissible under special conditions, such as wartime, or when it was otherwise physically impossible to conduct as many individual confessions as were needed.

"Hamer asked me how could I do this?" said Bishop Sullivan. "I replied to Cardinal Ratzinger, 'Look, this is going on all around the country. It's not my fault that you created a new way of dispensing absolution. You are talking as if we're the only ones who are doing it. And we only do it before Christmas and Easter. If you are a priest with a thousand parishioners, how can you function? Finally, I got irritated. "You put it in the book," I said. Ratzinger looked at me and said, 'You're right.'"

Nevertheless, Cardinal Ratzinger insisted that Bishop Sullivan cease the practice. Accordingly, Bishop Sullivan instructed his then-chancellor, Monsignor Pitt, to send out a memoranda to all priests in the diocese that there was to be no general absolution under any circumstances.

"The practice of giving general absolution," explained Pitt, "went back to 1975, when Bishop Carroll Dozier in Memphis did a big general absolution in the coliseum with all kinds of people there. Rome went wild. Dozier told Rome, 'I don't work for the Curia. The Curia works for me.' Then Walter started doing it and it was very popular. People came. And it was done quite well. But under John Paul II they had this big push called 'The Year of the Priest,' and they pushed two things—individual confession and perpetual Eucharistic adoration. Individual confession strengthens the power of the priest over the people and general absolution weakens it. Walter told me to call the priests and tell them to stop doing it. He was in enough trouble as it was."

That "trouble" is contained in three blue bound volumes of letters, newspaper clippings, editorials, and related matter that cover the period of the papal investigation from just before its inception to its end, which was never clearly defined. Unlike

Bishop Hunthausen, who was eventually sent a letter of commendation from the Vatican, praising him for his fidelity after his investigation was over, Bishop Sullivan received no such absolving document. Instead, there was silence—and from his fellow American bishops a surprising lack of collegiality and moral support.

"It wasn't just me and Hunthausen who were being criticized," said Sullivan. "A lot of us were being criticized. The bishops were nervous about it. Those were personally upsetting days."

Father Jim Griffin came to work for Bishop Sullivan as his driver shortly after the investigation began. He observed close-up what effect the investigation had upon him. "The biggest toll on Walter was after the investigation ended. To me it was apparent that he had to curry favor with Rome. They were always after him, trying to catch him out.[61] He was certainly honest. He loved being bishop, and I think he loved his priests. But he was always being told how to do things, to make monsignors, to let deacons be ordained, to allow the Latin Mass."

The clamor for a return to the Latin Mass, where the priest celebrates the liturgy with his back to the people, seems to be one of the more sincere complaints, a direct reaction to Vatican II, which explicitly directed that the Mass be performed in the vernacular of the people. This was a radical change from two thousands years of using Latin as the *vox populi* around the world, and many Catholics longed for a return to it. The bishop conceded that the transition had been unnecessarily swift.

"There were a lot of valid complaints," Sullivan commented in a 1981 interview.[62] "Symbols are very important to people. What we did was we tore them all out. We kind of said to people, if not directly, then indirectly, all these things that were important to you are no longer important. People may not realize it but I've sort of changed my style a little in the sense that I am becoming more patient. You have to allow time with people. An idea or a thought has to germinate."

Sullivan decided to meet with all of the priests in the diocese to discuss it. "There was a lot of hemming and hawing, saying why do we want to give it to them," he said. "But the people who wanted it had as much a right to the Latin Mass as other people had a right to the English one."

Other complaints did not carry the same weight. One complaint, which could stand for many that were equally as microscopic, revolved around the matter of communion "crumbs."

In separate letters, the Roman Catholic Confraternity alerted the Vatican and Bishop Sullivan that at St. Augustine's Parish, Catholics were being told that "brushing crumbs from the clothing is acceptable when done in a delicate manner." Believing in the real presence, or transubstantiation of bread into the body and blood of Christ, this would be like brushing Jesus onto the floor.

"Your Excellency," begins a letter to Bishop Sullivan from Archbishop Noe at the Vatican:

> This Congregation has received a communication from Mr. Edward S. Gibbons, of the Diocese of Richmond, regarding particles of the consecrated host. I would inform Your Excellency of the matter. Enclosed please find a proposed reply of this Congregation to the writer. Unless Your Excellency deems it inopportune, I would be very grateful if the above proposed reply could be forwarded to Mr. Gibbons.[63]

"Do you agree, Bishop Sullivan," asked four signers of a letter on Roman Catholic Confraternity stationery, "that such instructions to the laity are acceptable?"[64]

"Dear Ed," responded the bishop.

I received your letter in which you expressed the desire for some additional clarifying information regarding the fragments from Holy Eucharist which might be a problem to some parishioners at St. Augustine's. I plan to discuss the matter with Father Carr, the pastor, and will ask him to take proper action.[65]

The bishop then sent Father William Carr the correspondence between him and the Roman Catholic Confraternity, suggesting that he hold a special meeting so that any parishioners with an issue about communion could have an open discussion, adding, "By all means don't over-react to the RCC; you have my full support." Carr responded.

Dear Bishop Sullivan:

The concern you bring to my attention is not an issue in St. Augustine's Parish. The faith-life of the parish is deepening as the staff gives their hearts and souls to good leadership and example. Hundreds are coming to our programs. Mass attendance has increased, the collections are up considerably.

Apparently an unhappy person or two has complained to someone outside the parish. I feel strongly that a public meeting would bring others from outside the parish who would use the opportunity to display their animosity towards the Church in general.

With that in mind I have written the attached bulletin announcement, which will run two weeks, and I hope, clarify any misunderstanding. "Town hall" meetings here in the past have turned into lynch mobs, and I would like to spare the parish and myself such an ordeal.

Sincerely, in Christ,

Bill

Carr attached his parish announcement:

When we made our transition from hosts to more substantial bread for Holy Communion, some asked: "What do we do with the crumbs that fall on our clothes?" Responding in the language in which the question was put, the bulletin ran an announcement entitled: "Crumbs?" to get the attention of those concerned. The correct terminology is "fragments" or "Sacred Particles" and one must be careful to give such fragments the most reverend attention. Such fragments large enough to do so should be consumed and not brushed from the clothing.

The Blessed Sacrament, source and summit, sum and substance of our Catholic lives merits our deepest devotion. . . . Should a parishioner remain concerned about the proper procedure, Father Carr's door and heart are always open to discussion.[66]

In a final note to Carr, Sullivan thanked him for his letter and commented that "in all my years of priesthood I have never seen this [falling of crumbs of the Eucharist onto clothing] happen. I have seen fragments fall on the ground."[67]

A more substantial complaint involved a priest from Norfolk, Father Vincent Connery, who wrote a letter to the editor of the *Virginian-Pilot* in September 1983 supporting women's ordination. Father Connery suggested that Pope John Paul II's recent speech calling on bishops to withdraw their support from any one person or organization supporting women's ordination should be a rallying cry for the opposition. "Perhaps," he wrote, "it is time for priests to think about what kind of leverage we might effectively wield on this matter. A selective strike might not be a bad idea."

The contents of his letter horrified a retired naval captain from Virginia Beach, who sent a copy to the apostolic nuncio, Pio Laghi, identifying himself as "a concerned lay person who has been exposed to the deviations and eccentricities from the norm of Roman Catholic Doctrine which are perpetuated within the Diocese of Richmond. . . . The past eight (8) years in this diocese have been a hotbed of revolutionary ideas in philosophy, theology and liturgy."[68]

Responding to a letter of inquiry from Pio Laghi on the matter, Sullivan wrote, "Our priests' council took a definite stand against any confrontation on the issue [of women's ordination]."[69]

The Vatican was equally as disturbed by Father Connery's outspokenness, and this time it was Cardinal Ratzinger himself who wrote to the bishop. Calling Connery's letter "a bitter display of public dissent from the Magisterium . . . ," he added, "Your Excellency is quoted as responding to the above by saying that Father Connery has 'a right to share his thoughts.' Public dissent from the Magisterium is not a right enjoyed by anyone. . . . I would ask Your Excellency in light of all this to direct Father Connery not to express himself publicly in similar terms in the future."[70]

Bishop Sullivan's letter to the cardinal manages to convey both obedience to the Church and loyalty to his opinionated young priest in the same letter. "When I noted that Father Connery had a 'right to share his thoughts,' I obviously did not have in view the question of dissent in the Church," he wrote. The bishop made a distinction between the First Amendment right of free speech and what he claims are his very clear statements on his support of the Church's teachings against women's ordination.[71] Sullivan's letter then took up for his priest:

> Father Connery is a fine priest and a zealous, gifted pastor. I had a lengthy meeting with him within two days after the letter appeared. I reviewed for him the official teaching and I rebuked him for his ill-considered action. Father Connery agreed not to make any further comments on the subject. In the two and one-half months since our meeting, [he] has obeyed me to the letter.

But it is in Sullivan's follow-up letter to Father Connery that Sullivan reveals his pastoral sensitivity to the priest himself.

> Dear Vince:

> Enclosed are copies of two letters that I sent to the Apostolic Delegate in regards to your statement on women's ordination.

> As I stated to you, in my letter of September 12, I did mention the fact that you were going to take some testing. I presume that this was at the House of Affirmation although I'm not sure if that is completely accurate.

> I hope that I have not embarrassed you in any way. This certainly was not intended. I wanted to soften the

reaction I would inevitably receive from the Apostolic Delegate.

Thanking you for your understanding of the matter, I am

Yours sincerely,

Walter F. Sullivan
Bishop of Richmond

Today Connery is no longer a priest. "The last I heard," said Pitt, "he had not gone through the laicization process."

The organized attempts to bring Bishop Sullivan to his knees were at their most intense for about six years, from 1979 to 1985. During that time, the bishop continued to pay close attention to his diocese, establishing new parishes, building schools, opening up homes for the elderly, presiding over Confirmations.

The troublemaking machinations of the Roman Confraternity siphoned off precious time and energy, which makes Sullivan's ability to perform so well in two separate circus rings impressive.

"I love a messy Church," Sullivan once said. "Life is messy." This is the remark of an extrovert with an abiding faith in the underlying order that runs beneath the chaos. But the constancy of the attacks, both by the Roman Catholic Confraternity and the ad hominem attack editorials in the Richmond newspapers, did not go unnoticed by his supporters. Rome heard from them as well.

Individual groups of Catholics protested the investigation, comparing both Sullivan and Hunthausen to the late archbishop Oscar Romero of El Salvador, who had also been persecuted by the Church for his opposition to right-wing enemies of the poor. The Reverend Richard McSorley sent a letter to the apostolic nuncio saying, "It would have been much easier to soft peddle the Peace Message in their terri-tories . . . but like their Master Jesus they didn't. . . . Jesus was harassed throughout His public life. . . . So are His followers, Archbishop Hunthausen and Bishop Sullivan."[72]

Both Richmond's diocesan Council of Priests and the diocesan Pastoral Council sent emphatic letters of support to Rome, asking that Sullivan be seen as a true prophet and leader, under whose care the diocese had flourished.

But it was not until a short, particularly vicious editorial appeared in the *Richmond News Leader* that the entire faith community in Richmond was galvanized into action.[73]

The editorial, entitled "Impossible Walt," spun off a recent comment of Sullivan on the Vatican-ordered investigations. The story quotes Sullivan as saying: 'This is happening all over the country. The letters are being sent to Rome. *It's an orga-nized effort to discredit the direction of the Church in the United States.*" (Italics are by the editorial writer, who then goes on to supply the bishop's meaning between the lines.)

"The direction of the Catholic Church in America is to the Left, and commendably so. I am in the vanguard of taking it in that direction. But there are these Neanderthals around— notably here in Richmond. They are rigid; they resist change. And they are trying to thwart me. . . . It doesn't matter that they pay the bills. . . . I am the shepherd; they are but the flock. I, and other shepherds who think as I do, am taking them in the proper direction. . . . "

The editorial concludes with a quote from *Alice in Wonder-land.* "There's no use trying," said Alice. "One *can't* believe impossible things. . . . As we write . . . we're trying, for the life of us, to believe Impossible Walt."

Individual priests erupted with icy anger. "As a priest of the same diocese for seventeen years, I take exception to your lack of historical awareness of the issues and disregard for the consequences of what can only be described as ill-considered action," wrote Father George Zahn.[74]

"You want Alice in Wonderland? You got it!" wrote Father Thomas Reardon.[75] "When Alice asks the caterpillar 'Where am I?' he responds: 'Who are you?' The claiming of our personal identity always precedes the understanding of ourselves by what we do. Who are you, Mr. Mackenzie? [Ross Mackenzie was the editorial director of the editorial page of the *Richmond Times-Dispatch*.] Bishop Walter F. Sullivan is not afraid to stand for who he is. What's your gripe, Mr. Mackenzie, what's your real gripe? We caterpillars would like to know."

But the immensity of the flag that flew above Bishop Sullivan's head was not completely unfurled until Thanksgiving Day, when a full-page ad appeared in both the *Richmond Times-Dispatch* and *News Leader* under the bold headline "In Appreciation of Bishop Sullivan."

Calling the "Impossible Walt" editorial unfair, distorted, and offensive, more than eight hundred people from all segments of the Richmond community are squeezed onto one page as standing four-square behind the bishop and deploring the attacks.

> Although not all of us agree with Bishop Sullivan on all issues, we support his right and duty to preach the word of God as he perceives it. A spokesman for the poor, the elderly and the handicapped and an advocate of unpopular positions, Bishop Sullivan challenges many of us to think about the issue of our day. Our community is strengthened by leaders like him.

It was an impressive, unprecedented expression of support. The following day, in another editorial, "Sullivan and the Ad," the editors simultaneously criticized Sullivan for "retreating to the loftiness of his position," and called Pope John II "one of the world's greatest living human beings."[76]

Until Bishop Sullivan was in his seventies, he always kept a tennis racket in the trunk of his car so he could pick up a game wherever there was a nearby court. One of his frequent partners was Apostolic Delegate Pio Laghi. They would play singles when they were both in Florida for the bishops' retreat. "Laghi was a very intense player," said Sullivan, "and I was very lackadaisical. He tried his darndest to beat me, but he never did. I think being left-handed gave me an advantage."

Sullivan's style of dealing with Rome was not unlike the way he played tennis. He was competitive. He did not give up. And if his style was unorthodox or "lackadaisical," the rougher the game, the more relaxed he appeared. Or so, to the outward eye, he appeared.

Publicly, Sullivan maintained that the investigation was really an attempt from Rome to see whether his request for an auxiliary bishop was justified, an explanation that Archbishop May publicly supported. In his "Tidings" column, Sullivan was upbeat, even euphoric about his second *ad limina* visit (the July 1983 trip was followed by another in December), calling it "memorable," the pope "very warm and friendly," and his visits to four different offices "valuable."

He was determined to keep his priests out of it. "One of the things I was very strong on was not wanting to share [the investigation] with my priests. I didn't want to get them involved or drag down the spirit of the diocese. But the aftermath of the investigation was long, drawn-out, and inconclusive. More than a year after May had sent in his report, Sullivan was still in ecclesiastical limbo, with no word from Rome about the outcome.

After a U.S. Conference of Catholic Bishops meeting in November 1984, the bishop wrote a letter to the conference chairman, Bishop James Malone, expressing his thoughts:[77]

Dear Jim,

This letter is of two-fold purpose: one, to express my sincerest thanks to you for the excellent first meeting. You are the best yet as presider at our Conference meetings. . . .

The second purpose of my letter is to share my private response with you on the report that you gave at the Executive session regarding your attempts to lessen tensions between Rome and the American Church. At your meeting in Rome, you apparently discussed apostolic visitations of certain dioceses in the United States. I was happy that such visitations were a matter for discussion. At the same time I was personally disappointed that no one has talked to me about my experience with the visitation. I have nothing but the highest praise for the kindness shown to me by John May. I cannot say the same for the actual process and my two visits with the Congregation for the Doctrine of the Faith.

After the executive session, I spoke personally with Ray Hunthausen. He also stated that no one has spoken to him about the apostolic visitation.

I'm not looking for sympathy or condolences. I have remained silent throughout the entire process which in my case seems to be without closure. Perhaps it is not the role of the Conference to be appraised of the situation. There are some aspects of the apostolic visitation which I find both unjust and if publicly known, quite scandalous.

Again, I thank you for your prophetic leadership.

> Yours sincerely,
> Walter

Bishop Sullivan then sent a copy of this letter to Bishop Hunthausen, who contested some parts of it. Hunthausen had, in fact, had numerous conversations with both Archbishop Roach and Bishop Malone, who had been very supportive. "I certainly do agree with you, however, regarding the entire process that was employed in the Visitation. I think it was flawed from the start and entirely inappropriate given the collegial nature of our church."

A few days later, Sullivan wrote Hunthausen thanking him for the clarification about the latter's experience, but repeating that nobody from the Bishops' Conference had been in contact with him.

> The whole process is shrouded in secrecy. A year and a half has gone by since the visit to Richmond was made. A year ago I was in Rome and completed all I was asked to do. I am beginning to find the experience a different kind of "mushroom cloud." Thankfully, things are going real well on the home front. I rarely think about the Visitation. . . . [78]

The bishop was reverting to type, being upbeat and optimistic. But perhaps his candor was the catalyst for action. Within weeks, he received a letter from his old tennis partner, Pio Laghi, with tentatively good news.

> Dear Bishop Sullivan,
>
> Following our recent conversation, I am writing concerning the matter of an auxiliary for Richmond.
>
> As I mentioned, I have recently received a letter from the Holy See in which it is suggested that the Apostolic Visitation, conducted in a pastoral and friendly manner, should be terminated. In due time a statement to this effect will be prepared and publicly announced along with the announcement of the nomination of an auxiliary bishop.[79]

Pio Laghi then submitted another set of possible candidates. The tug of war continued for the better part of the year until finally, on August 30, 1985, Pio Laghi asserted, definitively, that no candidates from the Richmond diocese would be considered.

Bishop Sullivan's extensive handwritten notes of the face-to-face meeting with Laghi the day before describes the situation between Richmond and Rome. From Laghi's perspective, the emphasis in Richmond is upon the local church but that "loyalty to Rome cloudy." The morality of the priests in Richmond is suspect, with "homosexuality evident among clergy." Laghi admits that most of the complaints to Rome have come from one source, that the diocese is very much alive, and Bishop Sullivan is "killing himself." The possibility of sending a co-adjutor, which is what Hunthausen got to oversee him, instead of an auxiliary bishop, had been discussed in Rome but decided against. Instead, Rome would grant the auxiliary bishop special faculties to oversee the seminarians, clergy, and liturgy, under direction of Sullivan.

Sullivan disagreed with the criticism that there was a lack of loyalty to Rome and the pope and defended the openness in the Richmond diocese where priests can express themselves freely without fear of reprisal. He denied that the diocese had called for the ordination of women and suspects that Rome was probably wary of the "Women Listening to Women" program in the diocese. He accepted the proposed solution that the auxiliary's faculties come from the bishop of Richmond, not Rome. With regard to who should be on the final list, Laghi acknowledged that the names Rome put forward weren't appropriate but that no auxiliary would come from Richmond.

Sullivan's conclusion: "Rome still suspicious of Richmond. No opportunity for dialogue on issues. Bishop Sullivan still not allowed to read the May report. Progress has been made."[80]

If there ever was any doubt about the bishop's tenacity, the next letter, on October 25, 1985, proves that Sullivan, so close to closing out the set on one court (the investigation) is not about to lose the set on another (the matter of getting an auxiliary bishop with no strings attached). In a blistering five-page letter, he absolutely rejected the Vatican's solution of an auxiliary bishop with special faculties.

He lobs one question after another over the "net." How would such a person relate to the recently appointed vicar for priests? Who would have the final word on disciplinary matters? Would the auxiliary have the final word, "thereby stripping me of any authority or influence over the priests of the diocese?" Finally, and dramatically, Sullivan declares that he would rather have no auxiliary bishop than one who would be such a source of tension.

Since I was told the Apostolic Visitation was completed, there must be additional issues that are still unresolved. I can only conclude that the Holy See doubts my leadership and competence, and lacks confidence in my exercise of the office of bishop. Suspicion and distrust decrease my effectiveness and drain my energy.

I sincerely request a further dialogue on these matters, since I think I am entitled to some explanation. My concern is not simply for myself, but for the good of the Church of Richmond. I would appreciate whatever help you can give to bring this matter to a harmonious conclusion.

Cordially yours in Christ,

Walter F. Sullivan
Bishop of Richmond

After one more round of names, which included a candidate whom Bishop Sullivan could accept, Pio Laghi finally wrote, on April 30, 1986:

Dear Bishop Sullivan,

I am writing to confirm that the Holy Father Pope John Paul II has appointed as your Auxiliary The Reverend Monsignor David E. Foley. . . . It is understood that you will grant him special faculties empowering him to deal with the discipline of the clergy in matters of doctrine, liturgical practice, and morality, and with the formation of the seminarians. Consequently, I would ask you to kindly let me have in writing your assurances that these special faculties will be expressly given to him, by means of a decree signed by you, on assumption of his duties.

On the surface, it would appear that Rome had won the match. They were looking for someone outside the diocese

(Foley came from Maryland), of a more conservative point of view (also true of Foley), who would be, therefore, a tempering influence. But equally as true was the fact that Foley and Sullivan had known each other since childhood, having been schoolmates at Blessed Sacrament School in Chevy Chase, Maryland, together.

"I grew up with Foley in Washington," said the bishop happily. "We were close friends. He was a monsignor at the time he was selected to come to Richmond, and I ordained him a bishop. I had confidence in him. He tended to be more traditional than I am, like wearing episcopal robes. But he was always very supportive. When he came to Richmond to be my auxiliary bishop, I invited him to go with me to the Homestead. There I gave him this thick book about the investigation. I thought he should be aware of the issues."

Foley served under Sullivan for eight years before moving on to become the bishop of Birmingham, Alabama. It was a harmonious relationship, for several reasons. They genuinely liked and respected each other and—before Foley arrived as his auxiliary bishop—Bishop Sullivan had done some homework. By canon law, it turned out that any special faculties Foley possessed were dependent upon the authority of the diocesan bishop who was, of course, Sullivan.

Pio Laghi himself came down to participate in Foley's ordination. "Your presence added so much to our connectedness to the universal Church and most especially to Our Holy Father, Pope John Paul II," wrote Bishop Sullivan in a letter thanking him for attending. In addition, he thanked him for taking care of a complaint from Norfolk with respect to "concern regarding the Eucharistic bread." Laghi had asked the correspondent to send any future letters directly to the bishop of Richmond.

The slings and arrows from the Roman Catholic Confraternity did not end on any particular day, but after the investigation was over several RCC members met with the bishop, he said, and cheerfully admitted that they had occasionally lied in the interests of their cause. The story of the priest celebrating in his summer shorts, for instance? They had made that up. They hoped the bishop did not mind.

An Addendum

In 1984 Peter Lee was elected Episcopal bishop of Virginia. Tall and patrician looking, with kind eyes and smooth, boyish features, he had earned the reputation of being a solid, middle-of-the-road churchman with an ability to bring all sides of an issue to the table for resolution. In a diocese whose roots go deep into the beginning of the seventeenth century in colonial Jamestown, Lee was a good fit, although clearly there was some residual worry.

"When I first came to Virginia," said Bishop Lee, "a number of conservative Episcopalians told me that they hoped I wouldn't follow Bishop Sullivan's pattern. I told them I am not as progressive as Bishop Sullivan."

Is it true, Lee is asked, that at one point he said publicly that he considers Walter Sullivan to be his bishop? "Yes," Lee acknowledged. "I do consider him to be my bishop. He is in every way a model of what a bishop ought to be in terms of his pastoral concern, his caring for the poor, the imprisoned."

That being said, Bishop Lee was aware that his Catholic colleague had been in hot water with his superiors in Rome, that his outspoken positions on peace and the immorality of war and nuclear weapons had inflamed a small group of Catholics in the Richmond diocese, that there had been a papal investigation of Sullivan's diocese.

"When David Foley was sent down to be Walter's auxiliary bishop," Lee said, "I asked him were you sent by the Vatican to help Walter or to watch him?"

Bishop Lee's own moment of truth lay ahead of him. Not until 2003, when he cast his vote for Eugene Robinson to be the first openly gay bishop in the Episcopal Church, did he experience the full wrath of conservative Virginia himself. Thousands of angry letters calling him a disgrace and a traitor poured into his office. At a forum held at the Virginia Theological Seminary he was publicly un-invited to preside over a confirmation class at a large evangelical Episcopal church in northern Virginia. A woman read from a letter that Lee had already received in private. "Our people are so distressed by your views that contradict the very clear teaching of Scripture that your visit this Fall would be painful and divisive." Five hundred people let out a gasp.

Suddenly, after a career nudging people toward *The Center Aisle* (the name of a daily newspaper he oversaw during an Episcopal convention), Lee had been hoisted upon the scaffold of his own convictions and it gave him a deeper perspective on himself. "Psychological studies of clergy show that we are people who like to be liked," said Lee, in a 2004 *New York Times* interview. And Virginians? How does Lee see them? "Virginians, on a positive level, are very polite and restrained," said Lee. "You can really say a lot of politically provocative things if you couch what you say in a polite, restrained way. Walter succeeded as a provocative bishop because he is also a very kind and gentle person. He shows up at the emergency room when your spouse is hit by a truck."

It was a distinction that many of Bishop Sullivan's adversaries were honest enough to own. After the *Richmond Times-Dispatch* had once again raked the bishop over the coals in an editorial, one conservative reader registered his anger. "While I do not agree with the bishop on his opinion of either Ronald Reagan or the nuclear freeze, there is no doubting his virtues, and, particularly, his virtue of charity. . . . An apology is in order."[81] "Bishop Sullivan is a good man," wrote another opponent of his peace views "and I am very fond of him as a person, but he is much too liberal for many Catholics, including myself."[82] The rest of the letter is a synopsis of how most conservatives viewed him.

> I see the movements of the liberal bishops and Pax Christi as an effort to weaken our resolve to properly arm ourselves to do this. They are attacking government credibility, as they did about Vietnam, to weaken our will, and to get us to leave others to the tender mercies of the communists.

Sullivan had weathered the charge of being un-American before. While the Bishops' Pastoral on War and Peace was still in draft form, he attended a panel discussion of the pastoral and said he didn't mind being at odds with the United States government. "We could stand here in support of Americanism, but I'm not so sure we'd be standing for Christianity. We love to talk about the age of martyrs but we have difficulty living it today."[83]

When Bishop Sullivan was first asked, for the purpose of this biography, whether there had been any particular crisis points in his ministry, he replied, "Not that I can think of. But I had a great desire to achieve because of my background. That I don't deny. I wanted to prove that I was as good as the others." As the project progressed, the bishop became more candid about the effect the papal investigation had upon him. "Pio Laghi told me people were writing to Rome and that Rome was feeding them, seeming to relish what people were saying. It was very traumatic because you feel very defenseless, you don't know where to turn. What were people saying? I didn't know." Not being able to read the report on him was one of the sources of his anxiety. "Finally, they gave me a summary. Pio Laghi told one of the priests that I should never have been investigated.

"It was much more of a strain than I'd ever want to admit. I didn't share it with anyone. I didn't share it with my family. I kept it to myself. And around that time I lost two wonderful priests, Charlie Kelly and Bill Sullivan. I don't know how I did any of it, good or bad. But I've always been an activist. I didn't have time to feel sorry for myself."

Near the time of his retirement, the bishop had an operation that removed his entire lower intestine. He suspects that there might be a connection between the tension he experienced and the pre-cancerous condition that necessitated the operation and regularly sends him back to the hospital for repairs and blood transfusions. "Those were upsetting days personally," the bishop concedes, "but it helped to know that I had the support of the people."

In 2005 the bishop went to Rome on a pleasure trip. Jim Griffin was with him and remembers walking into St. Peter's Square in Vatican City. "On the left side of the colonnade is the Holy Office, where one's orthodoxy was examined by Cardinal Ratzinger before he was pope. Walter gestured to the little yellow building and said casually, 'Oh, I've been there.'"

Chapter Eleven

A Shadow on the Cathedral

The bishop of a diocese is like the president of a university. Development, fund-raising, and public relations are important parts of the job. But his primary responsibility is to his priests who are, in effect, the bishop's faculty. "I must have heard him say ten times at various convocations that a bishop is only as good as his priests," said Father Jim Griffin. "He would tell us that we will touch people that we will never see."

It was not for want of trying that the bishop conceded his finite influence over his flock, a word he himself dislikes. He logged over thirty thousand miles a year on a series of automobiles that would eventually collapse from overwork as Sullivan traversed and retraversed the Richmond diocese, meeting and reinforcing his relationship with the parishioners and their pastors.

"At one time," said Father Pat Apuzzo, "there was a push out of Rome to put the brakes on the bishops who were always looking for the next best diocese. Rome said no, you're supposed to be married to your diocese, to be wedded to your priests, to stay with them. In this, Bishop Sullivan was ahead of his time. He has always had that pastoral relationship to his priests."

The bishop's management style mirrored his personality—nonjudgmental, with a light but controlling hand on the reins. "There was an atmosphere when he was bishop," said Father Robert Perkins, who at various times was rector or vicar to the clergy, "when you felt he was really looking to hear the input of his priests." Monsignor Bill Pitt agrees. "With Walter, there was this freedom. He'd come to the priests' council meeting in a sports shirt. It set the tone. But the main thing was that we were free to discuss things with him, to formulate our own agenda. We didn't realize how unusual that was at the time."

Bishop Sullivan was casual but clear about who was in charge. "In a clash of wills," said Apuzzo, "the bishop always prevailed," but when he clashed with Rome over the selection of an auxiliary bishop who would be given oversight powers over him, Sullivan wondered in a letter to the apostolic delegate, Pio Laghi, why such a thing was necessary.

"Perhaps," he wrote, "my style has not been forceful enough for the Holy See. I do believe, however, that compassion and calling priests to personal responsibility and maturity achieves far better results."

"It was one of the ways in which he was an outstanding bishop," said Apuzzo. "He understood the interdependent relationship. He would never waver in his loyalty. Whenever complaints were made against a particular priest—I'm not talking about sexual abuse, rather the Father So-and-So talks too much or has a drinking problem or doesn't pay enough attention to this or that—he would always give the priest the benefit of the doubt. The priest was always able to give his side of the story. It's not that he didn't understand that his priests were fallible, but he would say you've got to take the bad with the good. If I got rid of every parishioner and every priest who had a problem, the churches would be empty."

Monsignor William Carr, now pastor of St. Bridget in Richmond, once served as chairman of the Diocesan Priests' Council. "He was tight-lipped, keeping matters to himself, especially when it came to personnel. He formed opinions but was very discreet. I think personnel matters were most challenging to him. He wanted parishes to get the right priest assigned to them. This wasn't always possible and he found it frustrating. When the assignment wasn't working, he heard about it from the parishioners. Trying to be fair to both the priest and the parish was never easy."

"My point of view," said Bishop Sullivan, "is that you don't let things simmer. You address them as quickly as possible. Once one of our priests got arrested for solicitation in a public bathroom. He came to me. 'What are you going to do to me?' he asked. I said, 'Why don't I give you a hug?' He burst out crying. He was an alcoholic, and the alcohol brings out whoever you are. We had him put in an alcoholic treatment program. Afterwards I reassigned him. Now he is retired but he has been fine ever since."

"I was with him once or twice," said Monsignor Carr, "when problems with priests were presented. One particular priest came in to Sullivan and told him that he was an alcoholic and wanted to go for treatment, but he felt guilty about leaving his parish for a couple of months. Walter asked him. 'How long have you been a priest?' He said twenty years. Walter said, 'You have given us twenty years of your life. Let us give you a couple of months. We will take care of your parish.' Those kinds of remarks came spontaneously from him. I think the way he was treated in the seminary gave him a compassion for priests that he himself did not receive."

"There were times when I felt he was being too easy on a couple of priests," said Monsignor Pitt. "They needed more direction and less episcopal leniency, and he could be oblivious or naive about the clergy who didn't like him. I would say, to him about somebody, 'You know, he really dislikes you.'

And Walter would say, 'Really? Why?' or 'Oh, do you think so?' and then he would move on.' "

When the diocese split in two in 1974, the priests who elected to remain in the Richmond diocese tended to be more liberal than the priests who shifted to the new Arlington diocese. But not always. "There were times," said Perkins, "when Bishop Sullivan was much more progressive than they were, much more willing to take a stand. On the issue of nuclear war, for example, he was much bolder."

"I would say that the priests were very open to the ideas of Vatican II," amended Bishop Sullivan, "but I never asked them to preach on it. I did what I did out of my own convictions. I would set an example and they could follow me or not."

Some did. The bishop's willingness to take unpopular stands, said Father John De Giorgio, makes it "easier for me to take stands in homilies, even when I know I'll get grief in the parking lot."[84]

Some didn't. John Barrett assessed the priests as being in two camps. "There were the 'ins' and the 'not ins' but there were no 'outs.' The priests who were 'not in' were priests who disagreed with the bishop's style or direction, but they just said, 'I'm not into that' and went about doing their job."

"There are a few priests who have been hurt by Walter's decisions," said Father Jim Griffin. "But I never felt he was overly firm with me. When I was stationed in various posts, he always trusted me. But I'll tell you what he doesn't like, slackers and people on the pity pot. He'd say, 'Come on, Griffin, just do the job. You love being a priest, do the work.' The night before we were ordained he told us that he gets letters complaining about this and that with regard to his priests, but the only ones he takes seriously are the ones that say the priest treats his parishioners badly. He would say, 'You don't treat people like crap.' Actually, he used the word 'shit.' You show up and you love them."

Sullivan showed up for his priests as well. "Walter had a great sense of the symbolic," said the late Father Tom Quinlan. "When they got sick he would always try to visit them no matter where they were."

When Sullivan was bishop, the Richmond diocese developed a reputation as being a hospitable place for priests who were not happy with their own diocese, or vice versa. One of them, a Jesuit psychologist in New York, applied after Rome told the Jesuits that they couldn't be free agents. "They had to quit floating around and become part of a diocese," said Sullivan. "I told him he could use us. He's still floating around."

"Bishop Sullivan had a very close friend named Monsignor Charles Kelly, who died from cancer prematurely," said John Barrett. "Once I was discussing with him why so many priests in the diocese were from out of state. [In order to be admitted to a diocese other than the one in which a priest was ordained, he has to be granted permission by the receiving bishop.] Monsignor Kelly told me, 'Walter Sullivan will always give a priest a chance.' "

Oddly, the bishop was very resistant to giving priests the chance to become a monsignor. There was speculation that perhaps this was because he did not want to create jealousy or hard feelings among his clergy. But Barrett, along with others who were close to him, urged him to go forward.

"I told him that if you don't tell Rome that you've got candidates for a future bishop they'll look elsewhere," said Barrett. "I think that got through to him. Walter created fourteen recommendations. Thirteen made it."

In the mid-1980s, reports of priests sexually abusing children in the United States began to surface in the press and media. In 1984 New Orleans journalist Jason Berry heard rumors about a Louisiana priest pedophile. That led to his ground-breaking book *Lead Us Not into Temptation,* which verified that this was not an isolated instance. Between 1984 and 1992, at least four hundred other cases were reported, and a secret report in the Vatican's Washington, D.C., embassy warned that if a policy was not developed to handle the crisis, the Church would be in dire straits.

It was not, however, until early 2002, when the *Boston Globe* broke the story of a large priest pedophile scandal in Massachusetts that the attention of the entire country was irrevocably caught and held. Cardinal Bernard Law, under whose watch the abuse had occurred, resigned, and in June 2002 the U.S. Conference of Catholic Bishops met in Dallas to determine what should be done.

In Richmond, Virginia, Father Pat Apuzzo had just become director of diocesan communications when stories started appearing in the *Boston Globe.* "Long before that there had been cases here, and in 1992 Bishop Sullivan created a set of workshops for the priests during which he said to them, 'This is not ever going to be tolerated. If you do it, I'll be visiting you in jail.'"

According to Apuzzo, there was a protocol that the diocese followed. When a priest was accused of sexual abuse, Sullivan insisted upon being the person who informed him, not by letter or phone call, but in person. "He didn't want the priest to hear it from anyone else." A special panel was convened to interview the priest and the accuser, who wasn't always the victim, to get both sides of the story. Then, if the evidence had enough merit, the panel would go forward with its own full investigation.

In 1996 the former rector of St. John Vianney Seminary, an all-male Catholic high school in Goochland County, which Bishop Sullivan closed permanently for financial reasons in 1978, was accused by three former students who stepped forward to claim that he had sexually abused them in the 1970s. The priest, who denied all the charges, was placed on administrative leave from St. Michael's Church in Glen Allen, where he was a very popular founding pastor, while the charges were being examined.

The bishop eventually decided in the former rector's favor. "He had fired a coach, who was very popular among the seminarians, but he tended to be disruptive," said Sullivan. "Then he dismissed the coach from the diaconate program for the same reason. That was when he was told, 'We're going to get you.' Some of the seminarians made accusations that there had been improprieties. It was nothing specific, other than having had some of them in his room at night, having been with them in a motel or hotel during a trip, and a lot of sexual talk. I talked to a psychologist who said that if there had been sexual abuse, they would have told me exactly what happened the first time they spoke. Instead, the stories became more embellished with each telling. I felt it was very vindictive and I'm sure nothing would have happened if he hadn't fired the coach."

The priest was returned to St. Michael's to resume his duties after the investigation was over. According to the records, the former rector of St. John Vianney's was one of fifteen priests who have been accused and/or convicted of sexual abuse in the Richmond diocese as of 2012.[85] Charges against eight of those priests emerged when Sullivan was the presiding bishop.

The first priest admitted his guilt, paid for the victim's education, and was sent to a local men's prison to be chaplain, where he worked for many years until the victim took him to court, after which he was forced to resign from the priesthood, sentenced to indefinite supervised probation, and put on the sex offender registry. The second priest also admitted his guilt, was sent away for treatment, and when the victim then demanded that he go public with his crime, he was forced to retire from the priesthood without privileges. The third was originally investigated by the school where he was alleged to have molested some of the pupils, but he did not receive the full complement of counseling that was recommended. Nine years later, following the suicide of a young parishioner whom he was accused of molesting, the priest was confronted by these new charges, after which he committed suicide, too.

The priest who killed himself was Father John Hesch. In 1985 the bishop had received reports that he had been sexually inappropriate with a number of the boys at Sacred Heart–St. Augustine's School in south Richmond. where he taught sex education to upper-level elementary school pupils. "An accusation had been made," said Bishop Sullivan, "that he had been with a bunch of naked boys. I was ready to call him in but the school told me to back off, that they would take care of it. I foolishly agreed."

"The Church did not do enough," said Jacqueline Mishkel, who taught at the same school and went to the principal in 1985 after she heard stories about Hesch from the students. When the principal took no action, she went to church leaders. "I was such a good Catholic. I couldn't go to the authorities. All of this could have been stopped if someone had stepped in."[86]

"They told me that my son and other children were spreading vicious rumors about Father John," said one mother. "I was humiliated. My son was saying things about a man doing the work of God." When she confronted her son, she said, "He wouldn't talk to me. He just said, 'I just don't like him.' "[87]

Nine years later, a twenty-one-year-old man who allegedly was victimized by Hesch ten years before at Sacred Heart–St. Augustine School committed suicide. His parents were adamant about Father Hesch not attending their son's funeral. Bishop Sullivan wanted to know why, which is when he heard that Hesch had been accused of sexually molesting their son. Sullivan proceeded to investigate and on June 4, 1994, he confronted Hesch with the accusations. Hesch vehemently denied that he had ever done anything wrong. But four hours after the bishop confronted him, he walked into the auxiliary bishop's house where he had been living across from the cathedral and shot himself to death on the second floor. He left a suicide note that repeated his innocence.

"My sister Kathy was taking care of his dogs," said Bishop Sullivan's younger sister, Betty. "He was on the road but when he got the news he went right over there. The body was still in the house. When he returned home my sister said his face was completely white. He went upstairs without saying a word, kept it all to himself."

It was, in every way, a disastrous story, of decisions lightly made and signals not interpreted correctly through to the end. Father Perkins, who had been with Sullivan when he spoke to Hesch, said that they had tried to create a safe environment in which to present the evidence, but when Hesch shot himself he realized, too late, that no priest confronted with hard evidence of sex abuse should be left alone after the confrontation.

"I never realized he had a gun," said Bishop Sullivan, who decided to find out more about its provenance. "It turns out he had bought it in Washington, D.C., ten years ago. My guess is that if he had been confronted then he probably would have killed himself."

In a grisly juxtaposition of events, the head of the diocesan Office of Christian Formation and a good friend of Hesch, Gerry Van Ostern, had committed suicide sixteen days before Hesch. The cause: mental illness caused by being sexually abused by priests when he was a seminarian. Van Ostern's wife said that Hesch had been supportive of Van Ostern as his condition worsened and at Van Ostern's funeral Hesch wrote in the guest register, "At the end of the darkness there is only light."[88]

As for the alleged victim of Hesch's abuse, Sullivan met with the family of the young man who had committed suicide at least five times. "I made it a point whenever this would happen to meet with the parents and the families. I would reach out, get them psychiatric help, and we paid for it without question."

The fourth priest was an Australian who was accused of sexual abuse in the Richmond diocese and deported back to his Australian diocese, which paid damages to the priests' victims. The fifth was accused of sexual abuse, placed on leave, and eventually forced into retirement. The sixth was also retired after being investigated for sexual misconduct. The seventh was accused once of sexual abuse and nine years later, accused of "inappropriate behavior." Both times he was investigated, cleared, and reinstated.

The eighth priest was, once again, the former seminary rector. In May 2002 three of his former students at St. John Vianney told a diocesan investigative team that he had engaged in inappropriate behavior with them while they were students. Once again, the priest was placed on leave, and the sex abuse panel appointed a two-member team (Father Tom Caroluzza and clinical psychologist Dr. Therese May) to investigate the charges and draw up a report.

Ironically, before the report was finished, Bishop Sullivan had to fly to Dallas to attend a historic three-day meeting of the entire U.S. Conference of Catholic Bishops. The purpose of the meeting was single-pointed: to confront the massive scandal of sexual abuse of children by priests that had swept across the country and showed no signs of abating. It was the first time they had assembled *en banc* to acknowledge the scandal and come to grips with a solution.

"It was an eye-opener," said Sullivan. "SNAP [Survivors Network of those Abused by Priests] representatives were there. The ones they brought forward to make representations before us were the most injured. It wasn't a happy time. You had grown men crying. The bishops were all very guarded with each other, keeping things to themselves."

You can see that guardedness in a photograph of Sullivan on day two of the meeting, holding up a ballot to be collected. He is solemn and unsmiling, with downcast eyes, a white-haired man dressed in his Roman-collared black priest's suit, surrounded by other identically dressed white-haired bishops, none of whom wanted to be there.

"It was really awful," said Sullivan. "They brought in people who were basket cases. I couldn't believe how broken they were. You're taking away a person's identity. It's a trauma. It affects you to the core. When I returned home I met with all the priests and told them that if you do this I will visit you in jail. I'm not going to cover it up. It's an abuse of trust. The harm is unimaginable."

The U.S. Conference of Catholic Bishops adopted a youth protection charter in which there would be "zero tolerance" for any cleric who sexually abuses a child. It also called for preventive training for teachers and volunteers in Catholic schools. Subsequently, hundreds of sexual predator priests were removed from various dioceses around the country. There was no provision for supervision of the bishops, although every two years, beginning in 2004, there has been an in-depth review of records by a national review board, which is overseen by John Jay College of Criminal Justice in New York.

After returning from Dallas, Sullivan had to deal with the unfinished business of the former rector. The way he went about it underscored the reality that a new procedure was needed. The investigative team gave their report to Sullivan and Monsignor Perkins, who was chairman of the panel. Caroluzza and May would not discuss the contents publicly but they recommended that the bishop not reinstate him. Against their recommendation, the bishop did.

Some members of the sexual abuse panel maintained that they had never been allowed to read the report or the recommendation. When Dr. May was asked whether she was surprised that he was being returned to his parish, she replied, "Yes." Four lay members of the ten-member panel resigned in protest.

"I think there has been some confusion," said the bishop in a subsequent interview. "The investigation team should not have made recommendations. It's the panel who should have made the recommendations. By making recommendations [the team] bypassed the role of the panel. . . . I think improvements can be made. . . . It was a learning experience for all of us. Everyone acted in good faith."[89]

The original sexual abuse panel in Richmond was composed of ten members, five of whom were priests. After Dallas, diocesan review boards were required to have a mix of clergy and lay people. Bishop Sullivan went a step further and decided that he needed to create a review board composed entirely of lay people, whose qualifications did not have to include being Catholic. Charles O'Keeffe, who was already on the Pastoral Council, was one of the new appointees.

"I think he came to realize," said O'Keeffe, "that he needed to have a completely independent body make a recommendation to him." Serving with O'Keeffe was Bonnie Campbell, on the board with Sullivan of the Christian Children's Fund, Russell Palmore, who served as chancellor of the Episcopal Diocese of Virginia, Frank Ferguson, the assistant attorney general of Virginia, and James Meath, former president of the Virginia Bar, who was elected the chair.

Meath served on the board for a little more than two years. "There was a backlog of cases and some of the priests were dead, or the schools in which they had worked were closed. But before we got to work we all met at the Commonwealth Club for dinner with the bishop. At one point we asked that he be excused, or he excused himself, and the rest of us decided what we needed to be assured of if we were to take on the job. When the bishop came back into the room we told him that we needed complete independence, the ability to interview anybody we wanted, procure any documents we needed, and make any recommendation that we all decided upon. Our report would be just that—a report. The bishop could do with it what he wanted. But in all the time I was on the review board there was not one time that he did not accept our recommendations. Twice we referred a matter to the local court system."

Meath thinks that it was a relief for Sullivan to be out from under the responsibility of being the sole decider in these matters. When the bishop was asked if this was so, he said yes, that in the dioceses, like Philadelphia and Boston, where they did not have independent civilian panels, their dioceses suffered because of that.

The time he spent on the review board was a personally upsetting time for Meath, a "cradle Catholic" who had never seen the underpinnings of his own Church. Clearly, there was a lack of transparency. Priests were being moved around, sent here and there for treatment by a diocese whose leaders were trying to cope with a situation for which they had no manual and for which they were not educated or emotionally prepared to handle. "It wasn't in their wheelhouse," said Meath, who questioned whether the bishop always knew what was going on.

"There's a legal phrase," said Meath, "called 'plausible deniability' that refers to a higher-up official who is kept in the dark by officials lower down the ladder. Whether that was true with Sullivan, I don't know. But the whole Rube Goldberg labyrinth had come back to bite them.

"The first thing we decided to do was to have a spokesman, Pat Apuzzo, who was a very bright, with-it priest, who would be very up front with the reporters down at the cathedral who had suspected that things were being hidden from them. Apuzzo told them everything there was to know, and reporters began to realize that if the story stopped that was because there wasn't anything more to say. We weren't hiding anything."

The saga of St. John Vianney's former rector was still not over. In August 2002 two of his former students filed criminal complaints against him in Goochland County, the site of the alleged sexual abuse at St. John Vianney's in the 1970s. By the time the case came to court in March 2004, it had been plea bargained down to a misdemeanor charge. The priest took the Alford Plea (which maintains innocence but concedes

that the evidence available would persuade a jury to convict him of a criminal offense) and pleaded guilty to assault
and battery against two teenaged boys. He was sentenced to
two suspended year-long jail terms and placed on indefinite
supervised probation.

The court's decision overlapped with the diocese's sexual
abuse board's decision to put him on indefinite administrative
leave, which does not allow him to perform any priestly func-
tions for the duration. "I was the one who made the phone call
to the Commonwealth attorney with Bishop Sullivan's request
for them to investigate the allegations that wound up in court,"
said Apuzzo.

"We got all the reports that we needed, made our decision,
and he was gone," said O'Keeffe. "His behavior was not appropriate for the priesthood." By the time that had happened,
Bishop Sullivan, who retired in 2003, was gone, too. The former rector tendered his resignation to the interim administrator, Cardinal William Keeler.

The disconnect between the outstanding pastoral aspects of
Bishop Sullivan's ministry and his less-than-stellar treatment
of the sexual abuse cases that surfaced during his twenty-nine
years as bishop of Richmond is an uncomfortable reality. It is
made more so by the fact that Bishop Sullivan feels he handled
it quite well.

On the plus side, the diocese responded to every accusation and attempted to get to the bottom of it. There was one civil
suit (filed by one of the former rector's accusers), which was
dismissed because lawyers for the diocese successfully argued
that the statute of limitations had expired. There was no serious depletion of diocesan funds for legal costs, and compared

to some other dioceses, where there were criminally culpable bishops and cardinals covering up for their priests, the bishop's honesty has never been questioned. His judgment has. Even his most ardent supporters acknowledge that, in the words of one close friend, "He didn't get it. None of them got it."

Before the early 1990s, when bishops across the country reluctantly concluded that pedophilia couldn't be cured, offending priests in the Richmond diocese were sent to rehab centers, like St. Luke's Institute in Suitland, Maryland, with the expectation that pedophilia could be cured or controlled, like alcoholism. And despite Sullivan's vow that he would not tolerate sexual predators in the priesthood and would visit them in jail if he got wind of their activities, the bishop himself does not recall any specific times that he did.

"He was no better and no worse than most of the bishops in this country," said Dr. Therese May, who served on the diocese's first sexual review board. "But he certainly was no hero. I'd put him right about at 50 percent."

As this book grew and my knowledge, respect, and affection for the bishop increased along with it, searching for underlying reasons as to why he did not handle the sex abuse accusations better became a kind of ongoing mental parlor game. Why was it so difficult for Sullivan, who was otherwise so morally courageous, to deal with this issue correctly? The more I thought about it the more I realized that it was the wrong question. Better to ask what was it about Bishop Sullivan that made it so difficult for him to accept the possibility that a priest could be a pedophile? The answer is "almost everything."

This was a bishop who was reared in a home full of devout Catholic women in the 1930s and 1940s in a culture where words like "pedophilia" or "pervert" were as foreign to him as they were to every other parochial schooled, middle-class Catholic youngster growing up during that time. After the eighth grade he went off to a junior seminary, where his exposure to sexual deviance was limited by his own nature and the nature of his education, which drew his intellect along a particular path. That path emphasized the natural and supernatural laws and virtues that would help him be a good priest and preserve his imagination from prurient curiosity.

When Sullivan was ordained, he was forever precluded from the one experience that might have sensitized him to the victims of a pedophile. He had no children of his own. But as bishop he was, first and foremost, a father to his priests and a good father protects his children, even those who have may have done something wrong. In Bishop Sullivan's mind, the idea that one of his priests would prey upon real children was unimaginable. Therein lies the tragedy. His imagination failed him.

"There is nothing subtle about Walter Sullivan," said Charles O'Keeffe. "He's naive to a fault. He could not bring himself to believe that people could do that."

In Dallas, Sullivan struggled to get his mind around the terrible tales that the victims of priest predators sobbingly laid out before them. Intellectually, he did not doubt their stories. Emotionally, it was hard to get a grip. "I don't live in that world," the bishop said. "It had never happened to me. I just didn't understand."

Catholic theologians, who usually have a tightly reasoned explanation for every kind of human failing, speak of two kinds of ignorance: vincible and invincible. Vincible ignorance is culpable. We simply decide not to pursue the truth because it does not serve our purposes to do so. Invincible ignorance is another story. For reasons of circumstance, intelligence, temperament, or a combination of them all, we are incapable of scaling the wall that separates us from a truth we would embrace if we could see it. Bishop Sullivan suffered from the latter. His cultural background, his lack of firsthand experience, an instinctive impulse to protect the priests under his care, and a temperamental proclivity to see the best in everyone created a "perfect storm" of invincible ignorance.

But perhaps the most powerful barrier to the bishop's understanding lay in what writer Jason Berry refers to as "the self-protecting mechanism of hierarchial life, where crimes are translated into sins so that forgiveness can be dispersed. It is one of the worst deformities of ecclesiastical culture."[90] Nor did it help that one of the bishop's own had killed himself to avoid facing further accusations.

Perhaps the horror of it happening again stayed his hand. It does not take much imagination to imagine that.

Chapter Twelve

An Instinct for Brotherhood

In 1943 America was in the middle of a war, during which the Jews in Europe were being rounded up and slaughtered. How effectively and horrifically, no one grasped at that time. But that summer in Richmond, Sara November picked up her pen and wrote a letter to two of her Jewish friends from New York.

They had been so entranced with Richmond that they discussed the possibility of relocating there. "Apropos of our conversation about the set-up of social groups among our Jewish people in Southern communities," wrote November, "perhaps you would be interested in having me go into detail."

Sara November was the right person to give such a tutorial. A prominent Richmond artist with a national reputation (one of her paintings was selected to represent the United States in the 1939 World's Fair) she was a cultural and philanthropic force in the city. She had founded an art school for black children on Church Hill (Craig House) and an arts academy that preceded the Virginia Museum of Fine Arts.

November's husband, Israel, was equally formidable. A clothing manufacturer who had left New York to avoid the unions (he later became their champion), he was one of the city's major employers. Starting out with two floors in a warehouse, he gradually expanded until his company, Friedman Harry Marks, was the third-largest manufacturer in the world of men's ready-to-wear suits.

"My mother was fawned over by the erudite gentile establishment which would come up to her studio to watch her work," said her only son, Neilson November. "But it wasn't easy being Jewish in Richmond, and she wrote her New York friends a letter telling them how they had to behave in order to be accepted—particularly if you were a Brooklyn Jew with a New York accent."

"As I have observed it," wrote Sara November, "there seem to be about five groups. No definite lines, no definite divisions, each overlapping those closest to them." She lists them: the Orthodox Jews who emigrated from Europe and whose struggle to find their place in America left them little or no time to learn English or get an education; their children, who became the small shopowners, plumbers, and tradesmen in the community; the professional class of lawyers, doctors, and engineers; the offshoots of this group (into which she puts herself and her husband) who strive "to put beauty into their way of life—not artificially, not affectation—but by developing their cultural interests," and, finally, the philanthropists, whose lives are spent in "unselfish enterprise."

"As always," she adds, "there are those in this [fifth] group who contribute nothing to the community. Although born to splendid heritage, they are content to sit within the aura of their family name, smugly gauging the worth of others merely by the standards of birth. They are worthless except as a symbol of good taste in superficial behavior patterns."

November's letter is a small, brilliant essay on the social structure of the Jewish community in Richmond. Then, as now, they were a small sliver of the overall population.[91] Then, as now, their economic, cultural, and philanthropic influence was disproportionate. Despite Sara November's place of privilege, the conclusion of her letter reveals how new the feeling of being accepted as a Jew in a gentile world was:

I have had to learn all this myself. Never having lived in a rooted Jewish community, and having had mainly Christian friends, just as you two have, I found it rather interesting to learn what I have just finished telling you. However, it is a smug feeling being rooted. Until it happens, one doesn't realize how "dispossessed" we are. (Having to pretend to friends, meeting them away from home, not really *belonging* somewhere, gives the feeling of being a phony.)

As I said at the beginning, nothing is cut and dried about such a fluid thing as social relationships. There are no fences, no outlines—everything is in a constant flow of development and change. It all depends on oneself.

Let's hope we all keep developing together.

In a world at war, where Jews were being slaughtered and Europe's preeminent Christian, Pope Pius XII, was doing nothing to halt the trains rolling toward the death camps and the Final Solution, "Let's hope we all keep developing together" was a lovely concluding thought.

When Sara November mailed that letter off, Walter Sullivan was fifteen years old, a high school student preparing for the priesthood at St. Charles minor seminary in Maryland. It would be a long time before he grasped the horrendous story of the Holocaust, or the way in which his own Church (at best, Pope Pius XII was shockingly passive) had turned a blind eye, failed to come forward. But as soon as Sullivan reached the chancery he took steps toward his Jewish brethren.

"There was a time," said Jay Weinberg, a member of Richmond's Beth Ahabah Congregation, "when my temple did pulpit exchanges. It was a historic thing that happened. There we all sat, Jack Spong from St. Paul's Episcopal and Nick Dombalis from the Greek Orthodox Church, hearing about how Jesus was a Jewish rabbi, and how many of the prophetic injunctions, like feed the hungry and clothe the naked, are the same in all our religions. But when we invited Bishop Sullivan's predecessor, Bishop Russell, he said he couldn't do it. Catholic priests weren't allowed to sit on any altar that wasn't Catholic. When we asked Bishop Sullivan he said sure, he'd come. Sullivan didn't care. If he was convinced something was right, he did it."

That series of pulpit exchanges was one way in which Sullivan came into deeper contact with the Jewish community. But Rabbi Jack Spiro and Rabbi Myron Berman were an important part of the Tuesday morning breakfast club, the Ecumenical Social Concerns Alliance, and the Virginia Interfaith Center for Public Policy, all of which were created to turn prophetic injunctions into realities. The interaction also sensitized the Christians and Jews to each other's needs.

"In Richmond," said Weinberg, "the public schools would schedule football games on Friday nights during high holidays. The Jews found that very offensive. Our boys couldn't play in or go to the games. It was always Bishop Sullivan or Nick Dombalis who would say, 'Don't worry, we'll go to the school board, we'll fix this.' "

"Richmond was unique," Weinberg recalled. "It was in many ways much more broad-minded than other cities, and certainly more so than where I grew up in Portsmouth, Virginia. I think the reason why it was easier is because of a handful of people like Walter Sullivan who made it mighty easy to be Jewish in Richmond. He did the right thing when no one was looking."

In 1964, when he was still rector of Sacred Heart Cathedral, Bishop Sullivan attended a conference of Catholics and Jews who had come together to identify common community problems. One of the speakers, Dr. Joseph Lichten (a Polish diplomat who took part in the first Anti-Defamation conference), exhorted everyone to combine their talents and listen with attention and regard to each other. "We are born," he said, "with a veritable instinct for brotherhood. If we deny its fulfillment, we deny our very human nature."

Sullivan's ears were open for such a dialogue. "At my [discussion] table," he recalled, "was none other than Nathaniel Krumbein.[92] We knew so little about one another's traditions, but that was the starting point of a lasting friendship."[93]

Sullivan was ahead of his own Church. A year later, in 1965, during the last months of Vatican II, Pope Paul VI issued a declaration (*Nostra Aetate*) that exonerated the Jewish people from that old charge of deicide and called all anti-Semitism and acts of hatred toward the Jews deplorable. Publicly, the Catholic Church was beginning to repair the centuries of damage its prejudice against the Jews had done to them.

Later, when he became bishop, Sullivan appeared with leaders in the Jewish community before the General Assembly to speak on behalf of the Virginians who had no voice or power. "They were very much a part of our prison witness, probably because of the Holocaust," he said.

Once, when attending a service at Beth Ahabah, the bishop heard a Catholic priest preach on the subject of "When will the Jews forget the Holocaust?" The priest answered himself: "When Christians begin to remember."

"Those words touched me deeply," said Sullivan. "I knew then that our journey together was incomplete."[94]

Serendipitously, one of Sullivan's friends, Al Meyer, had just returned from a trip to North Carolina, where he had seen a monument to the Holocaust on the grounds of a Protestant church. He told Bishop Sullivan that he ought to do something similar. It just so happened," said Bishop Sullivan, "that the head rabbi from New York was in our office. I asked the rabbi what he would suggest that I do, and he said why don't you put a memorial of Rachel weeping for her children in front of the Cathedral."[95]

Sullivan liked the idea and set about looking for a sculptor. He did not have to look far. One of the best lived right in Richmond, Linda Gissen, the wife of Ira Gissen, the head of Virginia's Anti-Defamation League and a close friend of the bishop. Sullivan commissioned her to create a Holocaust memorial, dipping into his aunt's trust fund to pay for it.

On April 26, 1987, a bronze and copper figure of Rachel, surrounded by six tongues of flame, representing the six million Jews who were murdered, was installed on the grounds of the Sacred Heart Cathedral. Her fingers are pressed against her eyes as she weeps. Beneath her, on a stone, is carved one word, "Remember," in Hebrew and English. It was the first memorial to the Holocaust on the grounds of any Catholic church in the United States.

Present at the ceremony that day on the cathedral grounds was Jay Ipson, a Holocaust survivor who had escaped from Lithuania to America with his parents at the age of twelve. It was the first time Ipson had seen Bishop Sullivan. But Ipson was preoccupied by his father, who had come with him to the ceremony.

"What I really remember from that day was how my father felt really uncomfortable because his pain was far greater than mine. That morning, being inside a Catholic Church was more than praying for the souls of people who had died at the hands of Christians. He thought, here they killed us and now they're praying for us." When it came time to enter the cathedral, Ipson's father stayed outside. "If he were alive today, he would be accepting but then he thought that it was a service by non-Jews instead of Jews."

For many years, Ipson, who owned a wholesale auto parts business in Richmond, dreamed of one thing: the day when Richmond could have its own Holocaust Museum. In 2001 he was deeded for one dollar by the state an abandoned tobacco warehouse. "I didn't have any money to build it and someone, it might have been Neil November, suggested that I go to see Bishop Sullivan. So I went to the cathedral and asked to see him. His assistant, who I think was Father Apuzzo, said that the bishop wanted to come down and see me at the museum site."

In 2001 the Holocaust Museum consisted of a couple of wooden desks and some chairs in a partitioned-off room in the middle of a vast, empty warehouse. "The bishop came and after we had talked for a while he said, 'Jay, I was going to give you $5,000, but now that I see you and talk to you I'm going to give you $25,000—from my aunt's estate.' He didn't take it from the Church, but from himself."

"There is no end to my admiration for Bishop Sullivan," said Ipson. "Integrity means more than anything else to me and the way he is, outreaching and accommodating, is absolutely a gift from God. When we're together we don't talk about religion. We talk about the Holocaust, about human behavior."

Today the Virginia Holocaust Museum is a thriving, multipurpose museum, with an outreach program for teachers, online research facilities, and a performance hall where lectures, musical events, and films are presented throughout the year. In 2003 Ipson went back to Kovna, Lithuania, where his family lived, to duplicate the synagogue. "I got the original drawings, photographed the synagogue, and took a cabinetmaker back to the U.S. I also went back to the potato hole where my family had hidden after we escaped from the ghetto." That potato hole has been duplicated in the museum, too.

"Before I knew Bishop Sullivan," said Ipson, "there wasn't much of a relationship between the Jewish community and the Catholic community. My personal experience had not been a good one. If you're familiar with the history of World War II, you know that the Catholics were totally against the Jews. All the problems were blamed on the Jews. We had such a bitter relationship in Lithuania. If the Catholic Church had gotten involved, thousands and thousands of Jews would have been saved."

Ipson's own consciousness has undergone a gradual evolution. Before he came to the United States the only black people he knew in Germany were American GIs. "They looked to me to be very sharp and beautifully dressed. But then the prejudices of the people I was associating with started to seep in. I went with the flow." Now Ipson uses the museum to teach other people how devastating such prejudice can be.

"There was a big incident at Bishop Sullivan High School. They had a basketball game with Norfolk Academy, which had a significant number of Jewish students, and the kids from the Catholic school were really abusive. The principal of the Catholic school contacted the principal of Norfolk Academy, and I was asked to talk to the kids at Bishop Sullivan High School. I said, 'No, who wants to listen to an old man? Let them come here,' and so they did and the whole attitude changed. Now they come here every year."

In 2011 a church group from Tennessee came to picket in front of the Holocaust Museum. "They called to say they were going to do it because God hates the Jews." Ipson's first inclination was to lock up the museum and let them picket an empty building. But then he thought better of it.

"I said, 'That's not me.' So I got in touch with the Virginia Interfaith Center for Public Policy and with some of the Christian community and some rabbis. The next day when I went out to greet the picketers, about four hundred supporters from churches and synagogues in Richmond stood behind me in silence."

"I said to the picketers, 'Well, God must love this Jew because I am here. Would you like to come inside?' They folded up their picket signs and left. A couple of young Christian kids who came to support me took up a collection and raised $1,500, which they gave to us."

That same year, a traveling exhibit of Pope John Paul II's evolving relationship to the Jewish people in Poland came to the Virginia Holocaust Museum. "As Christians and Jews, following the example of the faith of Abraham, we are called to be a blessing to the world," the pope said. "This is the common task awaiting us. It is therefore necessary for us, Christians and Jews, to first be a blessing to one another."

In 2005 Bishop Emeritus Walter Sullivan was awarded the Neilson J. November Award, given by the trustees of the Virginia Holocaust Museum to the man or woman who exemplifies its mission: "Tolerance through Education." If there was any one person interviewed for this book who convinced me that Walter Sullivan's life was too full of equally large characters to be an oral history, it was the man who endowed the award.

Neil November is an energetic, smiling man with piercing eyes and the mental quickness of a stand-up comedian. We first met in his office at 3600 Broad Street on the sixth floor. It is a narrow, unpretentious space, like a dorm room, with a couple of desks and a lot of plaques and photographs on the wall, plus a collection of bronze eagles on a filing cabinet. November was waiting for me with his feet on a spare chair, semidozing. But there was nothing sleepy about him when he sat up and began to talk.

I asked him how he had gotten to know Bishop Sullivan. "Walter was looking all over the country for a sculptor who could create a Holocaust memorial. Then he bumped into my wife, who told him about Linda Gissen, who lived right here in Richmond. That's how I first came into contact with him."

November makes no pretense about his own religious convictions. "I'm suspicious of all religions, the Catholics in particular. As far as I'm concerned all of them are just enhanced superstitions to keep people feeling afraid. And almost everybody is anti-Semitic. I don't know why, but we've always been hated. Ignorance, of course, is the basis of it. But it's amazing to me that people will line up behind something and when they're told Jesus was Jewish they either don't hear it or don't believe it. Or they believe it for their own purposes. The evangelicals love us because how their story turns out depends upon how the Jewish story turns out."

Why then, given these strong views about the negative role of Christianity and the Catholic Church in particular ("Catholics have been more antagonistic toward us than most," he said), does November have such a strong affection for a Catholic bishop?

"Because this guy, Bishop Sullivan, is genuinely not anti-Semitic. He takes you for what you are, not for your circumcision. The other bishops are standard hubcaps. They quote from the Bible, and that's about all. But Walter is like a lightbulb. He can see through the trappings of his religion. He doesn't get weighed down by all of the ceremony and accoutrements, those things they carry down the aisle and trail smoke."

November's father gave him an eye for authentic, large spirits. "He infused me with his spirit of magnanimity. With over twenty-five hundred employees, he never fired anyone and would always find room for a worker who was a loyal employee."

This early example made a big impression on him. He taught November that pretentiousness was a barrier. "My father said I had to have my office on the floor. That way people could find me and lean over the railing next to my desk and tell me what was on their minds. No air conditioning. My father was too smart for that. Once I remember looking up from my desk and seeing a lady fingering her way across the wall until she found the staircase. She was suffering from dementia, but we found a place for her in the shipping department."

November, whose philanthropy has literally opened up the stage for thousands of Virginians (he has vowed to build, refurbish, and rename every theater in Richmond for his wife, Sara Belle), knows a generous spirit when he sees one.

"There is a stratum of people who live outside the restrictions of their religion," said November. "Bishop Sullivan is one of them. He really sees the people and their problems. That's how I feel about him. He doesn't let the Church stand in his way."

To ensure that *Rachel Weeping for Her Children* is never removed from the south lawn of the cathedral, November and several other members of the Jewish community recently put together a sizeable purse and gave it to the diocese, in Bishop Sullivan's name, so that the memorial will always be well-maintained. It is not the first time that the Jewish community in Virginia has indicated how seriously they take the presence of a Jewish memorial to the Holocaust on Catholic soil, or how deeply they appreciate the bishop for making it happen.

Shortly after *Rachel Weeping* was installed, Sullivan ran into some trouble with a home for the elderly they were building in Charlottesville. John Barrett, the diocese's chief financial officer, was in a quandary. "The street in front of the home had not been deeded back to Albemarle County. We were getting dangerously close to completing the project but had no way to get into the property." Then Barrett got a phone call from the owner of the property.

"He asked to remain anonymous, but he said, 'I'm going to give you ingress and egress to the property across my land. Otherwise you won't be able to use your facility.' I thanked him and asked him what the cost to us would be. He said, 'I'll charge you what Walter Francis Sullivan charged us when he put the monument of *Rachel Weeping for Her Children* on the cathedral grounds.'"

Just before Bishop Sullivan retired in 2003, a chair in Catholic Studies was established in his name at Virginia Commonwealth University. Dr. Eugene Trani, the legendary president of VCU, who transformed the university (and the Richmond skyline) during his tenure, spearheaded the drive for funds. A devout Catholic, Trani admits to having sat unhappily in many pews over his lifetime, listening to bishops and priests whose narrow vision he did not share.

"Many bishops of the Church are isolated, but he wasn't," said Trani. "That's what attracted me to him. He opened up the gates of the Church and it's what inspired me to raise money for endowment." Sullivan's friends in the Jewish community were very generous. "They put us over the top," confirmed Trani. "Their affection for the bishop is well known."

On Sunday, April 22, 2012, a soft, steady rain fell upon the umbrellas of the men and women who made their way up the steps of the Cathedral of the Sacred Heart. By two o'clock, they were assembled in the pews. It was the twenty-fifth anniversary celebration of the installation of the Holocaust Memorial. Linda Gissen, who created the haunting statute of an emaciated, sorrowing Rachel, was there. She was profoundly altered, the victim of Lou Gehrig's disease, and barely able to move, reclining in a hospital bed at the end of the first row. It was her day.

Ahead of her, to the left of the raised altar, was Bishop Sullivan. Time had altered him as well. When he commissioned Linda Gissen to create a Holocaust Memorial, he was fifty-nine years old, in the energetic, project-creating prime of his life, a dervish of activity. Now he was an old man, sitting quietly in a side chair following the program while his successor, the current bishop of Richmond, Francis DiLorenzo, presided over the service. But everyone in the cathedral had their eyes upon Bishop Sullivan. And everyone had their own individual story about their friendship with the bishop that brought them there.

Filling up the side pews to the right of the altar was an interfaith crowd of Bishop Sullivan's Catholic, Protestant, and Jewish colleagues. Seated in the front row was Father Tom Shreve next to The Reverend Fletcher Lowe beside Rabbi Emeritus Jack Spiro. When the cathedral choir opened with the lilting words from Brahms Requiem, "How Lovely Is Thy Dwelling Place," the faces in the pews were the loveliest part.

It was a carefully prepared program, weaving together violins, psalms, Jewish hymns, kaddish, and prayers. A cantor sang "Let my tongue be silenced, if I ever forget you." A rabbi read from Ezekiel: "I will take the heart of stone out of your flesh and give you a heart of flesh."

When Rabbi Emeritus Dr. Jack Spiro rose to speak, Jay Weinberg sat in his pew and thought back to the old interfaith pulpit exchanges at Temple Beth Ahabah. "When I saw Rabbi Spiro in the pulpit of the Catholic cathedral I thought to myself, well, well, we've come a long way."

In his "Spoken Reflection," Spiro referred to Rachel as the spirit of God. "God is also weeping," he said. Then came a "Music Reflection." A young woman stood with her violin and played the theme from *Schindler's List*, releasing a bright scarlet ribbon of sorrow into the air.

It was over all too soon, with people searching for their umbrellas, but reluctant to leave a warm cathedral for a wet gray day. Nobody was anxious to depart. Governor Tim Kaine and his wife, Anne Holton, taking time out from a senatorial campaign, stayed behind to say hello to the bishop. Jay Ipson in his trademark white cowboy hat chatted with Eugene Trani, the former president of VCU.

Friends from all segments of the bishop's life gathered around him and each other to celebrate a miracle, or at least something that had not been seen before. One man's gesture had filled a Catholic cathedral full of Jews who would not have crossed the threshold if Walter Sullivan had not been waiting for them, "with a heart of flesh," on the other side.

Epilogue

When the time came for Bishop Sullivan to retire, he was surprisingly capable of it. Relinquishing control is one of the most difficult of human acts and the perquisites of his office (for twenty-nine years the waves had parted whenever he entered a room) would leave when he did. But by his own admission, the responsibilities of the diocese, in particular the vexing, often wrenching personnel issues that followed him from one day to the next, were pressing down on him.

"I was ready to move on," he admitted. So, too, was Rome, which was not replacing retiring Vatican II "peace bishops" with more of the same. "When I submitted my resignation," said Sullivan, "it was accepted immediately." The bishop raised his eyebrows and smiled. "I wonder why?"

"People saw the bishop as a radical," said Kathleen Barrett, the CEO of St. Joseph's Villa, a large non-profit organization in Richmond that serves special needs children and their families. Sullivan is on their board. "There was a joke circulating before he retired that when he sent in his resignation to the Vatican there would be a fax waiting for someone to hit 'send' accepting it as soon as it arrived."

The people, however, did not let Bishop Sullivan go quietly. Throughout 2003, the last year of his term, there were goodbye events all across the diocese. "It was endless, all the parties that were held in his honor," reminisced Father Robert Perkins. "I told him that if you have one more farewell tour I'm going to scream. It was like Michael Jordan leaving the NBA."

"The bishop is greatly loved," confirmed Kathleen Barrett, who has known him since she was a young girl. "In raising money for the Villa today, the first thing people always want to know is whether the bishop is involved."

The Richmond diocese provides Sullivan with a house, health insurance, a secretary, and an office. "They have been very generous," he said, "and that's not true in every diocese." In return, Bishop Sullivan keeps a proper and respectful distance from his successor. "It's very important not to be critical," he said. "One bishop in the diocese is sufficient." The two men usually have dinner at least once a month. "I let him take the lead in conversation."

Today, the former bishop of Richmond, who worships at St. Paul's Catholic Church in Richmond, is a priest without a parish. But he continues to say Mass five days a week for the Comboni Missionary Sisters, unless he is ill. On Good Friday 2012, he got himself out of the hospital just in time to celebrate the Eucharist at Greensville Correctional Center in Jarratt, Virginia. And the previous December he kept his monthly date to say Mass for the residents of St. Mary's Woods retirement community. The elderly, like the imprisoned, have always been an integral part of his ministry. That commitment has not changed.

Monsignor William Carr has known Bishop Sullivan for a long time. "When I try to think of describing him, three words come to mind: 'priest,' 'passion,' and 'vision.' The words 'passion' and 'vision' go together. He was deeply passionate about peace and justice, the care of the poor, the marginalized people. He had a very warm embrace for the left out. He was against all the injustices that keep people on the bottom."

Carr learned about the "priest" part of the equation inadvertently. "I would ask him to go someplace, or do something, and he would often say, 'I can't do that, I've got a baptism,' or a wedding or a funeral. He had a broad parish that consisted of

Cathedral staffers, his ecumenical friends, and others. He'd go around Richmond quietly being a priest to people. There was no pomposity, no ceremony. He was being with people in their moments of joy and sorrow. It kept his feet on the ground." It still does.

St. Mary's Woods is for elderly people who do not depend upon the charity of the diocese. The carpets are soft, the room where everyone sat quietly waiting for Bishop Sullivan to arrive is hung with tasteful swags around the windows. It is a bright, cold December day in Advent. In the living room, two life-sized plastic reindeer flocked with snow hold a pair of artificial Christmas trees decked with lights in their antlers.

The bishop pulls up alongside the entrance, extricates himself slowly from his car, plucks a bag from the back seat, and walks slowly up the icy walk to the front door. Once inside, he floats an alb over his shoulders, screws a crimson skull cap on his head, and enters the room.

"Good morning," he sings out in a voice stronger than he looks. "We come together to be with the Lord in this holy season of Advent. The Lord is near. The message is no different. What is different is you and I. I'm eighty-three. So the question is, what are you looking for at this time in your life?"

The congregation of St. Mary's Woods is 95 percent female. They sit in their wheelchairs, or behind walkers, their faces turning toward the bishop, like sunflowers toward the light, as he shuffles slowly down the aisle. The bishop is elderly now, too. His questions are grounded in what he too is experiencing.

At eighty-three, he has had his share of middle-of-the-night tumbles on the way to the bathroom. He loses names, forgets where he is in a conversation, drifts off to sleep at an earlier hour in the evening. In the past year, he has made four trips to the hospital. But his friends have learned not to anticipate the plot. One minute he is flat on his back, connected to a monitor. The next minute, he is driving himself to West Virginia for the weekend.

As Bishop Sullivan moves through the parts of the Mass, the smell of tomato soup wafts into the room from the kitchen, where lunch is being prepared for the residents. Shouts of children at recess from the nearby parochial school come from the playground. A church bell tolls twelve o'clock. Then the Mass comes to an end. The bishop moves back down the aisle and stands at the door to say hello to people as they file out of the room. He clearly enjoys it.

"What happened to Caroline?" he asks one woman. "She's been calling me. She said she had to take oxygen and might not be here."

"How's your leg?" he asks another woman. "What did you do? Did you fall?"

Sullivan is still ministering to the people—and the people are still ministering to him.

"Bring him some roses," said his gardener to a visitor who was on the way to the hospital after the bishop had taken yet another tumble. "He loves roses."

The bishop's friends are intensely proprietary, always saying that their close relationships give them the right to speak on his behalf. But everyone close to the bishop realizes that no matter how much they want to "take care of the bishop," the bishop is still in charge and has every intention of living out his life on his terms until the end.

"I wish sometime he did have some limitations," lamented his sister Betty. "But you can't tell him anything. He has to decide for himself. Like the telephone. You can tell him he doesn't have to answer it, that someone else can do it. But at the first ring he has the phone in his hand. It feeds him."

There is a reason why the phone rings so often. The bishop is genuinely glad to hear from whoever is on the line. "Oh, hi," he exclaims happily, in a slightly adenoidal voice that his friends delight in imitating, "I was just thinking about you." And he's not kidding. He *has* just been thinking about you.

"For years," said Monsignor Bill Pitt, "everyone has told me that the bishop is such a people person, as if being a bishop and being a people person don't go together." But to conclude that Walter Sullivan is a sunny, other-directed soul whose temperament enables him to roll like a beach tire over a bumpy life would not be quite accurate either.

When asked about the hard times in his life, this most candid of men is usually silent or dismissive. But in searching for the bishop among his own papers, the Irishman who does not dwell upon his troubles dissolves and the man who loves Jesus appears. He is not, however, a romantic when it comes to Jesus. He understood who Jesus was and what being his follower involves.

In a homily on Palm Sunday, the happy day Jesus entered Jerusalem in triumph, Bishop Sullivan moved ahead to Good Friday when he was crucified. "We make a mistake in looking at Jesus as the confident martyr. Jesus did not die majestically. Jesus felt the absence of God. Jesus was the Son who died in disaster. The cross was a scandal, a disaster for Jesus. He endured all the suffering a human person could endure.

"God continues his presence through people. God is found today in the crosses and the dying of people who feel oppression. . . . We cannot make a religion out of the cross unless we experience God in the suffering of humanity. . . . People cannot experience God as long as they condone violence, or tolerate injustice, or acquiesce when human dignity and human rights are denied, or put trust in military armaments, or remain unresponsive to the plight of the poor."

He spoke these words on April 12, 1982, before a Baptist congregation in Chesapeake, Virginia, which is the most highly militarized corner of the United States. A month later, Sullivan received an honorary degree from Randolph-Macon College in Ashland, Virginia. "Like the true shepherd who is not afraid of wolves, he teaches with courage and clarity," read the citation accompanying his award.

Sullivan frequently refers to himself as a coward, who has no taste for getting arrested, or going up against the Holy Father when the pope was on the other side of an issue. He has never felt iron handcuffs on his own wrists, or experienced the inside of a paddy wagon. Nor did he ever step over any bright red lines that would have put him at odds with official Church teachings. "He has his limits," said Eileen Dooley, "and only he knows what they are." But his knack for diplomacy runs parallel to a penchant for speaking his mind.

On his friend Jean-Bertrand Aristide, the former Salesian priest who became the first democratically elected president of Haiti, he said, "He didn't do well because the U.S. didn't like him. He didn't do our bidding. He's like Castro. We made him into who he is."

For a while Bishop Sullivan met with a group of charismatic Christians in the Richmond diocese, but he never could understand them. "This one individual was speaking in tongues and I kept asking, 'What did you say?' Finally, they told me to be quiet. That's not my cup of tea. Let's put it that way."

When asked what he thought of the recent Vatican crackdown on the Leadership Conference of Women Religious for failing to be explicit in their opposition to abortion and contraception, Sullivan replied, "What about the priest pedophiles?"

Bishop Sullivan is a self-described "churchy person," but he puts some daylight between himself and the institution. "I was never a company man," he concedes. And despite his own acknowledged need to succeed and to be loved by others, he has never allowed those needs to obscure his sight of the cross that held the reason for his life.

Did Bishop Sullivan ever have a crisis of faith? Perhaps because his life has such a consistent testimony to what he believed, it never occurred to me to ask. But he answered it himself in an extraordinarily candid and passionate homily on the eve of his retirement.

The entire homily, which he gave on May 14, 2003, to celebrate his fiftieth anniversary as a priest and thirty years as bishop before a gathering of his priests, is full of affection for them, and somewhere in the middle of it, he addresses the subject of losing faith.

"I remember a seminary professor who contended that priests can lose their faith. I dismissed the idea then, but the thought has always haunted me. Yes, faith can diminish and even be lost so that in ministry we dry up or simply go through the motions or wait for the magic age of retirement. Diminished faith can lead to burnout, discouragement, and personal tragedy. I certainly support all the outside helps to keep us effective in ministry. But when we take away all the trimmings, at the heart of what we are about as priests there is the truth found in the words when we received the Book of the Gospels. . . . The bishop says, 'Receive the book of Gospels whose herald you now are; believe what you read, teach what you believe and practice what you teach. . . . ' "

"That," Bishop Sullivan concluded, "is what our priesthood and priestly ministry is all about. Our lives are driven and motivated by the love of Christ. Yes, we must be prudent and wise stewards, taking care of our physical and emotional health. Yet, ever before our mind and heart are the words of Christ to each of us: 'And you will be my witnesses.'"

Walter Francis Sullivan's own life of witness is drawing to an end. So, too, were the interviews for this biography. On one of our last working afternoons together, as we sat quietly in his living room, all conversation over, I asked him, on a whim, if he could define the word "evangelize."

"It means to proclaim the Gospel," he replied.

"And does it not also mean 'to convert'?"

"Oh, no," he shot back, "that's the role of the Holy Spirit. Your biggest proclamation must be your life."

The good bishop did not know it but he had just given me the right words with which to end this book.

On November 28, 2012, Bishop Sullivan was admitted to St. Mary's Hospital in Richmond. Diagnosed with inoperable liver cancer, he was told by his doctors that the date of his death was uncertain, but it would not be long in coming. "He's coming to terms with his mortality," reported Fletcher Lowe, who phoned that night with the news. "He asked me to speak at his funeral. I said I would, but he had to use all his energy to fight for his life, like he fought against the death penalty."

The next morning, when I walked into his hospital room, the bishop smiled wanly from his bed. "Give me a hug," he said. The bishop is not a physically demonstrative person, so I did not take him seriously and simply smiled. "Give me a hug," he repeated. I bent down and placed my cheek against his. He burst into tears.

This was new territory for the bishop. He loved his life and did not want to leave it. For the last few weeks of his life, he moved between grief and practicality. When Patrick Carlin, the cathedral's choirmaster, came to talk about what hymns the bishop wanted at his funeral, the bishop again broke into a sob. Carlin bowed his head, placed his hand lightly upon the bishop's chest, and waited for him to recover, which he did. There were details to be taken care of, his posterity to protect, and occasionally the bishop would reach for a pencil to write down the name of a friend or a passage from the Bible that he wanted to include in his funeral Mass of Christian Burial.

From the moment when news that the bishop was in extremis became public (Bishop DiLorenzo issued a diocesan-wide statement), people came in a steady stream into his hospital room to say goodbye: ex-prisoners who had been pen pals, nuns who ran his schools, priests, parishioners, the lay men and women who had worked tirelessly for him while he was the presiding bishop. They would approach his bed, their faces bright shields of love, take his hand, say how much they loved him, remind him of the highlights of their friendship.

The bishop, still very much the extrovert, was buoyed by their presence. He joked, asked questions, and when his cell phone rang, he would fumble for it among the bedsheets, press it to his ear, and say "Hel-lo-oh" as if he were standing in his kitchen making a peanut butter sandwich. Occasionally, the room would empty of visitors, during which time he would doze in and out of sleep. Once, out of the blue, I heard him say quietly, "Give me your blessing." It took me aback. "I would, Bishop," I blurted, "but I don't know how." He gave me instructions. "Just say, 'I bless you in the name of the Father, and the Son, and the Holy Spirit,'" and so I did, asking God to bless the bishop and all the people the bishop had blessed with his life.

When they brought him home from the hospital to die, the parishioners of St. Paul's Catholic Church held a prayer vigil and then walked, as a congregation, down the street to his house where they sang hymns outside his bedroom window. By then, the bishop was too tired to do anything but weep and wave to them from his bed as they filed, one by one, across his porch before leaving.

On the morning of December 11, 2012, two of Bishop Sullivan's closest friends, Monsignor Bill Pitt and Father Jim Griffin, came up from Virginia Beach to visit him. That afternoon, his older sister, Kathleen, was brought over from the nursing home for one last time to tell her brother goodbye. There would be no more visitors. At 5:45 p.m., the bishop died.

It was as if the world had been holding its breath. The day after his death, the first inkling of what his life had meant was celebrated in both the Catholic and secular press across the country. *USA Today* noted that among Bishop Sullivan's other stands, he had opposed the war in Iraq and handed out black armbands in the diocese when war was declared. The *Washington Post* blogged that he was deeply inclusive, stretching out his hand to gays, African Americans, Jews, and women. The *National Catholic Reporter* called him "everyone's bishop with a passion for peace." But it was Bishop Sullivan's old nemesis, the *Richmond Times-Dispatch,* that doffed its cap and bowed the most deeply when the paper received the news.

The morning after Bishop Sullivan's death, the *Times-Dispatch* devoted most of the front page to the news, calling him "the region's most powerful voice for ecumenicalism, peace and forgiveness." A week later, on the editorial page (a space previously reserved to flog Bishop Sullivan for his numerous sins against the conservative commonweal), there was an appreciation, titled "Rest in Peace," that was remarkable for its tenderness, bordering on contrition:

> Bishop Walter Sullivan led the Catholic Diocese of Richmond for 29 years. His visibility transcended his flock.
>
> Sullivan's stands on political and social issues generated heat. Editorials in the *News-Leader* and the *Times-Dispatch* disputed him. He responded with vigor and gave as well as he received. . . .
>
> Sullivan's tenure coincided with an era of clerical activism. . . . Congregations can argue over the placement of candles as well as the fundamentals of faith. Sullivan followed his lights. Time dims contention. Men and women are entrusted to do God's will on Earth. They will disagree on what that commandment means, yet the faithful often grow to realize that the life-or-death splits of specific hours were not as dramatic as proclaimed. The Eucharist supplies context.
>
> Bishop Walter Sullivan died Tuesday at 84. The community as a whole joins the Diocese of Richmond in mourning a shepherd and a lamb.

It may or may not have been a coincidence that the editorial was not printed on the day of his funeral but on the previous day, when the ecumenical community gathered to pay their respects.

The machinery of the diocese started to move in preparation for Bishop Sullivan's death the moment he received a terminal diagnosis. But even while he was making notes for his own funeral, Bishop Sullivan's power to determine how he wanted his life and legacy to be commemorated was dying along with him. The rumor, which turned out to be true, was that Bishop DiLorenzo was not going to allow Sullivan's chosen non-Catholic friends to speak during his funeral Mass.

Instead, Fletcher Lowe, representing the bishop's many Protestant colleagues, and Neilson November, from the Jewish community, were to be part of a separate ecumenical program during a prayer vigil for the bishop, the Office of the Dead the night before the Mass.

All afternoon on December 18, the Cathedral of the Sacred Heart filled slowly but steadily with mourners. The bishop's body lay, head pointed toward the altar, in an open casket. He was dressed in the bishop's full regalia of gleaming white vestments and mitered hat. Looking down upon him from the pulpit, The Reverend Lowe spoke for everyone when he said, "The words of the prophet Micah describe exactly who Walter was: to do justice, to love kindness, and to walk humbly with your God."

"Rarely does one have the privilege of knowing a man like Walter Sullivan," said Neil November, who followed Lowe. "He loved everyone and hoped everyone loved him."

Priests, deacons, and seminarians flanked the casket throughout the night, saying prayers for the bishop's soul, keeping vigil until the funeral Mass the next morning. No offense to the mortician, but the bishop's body no longer resembled him, which underscored the loss.

Before the Mass of Christian Burial began, it felt more like a family reunion inside Sacred Heart Cathedral. Priests, still in street garb, clutched their vestments against their chest like laundry, as they caught up with each other. Sullivan's inner circle of family and friends clustered in quiet groups toward the front of the cathedral. Further back, people took their places where they could. By the time the funeral Mass began, there was not a single space left. But when one surveyed the mourners it was clear from their expressions that everyone had a special knowledge of the bishop, considered themselves part of his real family. The bishop, in his long life, had singled them out, the way Jesus singled out his disciples, for his special attention. These were not mourners but heirs, coming to claim their inheritance.

There is nothing casual about a Catholic funeral. The Church intends, by its use of sign and symbol, to impress upon the faithful the timeless, God-given essence of its magisterium. By the time the plumed and caped Knights of Columbus, the visiting archbishop and bishops, vicars, priests, cross-, candle-, miter-, and crozier-bearers had moved down the aisle, the full weight and magnificence of the Catholic Church, with incense rising, was felt by everyone. Retired Archbishop Theodore McCarrick of Washington, elderly and resplendent in his red cardinal's cape, looked out upon the crowd like a figure from a sixteenth-century Florentine oil.

After the Mass was over, the pallbearers approached the casket, carefully lowered the cover, and carried off the Eleventh Bishop of Richmond to join his mentor and friend, John Russell, the Tenth Bishop of Richmond, in the cathedral's crypt. Bishop Sullivan's family followed behind. For several long minutes, while the congregation waited in silence for the funeral party to return, there was nothing to contemplate but the marble altar at whose base the bishop's coffin had lain. Morning sun clothed the bare altar with radiance. The bright emptiness emphasized what was no longer there.

Acknowledgments

The presumption involved in thinking anyone can capture another person's life on paper is considerable. But without certain individuals it would have been impossible. Bishop Sullivan has many friends and colleagues who contributed their time, information, and insights to the book. Among them are Sister Jean Ackerman, Steven Baggerly, Kathleen Barrett, John Barrett, The Reverend Jonathan Barton, Dr. Stephen Colecchi, John Dear SJ, Professor Joseph Fahey, John Gallini, Nancy Gowan, Joseph R. Giarratano, Jay Ipson, Robert Kline, Bishop Peter Lee, Marilyn Lewis, Dr. Therese May, Colman McCarthy, James Meath, Thomas Mellenkamp, Carol Negus, Bonnie Neuhoff, Steven Northup, Neilson November, Charles O'Keeffe, Robert Quirin, Donald Riley, Monsignor Thomas Shreve, Monsignor Michael Schmeid, Dr. Irving Stubbs, Dr. Eugene Trani, Jay M. Weinberg, and Pastor Hasan Zarif.

I am particularly indebted to Father Pasquale (Pat) Apuzzo, Monsignor William Carr, Eileen Dooley, Father James Griffin, Kathleen Kenney, Father Robert Perkins, the late Father Thomas Quinlan, and, finally, and most particularly, Monsignor William Pitt. Their close, in-depth association and knowledge of the bishop over the duration of his pastorate was invaluable.

The Reverend Fletcher Lowe and The Reverend James Payne were the persistent, insistent colleagues whose affection for the bishop turned the idea of a book about his life into a reality.

The bishop's younger sister, Betty Sullivan Hughes, not only made time for an interview, without which we would have no firsthand witness to the bishop's younger days, but she generously loaned me her extensive archive of magazine and newspaper clippings and photographs, many of which appear here.

William Greider generously gave permission to reprint large sections of his article on Bishop Sullivan in *Rolling Stone*. Without his permission, it would have been my impossible task to try to paraphrase it.

Justine Diamond and Pat Blair Funk performed the critically important task of listening to each chapter as it was completed. Every writer should have two such discriminating, truthful, and loyal friends.

Among those who generously contributed financially to the initial funding of the book are Mr. and Mrs. Cecil Brown, Mr. and Mrs. Vincent F. Callahan Jr., Mr. Connell and Mrs. McHenry-Connell, Louis Einwick Jr., Gerald Furst, Mr. and Mrs. William de Groot, Christian Hoeser, Mr. and Mrs. Stewart M. Kasen, Mr. and Mrs. Robert Kline, Mr. and Mrs. Martin Kuhneman, Mary C. Layman, Rev. and Mrs. J. Fletcher Lowe Jr., Richard Malek, Catherine Morhard, Mr. and Mrs. Edward Mulligan, Mr. and Mrs. Ed Murray, Mr. and Mrs. Joseph P. Nealon, Mr. and Mrs. Thomas Noone, Mr. and Mrs. Neison J. November, Mr. and Mrs. Charles B. O'Keeffe Jr., Dr. and Mrs. Paul Prince, Mr. and Mrs. Donald R. Riley, Thelma Robinson, Mr. and Mrs. Gilbert Rosenthal, Mr. and Mrs. Truman T. Semans, Mr. and Mrs. Lewis P. Sutzberger, Richard Vanderloo, Mr. and Mrs. Lester A. Wagner, Rembert G. Weakland, and Agnes B. Whitlock.

My husband, Ragan Phillips, was unfailingly supportive, reading chapters as they were completed, making insightful comments, and tolerating the long periods of time when our life together was put on a backburner. He is the real reason that the project was completed.

Robert Ellsberg, the publisher and editor-in-chief of Orbis Books, was an answer to a prayer. Already a good friend, he became the editor of this book. A more perfect editor could not be had!

Finally, I must thank the subject of this biography, Bishop Walter F. Sullivan. Being written about is a little like undergoing major surgery. It takes courage and trust to be at the sharp end of someone else's pencil. He never flinched or obfuscated when a question was asked. But most of all I thank him for being such an inspiration and deep pleasure to know. It is not too often that one meets a true follower of Jesus. It makes me want to know Him better, which is the effect that Bishop Sullivan had upon most people. His biographer is no exception.

Notes

Introduction

1. Manhattanville College of the Sacred Heart, in Purchase, New York.
2. *Richmond Times-Dispatch,* March 26, 1986.
3. Letter from McGrath to Charles O'Keeffe, March 28, 2000.

Chapter Two

4. "St. Mary Star of the Sea Turns 150," *Fort Monroe Authority,* September 20, 2010.

Chapter Three

5. From the *National Catholic Reporter* anniversary series of articles on Vatican II.
6. Joseph A. Komonchak, "U.S. Bishops' Suggestions for Vatican II," *Cristianesimo nella Storia* 15 (1994): 313–71.
7. Giuseppe Alberigo, *A Brief History of Vatican II* (Maryknoll, N.Y.: Orbis Books, 2006), 15.
8. Garry E. Adelman, *First Families: A History of Fairfax Memorial Park, 1957–2007* (Fairfax Memorial Park, 2007).
9. John A. Dick, "Cleric Who Shaped U.S. 'Pastoral Church' Dead at 99," *National Catholic Reporter,* January 21, 2009.
10. Ibid.

Chapter Four

11. Richard Henry Clarke, *Lives of the Deceased Bishops of the Catholic Church in the United States,* vol. 1 (New York: P. O'Shea, Publisher, 1870), 269.
12. *The Faith of Our Fathers: A Plain Exposition and Vindication of the Church Founded by Our Lord Jesus Christ* (1876).

13. John Tracy Ellis, *The Life of James Cardinal Gibbons, Archbishop of Baltimore, 1834–1921* (1951).

Chapter Five

14. Marie Deans, the founder of Murder Victims' Families for Reconciliation, was a death penalty opponent and a self-taught defender of death row inmates who had been poorly represented during their trials. Because of her work, all but two of the two hundred men she defended were saved from the death penalty. One of them, a mentally disabled death row inmate, Earl Washington Jr., was eventually exonerated, freed, and awarded two million dollars in damages by the state of Virginia. Deans died in 2011.

Chapter Six

15. *Richmond News Leader*, March 27, 1984.
16. *Today's Parish*, March 1983, 14.
17. Ibid., 13.
18. *Catholic Virginian*, January 22, 1982.
19. Anniversary Edition of "Pastoral Letter on the Powerlessness in Appalachia by the Catholic Bishops of the Region," 66.
20. *Victoria Advocate*, July 19, 1977.

Chapter Seven

21. *Richmond News Leader*, March 17, 1984.
22. *Daily Press*, November 28, 1984.
23. November 10, 1982.
24. "Tidings," *Catholic Virginian*, January 18, 1982.
25. Ibid.
26. "Catholic Meeting Gets Bad Review," *Washington Post*, September 1, 1978.
27. Ibid.
28. Letter to the editor from Walter Sullivan, *Richmond News Leader*, February 9, 1973.

29. *Norfolk Ledger-Star,* November 6, 1981.

30. "Tidings," *Catholic Virginian,* February 1, 1982.

31. Robert Blair Kaiser, *National Catholic Reporter,* May 18, 2012.

32. "Tidings," *Catholic Virginian,* March 23, 1987.

33. Letter to Archbishop Laghi from Charles B. O'Keeffe Jr., March 30, 1987.

Chapter Eight

34. Giuseppe Alberigo, *A Brief History of Vatican II* (Maryknoll, N.Y.: Orbis Books, 2006), 8.

35. "A Protestant Looks at Catholics," in *Catholicism in America: A Series of Articles from "The Commonweal"* (New York: Harcourt, Brace, & Co., 1954), 29.

36. Alberigo, *A Brief History of Vatican II,* 1.

37. "Tidings," *Catholic Virginian,* January 25, 1982.

38. In February 2012 the U.S. papal nuncio requested the current bishop of Richmond, Francis DiLorenzo, to investigate the Church of the Holy Apostles to ensure that the integrity of the *communicatio in Sacris* (the liturgical norms set forth if Catholics are to participate in rites other than their own) are being fully honored. The investigation was triggered by an article co-written by Holy Apostles' Catholic co-celebrant Father James Parkes and his Episcopal counterpart for an Episcopal magazine about the way in which the liturgy was celebrated at Holy Apostles. An investigatory team from the Diocese visited Holy Apostles in March. In November, Father Parkes was relieved of his duties and Monsignor Ray Barton came out of retirement to serve as the interim priest. Reached at his office at Holy Apostles, Barton confirmed that they were "looking for a way to revise the liturgy, particularly the liturgy of the Word, because right now the entire community is together in one room, but with two altars. We are looking at other options that would receive approval by Bishop DiLorenzo and still serve the community and put everybody at ease." The outcome is uncertain.

39. 2004 interview with Hans Küng by Laura Sheahan, for Belief-net.com.

Chapter Nine

40. Bishop Thomas Gumbleton, The Bishops' Peace Pastoral Letter 25th Anniversary, May 21, 2008.

41. *Norfolk Ledger-Star,* September 14, 1981.

42. *Roanoke Times & World News,* September 15, 1981.

43. Letter to the editor from Walter Sullivan, *Richmond Times-Dispatch,* May 7, 1982.

44. Hearings on the Full Implications of the Military Budget, March 31, 1982, Morning Session.

45. Unlabeled news article, March 22, 1982 .

46. Letter to the editor of *America* magazine, July 29, 1982, regarding Father John R. Connery SJ's article, "The Morality of Nuclear War Power" (*America,* July 10, 1982).

47. *Richmond Times-Dispatch,* January 24, 1982.

48. *Wall Street Journal,* June 9, 1982.

49. Mary McGrory, "Reagan's 'Father Knows Best' Didn't Play in Bonn or New York," *Washington Post,* June 15, 1982

50. Letter to the editor, *Richmond Times-Dispatch,* January 6, 1982.

51. Letter to the editor, *Richmond Times-Dispatch,* July 23, 1982.

52. Editorial ("Careful Bishops"), *Richmond Times-Dispatch,* February 4, 1982 .

53. The italicized material below is excerpted from Greider's article on Bishop Walter Sullivan, "The Power of the Cross," in the April 26, 1983, issue of *Rolling Stone.* Used with permission of the author.

54. Ibid.

55. Ibid.

56. Bishop Thomas Gumbleton, The Bishops' Peace Pastoral Letter 25th Anniversary edition, May 21, 2008.

57. One observer suspected that O'Connor was a mole for the Pentagon, claiming that he would go to dinner after the meetings and he would get up to go to the bathroom and make a phone call. The next day the *Washington Post* would have a Pentagon-placed story that dealt with what the bishops had just been talking about.

58. *Richmond News Leader*, May 6, 1982.

59. "White House Outreach to Catholics," in *Catholics and Politics:The Dynamic Tension between Faith and Power* (Washington, D.C.: Georgetown University Press, 2008), 175.

Chapter Ten

60. John Tracy Ellis, *National Catholic Reporter*, undated 1983.

61. Most of the letters in the bishop's files from that period bear out this observation.

62. *Virginian-Pilot* interview, September 13, 1981.

63. Letter from Archbishop Virgilio Noe to Bishop Walter Sullivan, March 14, 1984.

64. Letter from Roman Catholic Confraternity, Inc., to Bishop Walter Sullivan, March 14, 1984.

65. Letter from Bishop Walter Sullivan to Edward S. Gibbons, president, Roman Catholic Confraternity, March 22, 1984.

66. Letter from Rev. William H. Carr to Bishop Walter Sullivan, March 27, 1984.

67. Letter from Bishop Walter Sullivan to Rev. William H. Carr, April 11, 1984.

68. Letter from James A. Mulligan to Archbishop Pio Laghi, September 8, 1983.

69. Letter from Bishop Walter Sullivan to Archbishop Pio Laghi October 6, 1983. Monsignor Pitt, who headed up the priests' council at that time, disagrees with Sullivan's account. "I think Walter is fantasizing. [The priests' council] didn't say anything on the issue."

70. Letter from Cardinal Joseph Ratzinger to Bishop Walter Sullivan, October 26, 1983.

71. Letter from Walter Sullivan to Cardinal Joseph Ratzinger, November 22, 1983.

72. Letter from Rev. Richard McSorley to Archbishop Pio Laghi, September 9, 1983.

73. Editorial, "Impossible Walt," *Richmond News Leader*, November 2, 1983.

74. Letter to Ross Mackenzie, editor, *Richmond News Leader*, November 3, 1983.

75. Letter from Bishop Walter Sullivan to Bishop James Malone, November 20, 1984.

76. Editorial, "Sullivan and the Ad," *Richmond News Leader*, November 25, 1983.

77. Letter from Bishop Walter Sullivan to Bishop James Malone, November 20, 1984.

78. Letter from Bishop Walter Sullivan to Bishop Raymond G. Hunthausen, December 18, 1984.

79. Letter from Archbishop Pio Laghi to Bishop Walter Sullivan, January 17, 1985.

80. Taken from handwritten notes that Bishop Sullivan made of his meeting with Archbishop Pio Laghi.

81. Maurice B. Sullivan, letter to *Richmond Times-Dispatch* Forum, June 1, 1983.

82. Frank A. McDonnell, letter to the editor, *Richmond Times-Dispatch,* undated.

83. "Bishop's Arms Crusade Gets Lukewarm Reception," *Hampton Roads Virginia Daily Press*, March 7, 1982.

Chapter Eleven

84. From an article in the *Virginian-Pilot*, December 1, 1995.

85. www. BishopAccountability.org.

86. Mark Holmberg, "Mistakes Made in Handling of Hesch Sex Case," *Richmond Times-Dispatch,* July 30, 1994.

87. Ibid.

88. "Priest Shot Self after Sex Abuse Allegations," *Richmond Times-Dispatch*, July 13, 1994.

89. Interview of Bishop Walter Sullivan in *Richmond Times-Dispatch*, July 19, 2002.

90. Author interview with Jason Berry, January 13, 2013.

Chapter Twelve

91. 7,500 out of 193,000, AJStatistics, 1940.

92. A prominent Richmond retailer and chairman of the Virginia chapter of the Anti-Defamation League.

93. From a speech delivered by Bishop Walter Sullivan when he received the Virginia Anti-Defamation League of B'nai B'rith Award on May 25, 1988.

94. Ibid.

95. Rachel, mother of Joseph and therefore the mother of the twelve descendant tribes of Israel, is spoken of by the prophet Jeremiah in the Bible as weeping for an end to her descendants' suffering after the destruction by the Babylonians of the First Temple in Jerusalem. She begged God not to cause them to be exiled. God hears her plea and promises that, eventually, the Jews would be returned to their own land.

Chapter Twelve

91. 7,500 out of 193,000, AJStatistics, 1940.

92. A prominent Richmond retailer and chairman of the Virginia chapter of the Anti-Defamation League.

93. From a speech delivered by Bishop Walter Sullivan when he received the Virginia Anti-Defamation League of B'nai B'rith Award on May 25, 1988.

94. Ibid.

95. Rachel, mother of Joseph and therefore the mother of the twelve descendant tribes of Israel, is spoken of by the prophet Jeremiah in the Bible as weeping for an end to her descendants' suffering after the destruction by the Babylonians of the First Temple in Jerusalem. She begged God not to cause them to be exiled. God hears her plea and promises that, eventually, the Jews would be returned to their own land.

Index

About the Author

Phyllis Theroux was born in San Francisco and wanted from an early age to be a saint. When that ambition was thwarted, she turned to writing about saintly people, which suited her. Her essays in the *New York Times* led to a memoir, *California and Other States of Grace;* two essay collections, *Peripheral Visions* and *Nightlights: Bedtime Stories in the Dark;* an anthology, *The Book of Eulogies;* a novella, *Giovanni's Light;* a children's book, *Serefina under the Circumstances;* and another memoir, *The Journal Keeper.*

A writer for various national publications, including the *New York Times* and the *Washington Post*, and a columinst for two magazines whose titles do not reflect her expertise (*Parents* and *House Beautiful*) she was, for several years, an essayist on the *News Hour with Jim Lehrer.* The founder of Nightwriters, an intensive residential seminar "for people who need to write it down," she frequently holds one-day workshops on how to keep a good journal. The mother of three children and four grandchildren, she lives with her husband, Ragan Phillips, in Ashland, Virginia.